International Military Forces

A Study from the Arms Control Project

Center for International Studies

Massachusetts Institute of Technology

INTERNATIONAL

The Question of Peacekeeping

MILITARY

in an Armed and Disarming World

FORCES

Lincoln P. Bloomfield

with

EDWARD H. BOWMAN   HANS J. MORGENTHAU

HENRY V. DICKS   HERBERT NICHOLAS

JAMES E. FANNING   THOMAS C. SCHELLING

STANLEY HOFFMANN   BRIAN E. URQUHART

Little, Brown and Company

Published simultaneously in Canada
by Little, Brown & Company (Canada) Limited

PRINTED IN THE UNITED STATES OF AMERICA

FOREWORD

IN RECENT YEARS keen interest has been shown in the problem of international military forces. In the process it has not always been clear that there were two distinct meanings of international force. One refers to UN forces in today's armed, conflict-ridden world. The other has to do with international forces as part of schemes for "general and complete disarmament."

Linked by a common vocabulary, these two meanings are nonetheless profoundly different — as different as the UN Congo force of the early 1960's contrasted with the vision of a hypothetical world army able to enforce the will of the "community" on any nation however strong. This book grew out of the conviction that this question, in both its policy aspects, called for serious analysis.

In the first part of the book I have sought to lay out the problem of UN forces, both today and in a disarming world, as it seems to me to present itself to responsible policy-makers and scholars for improved understanding and new decisions. In doing this I have laid deliberate stress on the highly political nature of the issue rather than on the more technical problems of a primarily military and administrative sort.

My principal concern is with the present soundness and future prospects of Western policy, and if I appear critical of positions supported by my former colleagues in the Department of State it is out of no want of understanding and appreciation for their dedicated service. The proposal advanced in the last chapter of Part One can be charged with many shortcomings, but the only charge its author might resent would be that it was hasty or impetuous: it rests on laboriously constructed foundations some of which by one miracle or another may even have managed to affect policy.

Admittedly, a generalized sense of short-run caution verging on pessimism limits my own hospitality at the present for more elaborate, expensive, or revolutionary schemes for an international force. But it is a sense of greater optimism for the longer run that inspires the search for politically acceptable solutions which have a chance of fulfillment. My own position rests on the belief that this prospect is denied to utopias, whether they commit the Marxist's sin of abolishing history or the Western visionary's sin of abolishing man.

In this quest I also enlisted the talents of several highly qualified colleagues. One chief purpose in commissioning their papers was to have the benefit of the thinking of some who had not particularly focused their professional attention on international forces but who *had* thought deeply in other contexts about such subjects as military strategy and logistics, police functions, and the psychology of the soldier. Within these covers they share common quarters with others who have distinguished themselves in the area of international organization and politics.

Since the purpose is to illuminate the issues their approach, like my own, is generally friendly but critical. Each author has imposed his own particular logic on the material. The method was designed to scrutinize the problem through a variety of lenses, and the result, hopefully, is to open widely varying angles of vision into it.

In the second part of this volume, then, are several supporting essays. First the experience of the recent past is consulted. To do justice to the controversial and tangled Congo episode, as well as other postwar UN military and quasi-military operations, two parallel chapters are presented together. One reflects the view from inside the United Nations by a perceptive senior Secretariat official who was intimately involved in those operations, Brian E. Urquhart; the other represents an appraisal of the same events by a keen outside observer, Herbert Nicholas of Oxford University. Considered with these is an important technical problem — logistics. Edward H. Bowman and James E. Fanning apply the professional tools of logistical analysis to the highly unusual — but nonetheless exigent — logistics problems of international forces based chiefly on the Congo experience.

The second half of the symposium looks ahead to the possibility of international forces in a changed political and military environment brought about by a disarmament agreement. In the fourth and fifth papers two distinguished political scientists probe into some of the key theoretical issues in the complex relation of force and politics that are raised by any substantial version of international force. Hans J. Morgenthau focuses on those things that distinguish international "police" operations from the traditional concept of police in a community. Stanley Hoffmann tackles the problem through fundamental questions of political authority and loyalty in a political system.

Moving still closer to the so-far non-existent world in which armaments are significantly reduced, an imaginative analysis by Thomas C. Schelling speculates on the strategic problems that an international force would doubtless face whatever the national level of arms.

Finally, in considering a special aspect of international forces rarely investigated in the public print (or, for that matter, by governments) Henry V. Dicks reflects on his notable wartime psychiatric work with national soldiers to raise profound questions about international ones.

The Appendix supplies for convenience the most definitive statement on the subject by Secretary General U Thant and a few key documents representing landmarks in the recent employment of UN forces.

I am grateful to the Rockefeller Foundation, particularly Kenneth W. Thompson and Gerald Freund, for the support that made this research possible, including the opportunity to study the Gaza and Congo operations at first hand. I am similarly obliged to my fellow editors of the journal, *International Organization,* for their collaboration in bringing out the symposium portion of this material in an earlier form, to *World Politics* and *Daedalus* for permission to quote some passages from two articles of mine, and to the office of the UN Secretary General for authorization to reproduce U Thant's statement. Finally, I would like to record my debt to Richard W. Hatch and Irirangi C. Bloomfield for being helpful editors, to Donald R. Hammonds for ably representing a sympathetic publisher, and to Lisa Walford for being a patient and efficient secretary.

L. P. B.
Center for International Studies
Massachusetts Institute of Technology

TABLE OF CONTENTS

PART ONE

International Forces
Today and Tomorrow

PART TWO

A Symposium
on International Forces

UN FORCES AND LESSONS OF SUEZ AND CONGO

INTERNATIONAL FORCES OF THE FUTURE

Contents

Appendix

PART ONE

*International Forces
Today and Tomorrow*

One

THE MEANINGS OF INTERNATIONAL FORCE

Two sets of events in recent years have combined to give the subject of international military force prime importance. One was the dramatic creation of the several UN emergency forces. From the midst of the Suez crisis came the first true international force — the UN Emergency Force (UNEF); it can be seen today performing its tedious but useful patrol duty on the hot sands and in the dusty ravines of the Gaza Strip and the Sinai Desert and in a barren corner of the Gulf of Aqaba. Two years after Suez, in the tense summer of 1958, the UN Observation Group in Lebanon (UNOGIL) was created. And in July 1960 came the UN force in the Congo (ONUC). ONUC brought the United Nations to the verge of bankruptcy even as it was at the time containing the forces seeking to rend that turbulent land. None of these developments or those that followed was precisely envisaged in 1945 when the UN Charter was written with the expectation that the great powers would themselves furnish forces to the Security Council; it turned out that forces enlisted from the lesser, non-great powers were not only the best obtainable under the circumstances but also a potentially indispensable addition to the arts of peacekeeping.

This contemporary invention of a new form of military presence — the non- (or almost non-) fighting UN force contributed by the smaller powers — poses a host of questions for the foreign policy and strategy of the principal members. It has already stimulated some (but not enough) fresh analysis by a few governments of the need for stand-by forces and for improved international observation and fact-finding resources. The Congo experience alone has supplied material for permanent controversy — certainly enough to fill several volumes.

Alongside the UN problem another major political development has begun to raise still broader questions about the concept of international forces. Western acceptance of the package approach to "general and complete disarmament" carried with it a portentous corollary that both illuminates and bedevils the disarmament dialogue. The corollary, first enunciated by Secretary of State Herter in early 1960, has since become embedded in Western policy. Simply stated, it holds that general disarmament must be accompanied by a significant degree of world authority which in turn must have at its disposal a military capability that would grow during the disarming process to the point where, by the end of stage III, no state would be in a position to challenge it. In a word, it calls for limited world government (without labeling it that), backed by military power at the center designed ultimately to supplant national military power.

This revolutionary concept was advanced, one suspects, without full comprehension of its implications. Initially left unanswered were questions ranging from broad and obvious ones such as the kind of political world in which a world peace force could function, to the lesser but no less crucial ones about the sorts of people one could envisage serving in such a force, the kinds of real-life chores such a force would probably have to take on, and such possibly decisive issues as command and location (and thus vulnerability to control or seizure by individual nations).

There are, then, two large parts to the question of international force, one involving the painfully familiar armed world of self-help, nuclear deterrence, endemic crises, and weak international authority; the other the unfamiliar one of vastly reduced armaments, détente, quantum increases in international authority (and, it is argued here, nuclear deterrence and endemic crises as before).

As one tackles the several meanings of "international force" it is striking how little experience the world has actually had that could illuminate the future. Paradoxically, the type of international force that is most avant-garde, so to speak, is the type with the longest history. Groups of military men truly mixed down to the squad of foot soldiers, or the crew of a man o'war, have sometimes put in dazzling performances. Englishmen will not forget that Admiral Nelson's own flagship at the Battle of Trafalgar — H.M.S. *Victory* — was crewed by English-men, Scotsmen, Irishmen, Welshmen and various islanders, and the following: twenty-two Americans, seven Dutchmen, six Swedes, three Frenchmen, two Danes, three Norwegians, one Russian, three Germans, two Swiss, two Portuguese, four Italians, two Indians, one African, nine West Indians, and four Maltese.

Some would see the collective use of national power to suppress threats to the status quo of 1815 as an analogy to the world today: to others it would be ideologically far-fetched. Perhaps the six-nation international force that captured Peking from the Boxer rebels on August 14, 1900 is closer to the mark, even to its non-Western participants (the Japanese).

In 1910 the United States Congress suggested creating a commission which would study "constituting the combined navies of the world [into] an international force for the preservation of universal peace" in connection with arms limitation.[1] This early linkage of peacekeeping with disarmament reappeared in the aftermath of World War I in a French proposal for a joint military force under an international general staff, later renewed in more detail in 1932. It showed up in the closing months of World War II at the Dumbarton Oaks Conference of 1944 in proposals by both the Soviet Union and China for an international air force.

In pre-UN days the need for international enforcement power of some variety was sometimes voiced. But in the absence of any suitable international institutions individual nations sometimes believed themselves to be acting in the name of the non-existent — or at any rate non-operative — community. Theodore Roosevelt told the Congress that

> Chronic wrongdoing, or an impotence which results in a general lessening of the ties of civilized society, may in America, as elsewhere, ultimately require intervention by some civilized nation, and in the Western Hemisphere the adherence of the United States, however reluctantly, in flagrant cases of such wrongdoing or impotence, to the exercise of an international police power.[2]

[1] Cited by Arthur Larson in *When Nations Disagree* (Louisiana State University Press, 1961) p. 209.

[2] House Documents (4780), 58th Congress, 3rd Session, No. 1, p. XLI-II. Cited by Franz B. Gross, "The U.S. National Interest and the UN," *Orbis*, Summer 1963, pp. 369-370.

The closest thing to a genuine international force the world saw before the UN era was the 3300-man, four-nation force set up by the League of Nations to supervise the 1934 Saar Plebiscite.

The UN Charter, with its limited version of an "international police power," represented a shift in the legalistic, pacifistic, even millenial thinking that characterized the peace movement of the early 20th century. Whatever other misguided notions about the international political process the Charter may have embodied, it did incorporate some fresh insights into the relationship between peacekeeping and military power, insights the League of Nations Covenant had largely neglected in its preoccupation with disarmament. The 1945 Charter said a modest "Yes, but —" to disarmament. At the time it seemed sophisticated indeed in its acceptance of the legitimized role of force in support of the Charter principles.

The overwhelming obstacle this time was, we now know so well, the Charter's expectation of great-power collaboration in keeping the peace, combining elements of their military establishments on call of the Security Council for enforcement purposes. We have learned to live with the disparity between that hope and the reemergent reality of massive political warfare among the great-power blocs. The "Article 43 forces" were never placed at the disposal of the Security Council because such an act would have had to rest on a consensus that did not exist. From the onset there was thus not the single indispensable basis for the employment by the UN of significant force. It would have taken a politically cohesive directing body whose collective decisions would furnish the "law" in whose name the forces would act. (When the same organization, resting on the same fragments of true community, was required to deal with the Congo as though such an integrated system existed in fact, the complications were evident.)

It is generally supposed that if the superpowers had shared a common view of the established order in 1945 and had been prepared to defend outrages against it, the system would have worked. But one may fairly suspect that, even in such an unlikely event, the relationship between disarmament and international forces, between peacekeeping and enforcement, and between national sovereignty and multilateral power would still have been insufficiently understood — as it is today

— to the detriment of clear national policy and sensible international negotiations on the subject.

But that is in the realm of might-have-been. As it was, the Soviet leadership in the mid-1940's saw in the very notion of an international force in a predominantly non-Communist world a *prima facie* threat. There is evidence that this view still persists relatively unchanged. It is also likely that the fears of the hostile and sullen Communist minority of 1946 were magnified by the position taken by United States representatives in the UN Military Staff Committee which met in 1946 to negotiate the levels for the promised Article 43 forces. Even by contrast with its closest allies the United States seemed to be asking for an inordinately large force (e.g. 3,800 planes against the 1,200 proposed by the United Kingdom and France; 90 submarines against 12; 84 destroyers against 24).[3]

According to one observer these grandiose U.S. demands, coupled with the simultaneous American attack on the veto power, made the effort fruitless, particularly when the U.S. representative refused to discuss the forces question in conjunction with disarmament.[4] This is not to blame the collapse of Article 43 on the United States. It is to indicate the breadth of the gap that separated the two sides.

As virtually everybody knows, "UN forces" of one sort or another have been used in ten or so major postwar crises, and the statistics tell of both the modesty of scale of effort and the rather marvellous growth of wide-ranging peacekeeping activities. Fifteen countries contributed troops to the Korean action. Twenty-four offered units to the UN Emergency Force created in 1956 to enforce the ceasefire following the Suez invasion, and ten were finally accepted, supplying an average of one 500-man battalion apiece. Around 600 observers patrolled the Lebanese-Syrian border in 1958, with thirty observers of ten nationalities doing the same in Kashmir. One hundred and fifty members of UN Truce teams observed the Palestine War armistice. Twenty-nine countries offered troops to the ONUC force; at its peak strength of 19,000 or so in early 1963 ONUC contained elements from ten coun-

[3] *UN Security Council Official Records*, Second Year, No. 50, 149th Mtg. (June 30, 1947), p. 1177.

[4] Bernhard Bechhoefer, *Postwar Negotiations for Arms Control* (Washington: Brookings Institution, 1961), pp. 97, 98.

tries — predominantly African — plus supporting personnel from ten others. The UN Security Force in West New Guinea in 1962 consisted of 1,485 Pakistani ground forces and a small U.S. and Canadian air and sea support component. Two hundred observers served in Yemen in 1963. Panama, Angola, South Africa — the list may not be at all finished.

In attempting to approach systematically the problem of international forces one confronts an extraordinarily varied range of greater-than-national forces and their possible missions. If for the sake of analysis one accepts the concept of a continuum (without necessarily believing that one level will automatically lead to the next), the scale includes significant intermediate levels between the extremes of "the man with the binoculars" along the road between Damascus and Beirut, or in Kashmir or Yemen, and a world force possessing that paramount attribute of political authority, a relative monopoly of the means of physical coercion — Tennyson's "airy navies" in UN blue, as it were.

The very sharpness of the dividing lines on our hypothetical scale of international forces is the crucial point. For the chief threshold lies between the familiar kind of world of nation-states, each disposing of armed forces and subject only in limited ways to a higher law, and that very different political never-never land in which genuine power is centered in a supranational authority.

If one looks closely at the spectrum of international forces, six basic types seem to emerge: (1) the type or types that one thinks of as likely and politically feasible today; (2) a force organized on regional rather than global principles; (3) a stand-by UN observation and patrol-type force; (4) a standing UN observation and patrol-type force; (5) a stand-by fighting force; and (6) a standing fighting force. The last one can be divided into two basic sub-types: (a) a great-power contributed force with veto — an extension of what was put in the UN Charter in 1945 under Article 43; and (b) a force recruited from all sources, with no great-power veto. The last one is the model of the force that represents a true monopoly of coercive power in the hands of a central authority, i.e. world government. One can of course think of almost infinite variations on each basic model. And one can discern even more clearly both the salient thresholds and the discontinuities that represent sharp breaks with both past and present.

Some additional light is cast by considering the missions for which an international force might be designed, remaining attentive to the kinds of missions that represent the familiar and those calling for a revolutionary transformation in power and politics. Here also there is a range from minor to major, from cheap to expensive, from uncontroversial to bitterly contested.

(1) At the bottom of the scale are what can be called guard duties — policing the UN buildings and meeting rooms, including installations in the field; or bodyguard to the Secretary General (UN Field Service personnel so served in Leopoldville, and a personal guard was killed with Dag Hammarskjöld).

(2) Next is the function of observation and patrol. The man with the binoculars is a uniquely valuable asset, often worth as much as a platoon of infantry; but he is usable only when conflict has been suspended or stopped by agreement of the parties (or never really broke out). Here is the "eye-balling" task exemplified by the lonely sentries on the postwar border watches in Northern Greece, Palestine, Kashmir, Lebanon; the "presences" so useful for their psychological value, as in Laos and Jordan, and perhaps Cyprus and, some day, Berlin.

(3) Next is more militant enforcement of ceasefires and truces, for keeping the armed parties apart (but with far less actual military power than would be needed if they resumed hostilities). Here is the Palestine of 1949, Suez of 1956, and the Yemen effort commencing in June, 1963. Cyprus and Malaysia are good candidates here, too.

(4) Another brand of mission is internal policing and order-keeping, as in the Congo. It is guaranteed to be controversial because of inescapable involvement in internal partisan politics. And it is likely to keep the United Nations in turmoil because of great-power differences that are inevitable when the West seeks order and the East fosters chaos. East Africa and South Africa may be on this list.

At this point again an important threshold is crossed. For from (5) on, the missions involve combat for an international force. At the more modest end of this scale are internal disorder and civil war, and so far the powers, wisely or not, have not wished to entrust to the United Nations situations such as Laos in its acute phase or Vietnam. The scale ascends through the familiar categories of limited conventional wars to local nuclear and, eventually world-wide, strategic war. From the standpoint of political analysis it is axiomatic that the mission for an international military force must conform to the kind of political order that exists.[5]

[5] Stanley Hoffmann considers in detail in his chapter in Part Two the crucial relationship between mission and political context.

Two

WORLD FORCE AND WORLD ORDER

Western diplomacy increasingly insists upon a close connection between disarmament and an international military force sufficient eventually to enforce with coercive power the will of an as yet unspecified central authority.

In February 1960 the American policy was established when, as we have noted, the then Secretary of State Christian Herter responded to Khrushchev's call the previous fall for "general and complete disarmament." Mr. Herter first sought to place disarmament in the setting of a "more stable military environment." This goal called, he asserted, for measures to control two types of dangers of a continuing arms race: the danger of surprise attack, and the promiscuous spread of nuclear weapons. These initial arms-control measures would pave the way to "progressive, gradual, and balanced reductions" in national military forces. With the military environment thus stabilized, a "second stage of general disarmament" would be approached. Here the crucial political and institutional corollary to "GCD" emerges, and it is worth quoting in full:

Our objective in this second stage should be twofold:

First, to create certain universally accepted rules of law which, if followed, would prevent all nations from attacking other nations. Such rules of law should be backed by a world court and by effective means of enforcement — that is, by international armed force.

Second, to reduce national armed forces, under safeguarded and verified arrangements, to the point where no single nation or group of na-

tions could effectively oppose this enforcement of international law by
international machinery.[1]

In the fall of 1961 the United States and the Soviet Union undertook bilateral negotiations whose result, considered quite extraordinary
at the time, was a "Joint Statement of Agreed Principles for Disarmament Negotiations" which was circulated to all UN Members on
September 20, 1961. The relevant sections for our purposes were these:

> 2. The programme for general and complete disarmament shall ensure
> that States will have at their disposal only those non-nuclear ar-
> maments, forces, facilities, and establishments as are agreed to be
> necessary to maintain internal order and protect the personal security
> of citizens; and that States shall support and provide agreed manpower
> for a United Nations peace force.
> 7. Progress in disarmament should be accompanied by measures to
> strengthen institutions for maintaining peace and the settlement of
> international disputes by peaceful means. During and after the imple-
> mentation of the programme of general and complete disarmament,
> there should be taken, in accordance with the principles of the United
> Nations Charter, the necessary measures to maintain international
> peace and security, including the obligation of States to place at the
> disposal of the United Nations agreed manpower necessary for an
> international peace force to be equipped with agreed types of arma-
> ments. Arrangements for the use of this force should ensure that the
> United Nations can effectively deter or suppress any threat of use of
> arms in violation of the purposes and principles of the United Nations.[2]

That fall the United States submitted its own proposal for "General
and Complete Disarmament" to the UN Assembly. In it were these
provisions for the contemplated three stages of disarmament.

> A. States shall develop arrangements in Stage I for the establish-
> ment in Stage II of a United Nations peace force.
> B. During Stage II, States shall develop further the peacekeeping
> processes of the United Nations, to the end that the United
> Nations can effectively in Stage III deter or suppress any threat or
> use of force in violation of the purposes and principles of the
> United Nations:
> (a) States shall agree upon strengthening the structure, authority,

[1] Address to the National Press Club at Washington, D.C. on February 18, 1960.
Department of State Bulletin, March 7, 1960, p. 357.
[2] UN Document A/4879, 20 September 1961.

and operation of the United Nations so as to assure that the United Nations will be able effectively to protect States against threats to or breaches of the peace.

(b) The United Nations peace force shall be established and progressively strengthened.

C. In Stage III, progressive controlled disarmament and continuously developing principles and procedures of international law would proceed to a point where no State would have the military power to challenge the progressively strengthened United Nations Peace Force and all international disputes would be settled according to the agreed principles of international conduct.

The progressive steps to be taken during the final phase of the disarmament programme would be directed toward the attainment of a world in which:

(a) States would retain only those forces, non-nuclear armaments, and establishments required for the purpose of maintaining internal order; they would also support and provide agreed manpower for a United Nations Peace Force.

(b) The United Nations Peace Force, equipped with agreed types and quantities of armaments, would be fully functioning.

(c) The manufacture of armaments would be prohibited except for those of agreed types and quantities to be used by the United Nations Peace Force and those required to maintain internal order. All other armaments would be destroyed or converted to peaceful purposes.

(d) The peacekeeping capabilities of the United Nations would be sufficiently strong and the obligations of all States under such arrangements sufficiently far-reaching as to assure peace and the just settlement of differences in a disarmed world.[3]

When subsequently at Geneva the United States presented a treaty outline in detail, the same themes carried over. The outline specified a "United Nations Peace Force, which would be equipped with agreed types of armaments and would be supplied agreed manpower by states, would be progressively strengthened until, in Stage III, it would be fully capable of insuring international security in a disarmed world."

In detail, under Stage I the parties would agree on these measures:

(a) Examination of the experience of the United Nations leading to a further strengthening of United Nations forces for keeping the peace.

[3] *Department of State Bulletin*, October 16, 1961, pp. 653, 654.

(b) Examination of the feasibility of concluding promptly the agreements envisaged in Article 43 of the United Nations Charter.

(c) Conclusion of an agreement for the establishment of a United Nations Peace Force in Stage II, including definitions of its purpose, mission, composition and strength, disposition, command and control, training, logistical support, financing, equipment and armaments.

Under "United Nations Peace Force" in the Stage II section of the plan:

> The United Nations Peace Force to be established as the result of the agreement reached during Stage I would come into being within the first year of Stage II and would be progressively strengthened during Stage II.

And under Stage III,

> The Parties to the Treaty would progressively strengthen the United Nations Peace Force established in Stage II until it had sufficient armed forces and armaments so that no state could challenge it.[4]

Since Secretary Herter's speech, there has been little public exposition or exegesis by government officials of the official policy toward international forces in a disarming or disarmed world. Such references as there have been are typically in the context of modest urgings that the United Nations develop further its present capabilities for peacekeeping. One of the rare references to the longer-range proposal was made by Assistant Secretary of State Cleveland in 1962:

> At a later stage a larger international peace force with some experience behind it might be able to cope with actual hostilities between well-armed secondary powers.
>
> Only in the final and faraway stage of general and complete disarmament could an international force interpose itself in a conflict between great powers. But by making it more difficult for brush fires to break out, and by reducing the temptation for big powers to intervene when brush fires do break out, even a small, highly mobile police force could render more unlikely the escalation of little wars into big ones.[5]

---

[4] *Blueprint for the Peace Race*, USACDA Publication 4, General Series 3, May, 1962.

[5] Press release 160, March 12, 1962, see *Department of State Bulletin*, April 9, 1962.

The Western commitment is thus to some a form of world government, however ill-formed the notions of some of those pressing this policy. But the implications of such a policy are so grave and far-reaching that they require the most searching scrutiny, leading either to an informed opinion that would support the policy if it ever became operative, or to scrapping the present policy if upon analysis it is untenable.

The matter has been faced before in lesser form. The 1946 United States plan for the international control of atomic energy assigned the proposed international agency managerial control or ownership of "all atomic energy activities potentially dangerous to world security," plus "power to control, inspect, and license all other atomic activities." To carry this out would have required extraordinary powers at the center. But it was still some distance from even the Baruch Plan to the implications of political control of the world as a whole in present American disarmament proposals. Throughout the postwar negotiating period, even when programs were advanced for drastic reduction and limitation of armaments, there is no record of any concrete suggestion or even discussion of a supranational political organization that would exercise effective control in the world.

The current proposals for international peace forces backed by governmental-type powers, with all their unmistakable implications of an authentic world order, may not be taken seriously by many. Indeed, the usual responses to the idea on the part of politically sophisticated people are so invariably negative that the only wonder is that the United States thought it would make good propaganda to enunciate it. Some who are skeptical about disarmament will accept the troublesome political and institutional corollaries on the ground that "if you can believe that, you can believe anything."

But if one believes that significant moderation of the arms race is far too serious a matter to consign to a utopian paradise in which modern history reaches an end and a completely new political universe is wished into being, one will not accept such glib dialectics. It is worth while for three reasons to subject our proposals to serious analysis. On policy grounds it would be well to spell out with greater precision, if only for our own better understanding, that to which this country has committed itself. On grounds of sound scholarship it may be worthwhile to apply analytical methods to a problem commonly approached on the basis of hunch alone. (Finally, there is always the possibility that sophisticated people will turn out to have been wrong.)

What, in the highly unlikely event that United States disarmament proposals and, consequently, an effective world force were accepted, might it look like?[6]

To accomplish its mission, the international force, compounded appropriately of ground, sea, air, and outer-space elements, would have to consist of at least 500,000 men, recruited individually and wearing the international uniform. It would control a nuclear force consisting of 50-100 mixed land-mobile and undersea missiles averaging 1 megaton per weapon. The force would be stationed and deployed in territorial enclaves equitably allocated among continents and areas for minimum temptation and likelihood of seizure by any single nation. Ten air-transportable divisions trained for vertical envelopment, armed with the latest field weapons (including a modest supply of tactical nuclear weapons), and provided with transport and communications facilities should be able to counter an aggressive thrust across one nation's borders of the dimension likely under the circumstances. Beyond that, the strategic nuclear deterrent in the hands of the central authority would presumably deter conventional attack on a massive scale in the same fashion as in American hands it presumably deterred Soviet conventional aggression in Europe in the late 1940's and early 1950's. (The latter analogy rests of course on an unproved hypothesis, as does the whole doctrine of massive retaliation associated with preponderance in nuclear weapons.) We must also assume the force's ability to deal with guerrilla activities, but without high confidence.

It is obvious that an international force would be decreasingly capable of coping with higher levels of aggression involving several countries up to a point describable as true international civil war. It should, however, be understood that the choice is not between an international system incapable of coping with important threats and one that can deal successfully with every contingency in the spectrum. At one end of the scale the present international system has some capacity to cope even with Communist menaces. At the other end of the scale we can

---

[6] Thomas C. Schelling systematically explores the possible appearance, composition, and strategic problems of such a force in his essay in Part Two.

guess that there would be finite limits to the capacity of a supranational system to handle such maximum challenges as international civil war. A civil war, domestic or international, can gather such force as to end the preponderance at the center. The hypothetical system, while its capacities go significantly beyond those presently in sight, remains subject to the basic laws of political life.

What is the basis for the apportionment of forces that I have suggested between center and parts? Here strategic analysis supplies tentative answers.

Effective capacity to fulfill its mission connotes a relative monopoly of political power, accompanied by preponderant military force, at the center of the system. The word "relative" indicates that the power relationship between the center and the parts is one of degree. Some examples illustrate the equation. In the United States the people have the constitutional right to "keep and bear arms"; the government monopoly is legally abridged to this extent. In the Congo Republic during the most politically disturbed period the central army was outnumbered by the provincial forces, putting into question the existence of effective central rule. In Kuomintang China the military power of the national government was often balanced by the military power of the warlords; the writ of the government hence could not extend uniformly through the country. Thus under a supranational government the degrees of relative power as between center and parts can occupy a wide range. The most logical combination of forces poses at once the question of nuclear weapons. One fundamental consideration seems overriding.

Modern science and technology are essentially irreversible. They can perhaps be slowed down or even stopped either by some universal catastrophe or under a disarmament agreement that curtails the intensive allocation of economic and human resources to armaments. But the processes of fission and fusion and the design of engines of delivery cannot be unlearned. Moreover, assuming as we must that atomic power may become economical and fusion power — when harnessed — even more so, under total disarmament all of these technologies will be practiced in their peaceable aspects. Thus, however comprehensive the disarmament agreements, however much political power is transferred to a world government, and even if no significant amount of manpower is actually working on nuclear, chemical, and bacteriological weapons or on constructing military aircraft, ships, rockets, or space vehicles, there will always remain implicit in technically advanced societies the capacity to turn again to the production and fabrication of engines of war, probably with fair rapidity.

The very logic of effectiveness requires placing in the hands of the central authority military forces adequate to deal with breaches of the peace and acts of aggression through whatever means are necessary to preserve a preponderance of power at the center, even against the contingency of clandestine production of nuclear weapons. The conclusion is inescapable that the central authority, in addition to its conventional military capacity, will have to offset the inherent possibility of evasion by being equipped with nuclear weapons along with delivery systems adequate to deter any reasonable expectation of clandestine violation and consequent attempt to destabilize or even destroy the new system.

It can be seen that even under a radically designed system of authority in a disarmed world the problem of deterrence would persist, including some of the features that characterize it today. The situation facing the central authority would not be very different from that confronting the United States in its need to be equipped with forces, both conventional and nuclear, adequate to deter any likely combination of hostile forces. Indeed, this is the problem inside any society. But the special feature in the new situation would be an element of profound uncertainty. Today national military forces are designed to deter known quantities or qualities of war-making capability in the arsenals of other nations. But our postulated regime, even with a good inspection system, would be to a degree uncertain whether nuclear weapons were hidden or being secretly made, or some highly potent bacteriological agent being developed in an isolated laboratory, or some potentially commanding weapon secreted illicitly in the payload of a communication, weather, navigation, or other type of satellite. These possibilities, however statistically improbable, would pose anew the problem of deterrence in a different calculus, both for the general authority and for individual countries such as the United States in making their own calculations.

If this sort of world ever comes into being, a threshold will have been crossed for the United States, as well as for the other countries, from one historical condition to another profoundly different one. However many stages it passes through, however tacit or explicit the labels, however gradual or violent the process, there is a Rubicon that divides the Tuscany of basically untrammeled national sovereignty from the Gaul of meaningful supranational authority. Nothing could be more dangerous to sound thinking and planning than to elide this fundamental truth. By whatever process and under whatever name, the agency that is to control world affairs effectively requires in the most important ways the design customarily associated with government. A central authority with effective powers in the realms of disarmament and the settlement of international disputes, and with the capacity to deal with breaches of the peace and acts of aggression, and above all in possession of the most vital attribute of government — a preponderance of military power — is a government, however limited. To grasp the profound difficulty in securing American acceptance of this sweeping rearrangement of things, one only needs to recall that ratification of the UN Charter by the United States Senate was conditioned on having the veto power. Other Western nations such as France are more nationalistic than we. And the nationalist revolution in its purest form is only now sweeping the world south of the equator.

Even if American acquiescence in the implications of its own proposals could be assumed, it is surely unsafe to make the further assumption that the ideological and power struggle between communism and the West will not continue indefinitely. This throws into question any program requiring that both sides subordinate themselves, their power, and their ambitions to a supranational authority. That is of course the central dilemma of world politics today, and it applies with ultimate force to the proposition of world government. The logical trap is completed with the familiar paradox: given an unabated continuation of Communist dynamism, the subordination of states to a true world government appears impossible; but if the Communist dynamic were greatly abated, the West might well lose whatever incentive it has for world government.

If, to test our hypothesis further, we assume that the West would favor a world under the effective control of the United Nations, the operative question is then how to transform and tame the forces of communism. Such a transformation is theoretically possible, but only under two conditions. The first is that through evolutionary processes Communist doctrine becomes drained of its messianic quality, foregoes its imperialistic ambitions, and comes to accept the notion of a higher authority — a notion totally irreconcilable with its tenets. The other condition, which puts the possibility within a more foreseeable time span, is a crisis, a war, or a brink-of-war situation so grave or commonly menacing that deeply rooted attitudes and practices are sufficiently shaken to open up the possibility of a revolution in world political arrangements.

If we can for the sake of analysis make the further assumption that one or the other of these conditions has come about and that the Communists — both Occidental and Oriental — have consequently been brought to a significant mitigation of the force of their doctrine, what kind of political environment could then be foreseen?

Remember, we are assuming a world in which relations between East and West are characterized by significantly higher degrees of mutual trust, internationalist spirit, and unaggressiveness. But there is little in history to justify the belief that without the Communist threat in its present form the world political environment would be inherently stable. We have postulated by necessity a willing acceptance of limited world government by the great powers. We then have to postulate further either its acceptance by or imposition on all other nations.

This at once sets up future instabilities. Today the prime foci of instability are actually in third areas and center on economic disparities and nationalistic strivings for independence, factors which Soviet and Chinese policies purposefully exploit. There is no reason to assume the disappearance under limited world government of the dynamic factors — the intergroup competitions, the racial and ethnic tensions, and the economic disparities — that permeate human history and create the conditions for political upheaval. History, short of catastrophe, is not discontinuous. To paraphrase von Clausewitz, limited world government may be regarded, at least in part, as a form of international conflict carried on under institutional arrangements other than unlimited state sovereignty. Thus as international stability is restored under benign forms of world order, detailed disputes of a chronic or secondary nature can be confidently expected to re-emerge. The new regime will then be faced with a continuous agenda of problems stemming from political ambition, inequalities, avarice, irrational behavior, the inhumanity of man to man, and the use or threat of violence to achieve political or social ends. This prospect can be ruled out only by the untenable assumption that history will have run its course and an end put to its dynamic, refractory, and otherwise troublesome qualities. Thus a world government, even if it could be created, would be subject to continuing pressures, the most exigent of which could lead to civil war on an international scale.

The crucial difficulty then is to ensure that no large-scale civil war can take place to test the "union," for war on a major scale would gravely threaten the system. It would revive the production and, given the instability of such a situation, the probable use of weapons of mass destruction. In any event such a war would be no more tolerable under a world government than it would be today, and for precisely the same humanitarian, social, and economic reasons.

But here the model runs into one of history's most vexing dilemmas. War is the traditional means for changing the international *status quo* in the absence of effective provisions for peaceful change. When war is not possible — and when no such provisions exist — the traditional consequence is injustice, which in turn breeds even more ungovernable instabilities and ensuing violence. Perhaps the most sobering consideration about world government is the nightmare prospect of world order at the price of world tyranny — a kind of global Holy Alliance to preserve the *status quo*. Flexibility and capacity to adapt to change in time and with foresight become absolute imperatives in view of the probable nuclear monopoly in the hands of the central authority.

To achieve the necessary viability and durability, then, the world authority must solve the problem that has pervaded all modern history, and accommodate the dynamic forces making for change without allowing them to lead to war. Specifically the system must, through its legislative action, its executive implementation, and its judicial interpretation, allow for changes in fact, in law, and in the system itself. Without a genuine breakthrough in this realm of peaceful change in which man has by and large so far failed, with persistently tragic results, nothing else about the world order has any meaning in terms of either the efficacy of the system or the values by which we would wish to continue to live.

Even allowing that such a breakthrough were possible, the chances of conflict over the one legitimate stock of decisive weapons that would remain make us think twice about centralizing such power. To do so would contradict everything we have learned since Montesquieu about diffusion and balance of power, plural centers of action, and multiple and diverse components of strength. It would make possible tyranny at the hands of a world force legitimately possessing a relative monopoly of the means of physical coercion. Such tyranny on a world scale could make local tyrannies look relatively desirable. One can only conclude that nuclear weapons are necessary to the very concept of world police power but too dangerous to entrust to an authority not characterized by diffused power, pluralism in the chief forces of society, and a multiple balancing of interests. For the single most vital decision about international forces in a disarming world would concern the location, management, control, accessibility, and manning of powerful weapons. NATO's problems in the 1960's of "fifteen fingers on the trigger" pales into comparative insignificance alongside the prospect of 120 or so nations sharing control of a world force so equipped.

In directing a series of political-military simulations designed to illuminate some problems involving international forces[7] the author was struck by another problem of weapons technology that needs to be thought of in considering the relation between disarmament and peace forces. It is likely that the formulas proposed by the great powers for across-the-board disarmament will have the side effect of destroying certain local power balances, such as those involving Israel, South Korea, Turkey, or Iran, all of which today maintain armed forces high in proportion to population in order to balance far more populous hostile neighbors. To impose in such special situations a formula of "forces for internal security only," as present Western disarmament plans envisage in "Stage III," might tempt the country in question to seek "equalizers" in the form of unconventional biological, chemical, or radiological warfare capabilities.

Moreover, the logic applies equally to the broader picture. If a small Israel would feel the need of such "technological equalizers" to stand

---

[7] See Lincoln P. Bloomfield and Barton Whaley, "The Political-Military Exercise: A Progress Report" (Cambridge, Massachusetts: Massachusetts Institute of Technology, Center for International Studies, August 16, 1963).

off far more populous neighbors, or Turkey, Iran, or Korea to hold back a traditionally voracious Russia or China, what about a modest-sized international constabulary faced with the manpower potential of teeming millions in every continent? At the least, planning for such a constabulary should consider novel technical means to keep the peace, techniques aimed at offsetting the danger of overwhelming hostile ground strength. A prime target of the international peace forces, in other words, would be not cities but the human system.

Just as a smaller NATO force sought to equalize larger Soviet forces in Europe in the 1950's by developing a tactical nuclear capability, so an international force in a disarmed world would need exotic forms of protection against its likely adversary — unfavorable numbers. Nerve gases, tranquillizer dart guns, psychochemicals, and other temporarily disabling or paralyzing organic agents all may be high in the armorarium of an international police. They pose for the scientist and weapons designer a rather special set of requirements which he should begin to take seriously. For at least arguably such agents of persuasion and coercion would be likely to do the job in more appropriate and humane ways than more conventional military weapons whose efficient use depends upon the existence of the very kind of military targets that disarmament planners assure us will be outlawed.

Three

INTERNATIONAL FORCE IN A DISARMING –
BUT REVOLUTIONARY – WORLD

So far we have been discussing international force in its ultimate meaning — as the expression of coercive power in a world order characterized by total disarmament, the rule of law, and centralized political authority.

But general disarmament plans, like weapons of mass destruction, supply excessive solutions to problems, and, like those weapons, they tend to leave unanswered many highly pertinent questions about lesser conflicts, low-level disorders, ambiguous enemies, and local policing jobs. By and large, strategic planners have come to recognize this weakness in military doctrines, but it is not certain that the planners of general and complete disarmament (GCD) yet recognize that a blueprint geared to the deliberate violation, the great war, the two superstates in hostile confrontation, may turn out to be quite irrelevant to the real problems of a disarmed or even semi-disarmed world. At best such a blueprint is bound to be deficient until it comes to grips with disorders other than classic open encounters of two states — that is, with the painfully familiar gamut ranging from civil war fomented in a great state by outside agents to the purely internal breakdown of law and order in a small state.

The point is not whether these problems are more numerous or more likely to occur than classic open interstate conflict. It should be enough to recognize the quality of the age we live in. It is revolutionary in two literal senses. One is the sense of communism's social, economic, and political assault on the established order. The other sense is the continuing revolt of the emerging nations against foreign domination (real or imagined) before, during, and in many cases after independence. In a more figurative sense the future, like the present, will be revolutionary: virtually everything is likely to change — mortality, health, weapons, travel, communication, art, knowledge, the cosmos, and, *ex hypothesi,* political ideas. Specific revolutions may ebb and flow. But this truly systemic revolution (if I may borrow the phrase from Messrs. Strausz-Hupé and Kintner) is guaranteed to keep the political world dynamic through the foreseeable future. Disarmament planning which fails to take account of this dynamism does so at its peril.

A general disarmament agreement might well have a profound effect on the cold war. My own views have been criticized by some as overly pessimistic for failing to assume a dramatic transformation in East-West relations in an atmosphere of disarmament. But even if there is such transformation in East-West relationships, what the critics of excessive "realism" cannot legitimately assert is that GCD is also bound similarly to transform the range of lesser conflicts and disorders, at least for a very long time to come. The instabilities we must plan to live with are bred of historical conflicts, racial discrimination, economic disparity, and other deep-seated political and social factors, all of them producers of revolutionary situations with which any society, large or small, armed or disarmed, must cope.

To point to this phenomenon is not necessarily to decry it. But we should be clear about the special problems of peacekeeping it brings. Some of the changes we can foresee in both East-West and North-South conflicts are likely to be beneficial and ultimately favorable to a peaceful world. When the Portuguese colonies, the sheikdoms in the Persian Gulf, and the island dependencies in the Pacific finally find their ultimate political status, the instability caused by colonial rebellions will cease. Such present candidates for revolution and disorder in the form of pre-independence conflict as Angola may then become *status quo* powers. But one of the accompaniments of decolonization is the development of situations in which the enemy is within, and the problem of internal disorder may or may not be an improvement over colonial antagonisms from the international community's standpoint. (I happen to believe it is, but the remedial chore for the community may be even more difficult.)

By the some token the Messianic quality may drain out of Soviet world policy as affluence and concern with mass consumption make the revolutionary doctrine increasingly inappropriate. Disarmament may accelerate this process. But while this is happening, new opportunities may open for the Soviet-dominated peoples in Eastern Europe and Soviet Asia to assert their independence — a process that might be extraordinarily dangerous and bloody as well as gratifying to all free men.

The third category of potential disorder is endemic and not likely to be affected by disarmament. There is nothing in the historical record to suggest that the incidence of insurgencies, civil wars, and other local instabilities will significantly diminish merely because the great powers have agreed to restrict their strategic power. On the contrary, in such a situation the importance of local instabilities would doubtlessly increase until eventually it became the chief object of concern to the international community.

And of course there is always China to confound future calculations. If the Soviet world program were to pull in its horns, we can be confident of the dynamic and destabilizing quality of Chinese policy even if China were a party to an arms limitation agreement.

For these various reasons we can assume that local instability will be a crucial problem in a disarming world; that in that world only some aspects of the world situation will be affected by the agreement while others will remain unchanged. These two layers of reality are made vivid if we use the image of a world map overlaid with cellophane of the sort on which military planners chart their dispositions with a grease pencil. The underlying reality is that of the world map. It is the real world of geography, of national territory, of people, of states. All of these have their pasts, their ethnic characteristics and racial memories, minority relationships, national hopes and fears, geographic neighbors, and historical relationships with those neighbors and with other countries. This map remains essentially unchanged even if one assumes the signing of a treaty on GCD and, beyond that, the creation of an international military force to keep the peace.

The other layer — the plastic overlay, so to speak — represents those changes in the military and strategic situation created by an agreement on disarmament, along with the international order that accompanies it. The overlay does not and cannot replace the map, as some utopian thinkers would have us believe. To some extent it imposes new conditions on the map, particularly in terms of the strategic "reach" of great powers such as the United States and the Soviet Union. At a minimum, GCD implies alterations within the coalitions that now confront each other, specifically in the relations between the United States and Europe, and undoubtedly in the relations within the Communist bloc. Most importantly, whatever the political overlay when GCD is agreed to, it would undoubtedly alter in presently unforeseeable ways as the program goes successfully from one stage to another of disarmament.

For the vast majority of countries and peoples, however, in the first stages of GCD the overlay would remain essentially blank. For them reality would continue to be the land, the people, the racial memory, the boundary with the neighbor, rather than the shift in the military environment affecting first of all the nuclear powers. For three out of four human beings the only change GCD will bring will be in the mathematical chances that their particular country would be involved in a great-power war, that they as individuals would be killed or maimed in such a war, or that their descendants would undergo genetic mutations as a consequence of atmospheric radioactivity. It may be argued that GCD would bring untold economic benefits to the peoples of underdeveloped countries as a result of savings, and it is to be devoutly hoped that the $130 billion or so spent today on the arms race would be diverted in part at least to their crying needs. But one cannot automatically assume that here, and if one did, it would not significantly alter all of the projections of political instability that concern us here.

LOCAL INSTABILITY AS A FACTOR IN WORLD POLITICS

In trying to estimate the extent to which local instability would be a significant factor under GCD and to explore the means of dealing with it through an international force — including the paramount question of political control of such forces in this kind of situation — history must be our primary guide.

In what might be called the UN era — the period from 1945 through at least the middle 1960's — the armed world could be regarded as existing on two levels. In terms of the detailed agenda of international business, particularly as the United Nations was required to deal with it, the fundamental level of reality involved first of all the breakup of Western colonial empires and the substitution of native leadership for the white European rulers of the past. The "overlay" of the period was the cold war and the threat of widespread annihilation growing out of the nature of strategic weapons. Berlin, Korea, and Cuba were problems of the very first importance. But quantitatively the great majority of situations with which the international community, such as it was, had to deal were to be found on the underlying map rather than on the overlay.

The following tables, not intended to be exhaustive, illustrate some of the kinds of local disorder and governmental collapse in the "UN era":

Basically Internal [1]

The abortive uprising in East Germany, June 1953.
The three-cornered civil war between the British, Greek, and Turkish nationalities in Cyprus, 1954-1959, and again in 1964.
The Algerian Civil War from the early 1950's to 1962.
The Hungarian revolt against Soviet rule, 1956.
The overthrow of the monarchy and the Nuri government in Iraq, 1958, and of its successor in 1963.
The Castro revolution in Cuba against the Batista regime, 1959; i.e. the phase of purely internal revolt.
The military mutinies in East Africa, 1964.

This first category of "Basically Internal" disorders includes situations where outside influences may have been present but were not highly significant. In the following category the instability is still predominantly internal but is significantly affected by outside power,

---

[1] Earlier historical examples which are provocative because of their special circumstances might include the Russian Revolution, which led to Allied intervention in Northern Russia in 1918 when British, French, and American troops occupied Murmansk and Archangel until 1919 for a variety of muddled reasons, one of which, simply stated, was the belief that a dangerous vacuum had been created which outside forces must fill. Another had to do with an internal vacuum which was not filled by the outside: Weimar Germany in the last years of the 1920's and the early 1930's.

force, or influence; at a minimum the extent of external involvement is ambiguous.

Externally Abetted Internal Instability

The postwar Communist insurgent movements in both the Philippines (Huks) and Malaya.

The former French Indochina, 1953 to the present — both the earlier Communist-led anticolonial war against the French and the subsequent insurgent activities of the Communists against the legitimate governments of both Laos and South Vietnam.

The American-influenced civil war in Guatemala in 1954, resulting in the replacement of the Arbenz regime by one more to United States taste.

The election campaign in Lebanon in 1958, which included features of religious and minority strife, plus charges, never fully substantiated, of infiltration by subversive Nasserite elements from Syria.

The civil war in Yemen beginning in 1962, with the Arab world split between supporting royalist or republican factions.

In the next category the crucial factor in the internal disorder is extrinsic rather than intrinsic. Opinions can of course differ as to the relative degree of both.

Externally Created or Controlled Internal Instability [2]

The Communist *putsch* which overthrew the Benes government in Czechoslovakia, 1948.

The vacuum created in the Dutch East Indies in 1946-1947 by the withdrawal of Japanese power, the inability of the Dutch to restore fully their own authority, and the victory by the nationalists leading to the creation of the then United States of Indonesia.

The instability of the Hashemite Kingdom of Jordan in the face of Egyptian subversion, hostile propaganda, and indirect aggression, following the withdrawal of British power, and later, its acute instability in 1958 when Iraq collapsed.

---

[2] Two other cases outside the present scope are interesting: the first is the Irish disorders, reaching a peak of violence between the Sinn Fein and Black and Tans during the early 1920's; the other is a case of predicted internal outbreak which did not happen, for reasons which are instructive: the former Belgian trust territory of Ruanda-Urundi, which became two independent states — Rwanda and Burundi — in 1962 to the accompaniment of sharply diminished disorder and tension.

The collapse of the former Belgian Congo on independence in July
1960, to the extent that it was caused by the hasty and unprepared
withdrawal of Belgian power and authority.

The 1961 attempt by Iraq to create a situation in Kuwait that would
force British abandonment and (presumably) Iraqi acquisition.

GREAT-POWER ATTITUDES TOWARD LOCAL STABILITY

An analysis of the role of an international military force in a disarming world runs the risk of being too abstract. Two factors help to make
it concrete. One is the element of continuity in the basic national policies of the major powers. The other is found in a listing of cases for the
future that we can presently foresee.

The policy of the United States in the "UN era" has been the policy
of a rich, stable, and powerful state relatively content with its lot in the
world. Traditionally the policy of such a state is to favor the *status quo*
and oppose revolutionary change, if not all change. Consequently one
of the most difficult questions for American policy is the extent to
which a *status quo* power can act in support of revolutionary or otherwise destabilizing forces.[3] One of the great insights which Americans
are still painfully struggling to master is the extent to which, while
opposing Communist take-over movements, it is possible to support
genuine indigenous movements for national independence, civil liber-
ties, or economic justice even at the cost of temporary disorder. Even
here American policy is gambling that stability will soon follow and
that ungovernable forces of revolution will not be unleashed.[4] Compared to Communist strategy, the central theme of United States policy
is stability. This strategic concern manifests itself in a wide range of
policies, from interest in arms control to support for UN pacification
efforts in the Congo; from the Alliance for Progress to a lamentable
indifference to the future development of American dependencies in
the Pacific; from criticism of Portugal's colonial policy and South
African *apartheid* to pointed reassurances to the Soviet Union in No-

[3] The extent to which that apparent paradox represents reality and the extent to
which it is a caricature is examined in detail in Lincoln P. Bloomfield, *Evolution
or Revolution* (Cambridge: Harvard University Press, 1957).

[4] This thesis is elaborated in detail in Chapter 2, entitled "Strategic Doctrine
and National Interest," in Lincoln P. Bloomfield, *The United Nations and U.S.
Foreign Policy* (Boston: Little Brown and Company, 1960).

vember 1956 that the United States was not about to intervene in the Hungarian revolution.[5]

Taken in the large, it is no less true that both the Soviet Union and Communist China have in varying degrees adopted policies toward the non-Communist world designed to be destabilizing; in a nutshell, this sums up the East-West conflict in action. The avenue toward Soviet control, except in the few cases where parliamentary means seemed promising, has, according to reiterated Communist doctrine and action, lain in disorder, loss of confidence, despair, fear, and finally the collapse in chaos of the "feudal" or "bourgeois" regime, followed by take-over by well-disciplined and well-organized Communist cadres. China, *mutatis mutandis*, has vigorously pursued policies of this sort where it could.

Yet it is also true and equally consistent with Communist doctrine that tactics vary in different situations. The *front populair* is a well-established strategem on the road to power, and so is support for a bourgeois leader—a Nasser, Nkrumah, or Sukarno—who would hopefully prove to be the Kerensky of Egypt, Ghana, or Indonesia. And unquestionably there have been instances where for overriding strategic reasons Soviet policy has supported programs which fit into the Western stabilizing approach — technical assistance, aid to established regimes, unencumbered help with capital formation, even an occasional Austrian settlement or the ones subsequently attempted in the contested nations of former Indochina. The position of both the Kremlin and of the Indian Communist Party toward Peking's obviously destabilizing activities on the Sino-Indian border illustrated the growing gulf between the two interpretations of historic duty, as did Moscow's underplaying of help for Algerian rebels in favor of good relations with General De Gaulle.

There is one realm in which Soviet policy is inordinately conservative and, in the end, biased toward stability. It rests on the unwillingness of present Soviet leadership to accept the consequences of an all-out thermonuclear war. Soviet policy, for example, was profoundly destabilizing toward Egypt in 1955; but it became profoundly stabilizing in

[5] See speech by Secretary of State John Foster Dulles to Dallas Council on World Affairs, October 27, 1956, in *Department of State Bulletin*, November 5, 1956, p. 697.

late 1956 when the Near East threatened to become a serious theater of major-power warfare. Soviet policy was perilously destabilizing toward Cuba in 1959-1962; it turned at least temporarily stabilizing when the Soviet missile gambit was refused by President Kennedy.

If for the sake of our analysis we sum up over-all American and Soviet strategies in oversimplified terms, they might run as follows: With respect to real or potential situations of local instability the United States has been conservative, but its tactics seem to be increasingly "liberal." That is, the paramount American strategy has been one of seeking stability, at times regardless of the cost in image or ideology. But with time (and perhaps increasing wisdom) the United States may be prepared to run risks of short-term instability in order to achieve a satisfactory long-term result. Soviet strategy, in its essence, has been destabilizing, but over time it may be adjusting pragmatically to declining prospects, and compared to Chinese revolutionary *élan* it may seem increasingly "conservative." Above all, in its tactics the Soviet Union may be prepared to sacrifice important targets of opportunity if risks of general war appear too high.

What would be the effect of GCD on these strategies of the superpowers? What would it do to their present and historic approaches to stability and instability? If GCD were to be agreed upon in the foreseeable future, it is obvious that there would be no dearth of situations implying disorder, discomfort, turbulence, and potential danger to the United States, and by the same token offering to Moscow or Peking opportunities of potential vulnerability to Communist manipulation and possibly ultimate control. The most crucial question is whether a lessened fear of war, specifically of local situations escalating into general nuclear war, would alter those basic strategies in significant ways.

A case could be made that United States national policy might change in appreciable ways if general war appeared to be less likely or even less dangerous. Possibly the United States would feel freer to oppose Communist forces on the ground in such places as southeast Asia and central Africa — even in eastern Europe. In other words, at least in theory the policy consequence of GCD might be a new destabilizing American policy vis-à-vis the Communist empire. Similarly, the Soviet Union might adopt different policies if relieved of the fear that all is jeopardized by carrying a high-risk policy too far. Russia might become more sanguine about war, less likely to stay out of Suezes, to retreat from Congos, or to draw back from the ultimate consequences of a Cuba or a Berlin.

But this may not be the correct interpretation of the situation. It rests on the common assumption that in a situation of significant disarmament the United States and the Soviet Union would both be essentially relieved of their fear of war. But would the consequences of war really be less dreadful and unacceptable than at present?

In stage I, when there would remain up to 70 per cent of previous strategic nuclear delivery systems, obviously little would have been done to reduce to relaxed proportions the consequences of nuclear war between the superpowers. In stage II, when there would remain up to 30 per cent, the powers might still deter each other by adopting countercity strategies, aiming their remaining weapons in such a way as to make a nuclear exchange in some ways even less tolerable than with a greater number of weapons aimed in accordance with a counterforce strategy. And in stage III, even though weapons of mass destruction were finally to be eliminated, a new situation might arise involving remarkable vulnerability of both sides to secretly hidden caches of rockets, or to the surprise introduction of new terror weapons (bombs in orbit, military lasers, secretly unfrozen bacteriological or psychochemical weapons previously dry-stored, etc.). In short, the new fear would be of secret or sudden rearmament.[6] In the modern world, as compared with the 1920's, a rearmament race could be catastrophic; certainly the marginal political and strategic effects of any surprise — military or technological — would be more drastic than in a highly-armed world. Perhaps then we cannot be so certain that GCD as presently envisaged would necessarily remove the constraints now limiting both Soviet and American policy. Perhaps it is not so obvious that they would drastically alter the policies they now follow toward situations of local instability.

What can now be said about the approach to instability on the part of the world organization that would come into existence under GCD? What sort of positions would the new international order be likely to take with respect to subversion, indirect aggression, civil war, and

---

[6] This point was well made by Thomas C. Schelling in "The Role of Deterrence in Total Disarmament," *Foreign Affairs*, April 1962, pp. 392-406.

breakdown of internal law and order? Would those positions and the constraints on them be very different from those taken by the same nations in the United Nations at present? Should we assume that with GCD there will have come into existence a genuine international community resting on a real consensus? What is the relation between that degree of consensus and the stake in stability which the international order will have? How would that order express a policy toward instability, particularly if its component parts differed about the merits of individual situations? Would it depend entirely on the great powers? Would it, *per contra*, depend far less on their will and wishes than it does today? These are the questions that go to the meaning of an international military force in a disarming world.

Before turning to the concrete application of that question we shall look briefly at the categories of relevant problems a future disarming world might face and see if the comparisons and contrasts with the past and present shed any light.

LOCAL INSTABILITY UNDER DISARMAMENT — SOME SCENARIOS

The same three categories used earlier to describe present situations of local instability can now be employed for the near and middling future. One reason for these illustrations is to underscore the point that it is not impossible to try to become specific about a disarming world one, two, five years after an agreement is signed. There is no need to lump together into one unpredictable mass stages I, II, and III, and history affords ample evidence that along with unpredictability is a fair amount of continuity. The examples given thus represent evolution out of contemporary revolutionary movements, both Communist and non-Communist.

Basically Internal

(a) The chief cause of internal disorders will doubtless continue to be the multiple and complex revolution of the non-white peoples. The revolution in one of its aspects is against the dominant position of the white European West; in another it is against their own traditional past. From the history of past revolutions one can predict that this particular one may also eventually be at war with the very conditions that gave it birth and with the policies and people that carried the revolution through its perilous early stages.

(b) In the nation-building process we can anticipate that the simultaneous seemingly contradictory processes of fragmentation and unification will continue, with destabilizing results. Africa, with some 2,000 tribal and other local groupings, can be looked to as a continuous source of potential disorders as peoples within essentially artificial state borders search for their nationhood.

(c) Another potential source of internal disorder arises from the peculiar structures of internal rule with which many emerging countries have commenced their independent existence. Where the sinews of government are lacking and the sophisticated institutions of democracy in the hands of inexperienced people may produce a travesty of Western forms and an obstacle to consolidation and administration, only a rash man would predict a future of stability or even viability. When some of the one-party governments lose the momentum of their initial popular support, with no real provision for orderly transfer of power, trouble is certain, particularly if strong military figures emerge.

(d) In the Communist world the same issue of legitimacy makes for maximum instability in a succession crisis, with incalculable results if party discipline should ever fail to force together all contenders for the throne at that moment of maximum danger. We do not need to linger over other revolutionary possibilities within the Communist camp, itself subject to non-Marxist laws of maturation and evolution no less than everyone else.

(e) A new phenomenon of the 1960's may yield a form of future instability whose dimensions we are now only beginning to measure. This is what can only be called neo-imperialism on the part of some of the new countries themselves. Examples are Indonesia's acquisition of West New Guinea, complete with Papuans, and its avaricious "confrontation policy" towards Malaysia, as well as India's retention of Moslem-populated portions of Kashmir. Nkrumah's Pan-Africanism, Nasser's Pan-Arabism, and Ben Bella's dynamic external support programs have imperial overtones. And Communist China's Pan-Asianism is surely in this category as that nation seems to be beginning once again the bloody cycle of imperialism in southeast Asia.

(f) The seeds have already been sown for perhaps the most potentially explosive form of instability and disorder of all — that which may take place in the multiracial societies of southern Africa. Without statemanship, vision, and mutual tolerance of an order that seems totally lacking today the explosion in Southern Rhodesia and the Republic of South Africa is only a matter of time.

(g) Perhaps the chief lesson of history is the impossibility of foretelling in any significant detail the way present trends may unfold. Nevertheless, a partial list of candidates is highly suggestive:

> Succession crisis in the Soviet Union leading to civil war, and possible secession movements in Georgia, Bessarabia, Ukraine, etc.
> Revolution in some part of the Soviet East European empire, most likely East Germany, Hungary, or Poland.
> Disorders in Red China stemming from hunger, discontent, revulsion against Communist rule, or the growth of a new secret movement in the Chinese revolutionary tradition (Boxers, Kuomintang, communism).
> Racial wars within the "white redoubt" — Southern Rhodesia and South Africa.
> Revolution in Portuguese colonies of Angola and Mozambique, in British Guiana, in the United States-administered Trust Territory of the Pacific and American Samoa; nationalist revolutions in South West Africa, West Irian, etc.
> Failure of new countries to resolve their transition to real independence without civil war; disappearance of moderates between extremist wings of parties.

Externally Abetted Internal Disorder

The possibilities here are virtually infinite. Whenever internal disorder real or potential exists in the disarming world, we must assume that the Soviet Union, Communist China, or both will attempt to exploit it to the ultimate benefit of the Communist cause. Such power as is possessed by some of the newer societies will doubtless be employed in their own ideological crusade: *vide* Algeria's offer to the Congolese government in October 1962 of all the troops necessary to crush Katanga;[7] Indonesia's offer to volunteers in several postwar crises, such as Suez; Nasser's policy in the Yemen revolution; Castro's designs on Central and Latin America; and the meddlesome attempts by the

[7] *The New York Times*, October 23, 1962.

Casablanca powers to pursue a separate line in the Congo in 1960-1961 with forces ostensibly contributed to the UN operation.

It is inconceivable that any GCD treaty in the foreseeable future could seriously dispose of the desire, the capacity, or the intention of some countries to undertake limited intervention, whether called "helping our friends," "assisting national liberation movements," or "answering a call for assistance." Even at the very lowest level of national armaments it will still be possible to lend a group of internal security police to help a neighbor restore local order, or to help police an election, or to rescue one's nationals who are besieged in the consulate.[8] It will still be possible to broadcast messages of support and sympathy, if not downright calls to revolution, to other countries and still stay within an injunction (which incidentally is now lacking in any draft disarmament plan) against hostile or inflammatory propaganda. For example, it is virtually certain that the United States would not tolerate a prohibition on the broadcast of factual news, reports of UN proceedings, and the like. Yet these constitute "inflammatory" and even "revolutionary" propaganda in some societies even today.

Thus, even if we rule out under GCD the possibility of unilateral intervention by a formal military establishment, there remains a great capacity for affecting situations of local instability even within the changed rules of political life under such a treaty; such intervention will doubtless appear to one state or another, and even to large majorities of states, as legitimate and consistent with disarmament.

Externally Created or Controlled Internal Instability

Will the obvious cases under this heading — deliberate, purposeful subversion and indirect aggression by the Soviet Union, Communist China, or both, as in Laos and Vietnam — continue under GCD? There are those who believe that GCD "has to mean" the end to such expansionist policies; that by the act of agreeing to a significant re-

---

[8] In October of 1962 it was reported, undoubtedly apocryphally, that units of a 22-nation "International Combat Brigade" were in Cuba to defend her from a United States invasion. The countries listed by the Cuban newspaper *Revolución* as participating were Algeria, Argentina, Bolivia, Brazil, El Salvador, Ethiopia, Guatemala, British Guiana, Nicaragua, Panama, Paraguay, Peru, East Germany, the Dominican Republic, Senegal, the Soviet Union, South Africa, Venezuela, and North Vietnam. (*The New York Times*, October 24, 1962.)

versal of the arms race the Communist powers will see the world differently and thenceforth refrain from pursuing the struggle by unacceptable means. Those who believe this tend to assume that any struggle which does go on will be pursued by means which we consider legitimate, in political and economic fields in which competition follows the ground rules we are used to, and in which we should be glad to compete.

Communist agreement to GCD would doubtless imply the conviction that Communist aims could no longer be effectively pursued in an open-ended and increasingly exorbitant arms race in which the West was likely to maintain its lead. No doubt such a decision, even if made for highly ideological reasons, would cost the Communists a high price — so high that, if something resembling the present Western plan were accepted, it might succeed in introducing some genuine restraints into Communist policy and thus reinforce liberalizing trends in the Soviet outlook. Inspection, enforcement procedures, peacekeeping machinery, and above all the increasing loss of freedom to manipulate threats of force (both because the force is diminishing and, more important, because the relative Communist military weakness becomes known publicly) would be costly politically, strategically, and ideologically.

Nevertheless the burden of proof is upon those who believe GCD would signal a reversal in the political movements, whether Soviet or Chinese, which hitherto have consistently spoken and acted as if their international aims were unlimited (the classic criterion for imperialism). My own belief is that if GCD should come about within a reasonable time span, i.e. within the next decade, we would not be entitled by any empirical evidence to believe that the Communists had foregone their expansionist aims and meant to play within Western-type ground rules. Indeed, it would be foolhardy to assume that the costs enumerated above would not have been considered and discounted by the Communists. For planning purposes I therefore assume continued and possibly even stepped-up efforts at subversion and indirect aggression and a potentially burdensome agenda of cases of local instability requiring remedial action if they are not to infect the international body politic.

The Sino-Soviet dispute ought to be projected into the future in terms that are significant for our analysis. Under one plausible hypothesis the dispute will become worse, the cleavages in ideology will widen, and — as often happens when alliances break up — differences between the states as states will reassert themselves. Thus one could envisage China and Russia renewing a policy of mutual suspicion in territorial rather than purely doctrinal terms. Outer Mongolia and other parts of Soviet Asia could become loci of acute instability, fomented by a Chinese government no longer content with Russian hegemony and influence, or other border regions (Sinkiang, Chinese Turkestan) where Russia became aware once more of the possibility of subversion along *her* borders and adopted a traditional policy of, so to speak, political pre-emption.

THE APPLICATION OF INTERNATIONAL FORCE

We have now set the stage for considering the actual application of international peacekeeping capacities to local instability problems in a disarming and disarmed world. By putting this range of problems in a disarmament setting we have introduced several constraints most of which have already been mentioned in passing — the lower level of strategic military power available to the largest nations; the changed atmosphere that will accompany, or at least follow, agreements to reduce weapons and military forces; the possibility that Communism's aims will remain unlimited, hostile to the non-Communist world, and capable of using any remaining means of achieving those ends; and the threat of a rearmament race. A related factor I have not mentioned is the substantial *arrière pensée* we can assume on the part of military leaders of all major nations in a disarmament agreement, wholly apart from ideology.

The final constraint is the deterrent and possibly punitive power of an international military force in the face of threats to stability of the sort we have been discussing.[9]

Such planning as has been done has tended to start with a hypothesis that may be questionable. It is that since under GCD national armaments are to replaced by international forces, it follows that, during and increasingly toward the close of the disarming process, international forces will be expected to cope with all "military" problems, including

---

[9] Hans J. Morgenthau develops in his essay in Part Two a theoretical approach to the relation between police power and maintenance of the *status quo*.

those caused by local instability. The only way to test this hypothesis is to pose the crucial questions and see what evidence may be adduced to help supply tentative answers.

From our particular point of view the crucial questions are two: whether and how the proposed structure of international peacekeeping can in fact cope with the problems involved in local instability; and how the process of actual decision-making — that is to say of political control of the use of military power, both at the international decision-making level and at the level of actual operations on the ground — will operate.

To examine the first question requires some still newer categories. To find out whether and how an augmented international organization can cope with problems of local instability, we look to the political processes of the institution itself. The key to these processes in any future institution we can foresee at this time is the position of the principal states. Unless one envisages some future political Lilliput in which the midgets dance freely over the bound bodies of those possessing significant national power, the great powers will largely dominate the strategic scene. Until late in stage III of GCD this seems the only prudent hypothesis.

The categories of great-power involvement in the relatively low levels of local violence we are here considering are three:

Great-Power Agreement

The easy category of disputes in the modern world is that in which the United States and the Soviet Union are in agreement. The Suez episode of 1956 illustrated dramatically the force of such agreement. The two superpowers, once in accord, can endow the United Nations with all the powers it requires to subdue a small-scale conflict. This, the dream of Chapter VII of the present Charter, would apply equally well in a disarming world in which both powers concurred on the need to dispatch an international force to deal with a given situation of local instability. The decision-making process in the organization would be operating under its most favorable conditions, at least in our recent experience. The force in the field, if it ran into difficulties, would presumably be backed up with the overwhelming power of the two.

However, this picture has some darker tones to it. First, it will be recalled that when Soviet enthusiasm for exploiting the disarray of the West in Suez further inspired it to make the obviously mocking proposal of a joint Soviet-American force, the United States instantly drew back and reaffirmed the underlying strength of its attachment to Britain and France; the "aggressors" were our friends, and the matter was not to be carried to the point of humiliating, degrading, or otherwise punishing them. Also, as shown in the Congo, a joint decision to apply an international force to a local situation can quickly evaporate if in practice it comes into conflict with the larger strategic aims of a great power. The Soviet vote in favor of the Congo force did not stop it from castigating the operation within weeks and proceeding to a long-term campaign of attempting to sabotage not only the UN operation in the Congo but also the United Nations itself.

It is possible and even likely that because of its special nature a local disorder involving highly complex internal politics, racial enmities, or shifting international coalitions (the Congo model) could remain intractable to easy settlement even if an international force were introduced with full agreement among the principal powers. Even when the Soviet Union and the United States pursued the same policy in 1947 toward the creation of Israel and in favor of the Israeli side in the first Palestine war, this had little or no effect on the long-term prospects for settlement of the basic dispute. (Agreement between the two did, however, partition the land, create cease-fire machinery, and in 1956 produce the first real UN force.) Similarly, when the United States and the Soviet Union took essentially parallel positions in the late 1940's in favor of a Kashmir settlement, it had little visible effect on the underlying tensions growing out of deep-seated causes such as communal conflict. (But the UN observer group did have an effect on the continued cessation of hostilities.)

The two superpowers can be in harmony under GCD — indeed, by customary reasoning, ought to be in greater harmony in view of their attachment to an arrangement whose overturn would mean renewal of a dangerous arms race — but what if other "great powers" demur? France in the West and China in the East seem the likeliest candidates for breaking a great-power common front.

Finally, and perhaps most ironically, if the Charter dream of great-power unanimity were to become a reality in view of the high stakes the principal powers believed they had in preservation of the new order, the countervailing sentiment of the smaller powers might well reassert itself with the materialization of their 1945 nightmare of solid great-power hegemony.

With full appreciation of these complications, United States-Soviet cooperation in a disarming world could well provide the basic political precondition for an international decision to intervene with force in a situation of local instability, particularly a situation of such universal concern that British or French or even West European opposition would not appreciably deflect the decision.

Easiest of all would be a decision to intervene in the Portuguese colonies of Angola and Mozambique if indigenous forces succeeded in creating ungovernable turmoil for the Portuguese, or if the Portuguese pulled out as a consequence of the fall of the Salazar regime, or if in either case an Algerian-style situation arose between the Africans and the growing number of *colonos* (who appear determined to hold out regardless of what Lisbon might do). South West Africa might also be an overwhelmingly agreed-upon case if the South African control slipped and disorder permeated the unhappy mandate.

A conflict in Southern Rhodesia in which the outnumbered whites lost control over the situation would pose exquisitely difficult problems for the international community. Appeals from the whites would undoubtedly be met by South Africa and would confront the United Kingdom with painful choices. Appeals from the blacks would be met enthusiastically by Africans and Communists. But such an explosive situation would clearly require an international military presence as a *force majeure* to end bloodshed and restore a semblance of order, and the dangers of the situation would undoubtedly result in widespread political support for the force.

Some Great-Power Disagreement

One can imagine cases in which it might be considerably more difficult to form an effective constitutional majority for an international force to deal with a locally unstable situation even if a majority of small countries favored it. If the United States or the Soviet Union objected mildly, a force might still be created and used. But until some later stage of disarmament the force would not be a standing one and would therefore have to be raised. The attendant difficulties of finance and logistical support, particularly airlift and sealift, would give the great powers an effective veto even if the latter is not written into the procedures.

The United States could probably have its way in a politically clear-cut case requiring peace forces even where the Soviets objected, if Soviet objections were not strong enough to imperil the entire disarmament structure. A Soviet proxy aggression through indirect means, *à la* Greece in 1947, could perhaps be met with a UN presence to inspect and even drive out the aggressors, assuming that the Soviets valued the agreement highly enough to be willing to cut their losses once they were found out or effectively opposed, as in fact they have done in the past in Greece, in Korea, and in Cuba.

Violent objections by secondary powers to the point of also jeopardizing the agreement could make it difficult, if not impossible, to go through with an international action. Even with Algeria out of the way, France has indicated profound hostility to international forces for peacekeeping. Communist China, even if somehow persuaded or coerced into a GCD agreement, is unlikely to support "bourgeois" political-military actions, at least some of which would deal with situations termed "wars of national liberation" in the Communist lexicon.

It may be the British who would be forced into the cruelest dilemma by the possibility of international military action, and the United States along with them. Agitation concerning Oman and Aden could in the end assume the coloration of independence movements with or without Yemeni or other manipulation, posing for the United States the question of whether to follow the majority seeking to supplant British power through a UN force designed to smooth the transition from colonial insurrection to independence (or association with another state). It is not clear that the United States would have sufficient political power to control the situation in the international organization without taking the ultimate risk of breaking up the arms agreement. British Guiana might become another soft spot requiring international power to fill a vacuum; here British objections might not be so great. But the United States would for the first time face the prospect of an international force introduced into this hemisphere. It might well prefer an OAS force; but it might not care enough to insist on frustration of or opposition to the international political system.

Violent Great-Power Disagreement

I have suggested that the crucial factor in GCD would be the feelings with which the major powers regarded the prospect of renewal of the arms race and the ways in which they construed their security in the light of that prospect. It was all very well in our time for the Russian bluffs to be called in Greece, Korea, and Cuba, and for the Soviets to cut their losses with fair grace. But another satellite uprising could create wholly new priorities for the Soviets. The rest of the world community might this time favor UN intervention in a collapsed East Germany or a strife-torn Albania. The Soviets would have to measure the consequences of a repressive unilateral intervention against multilateral action with its equally unpredictable consequences.

We are thus reminded of the difficulty peacekeeping machinery has in coping with internal collapse or subversion in which a great power believes it has an overwhelmingly important stake. One can imagine a "war of national liberation" in Latin America opening to Moscow — or Peking — hitherto undreamed-of prospects; local disorders in Outer Mongolia or Sinkiang as a result of a renewed power struggle between China and Russia, with one power favoring international intervention for "policing" purposes and the other bitterly opposed; a systemic disorder in the Communist world posing for the West opportunities involving the very political future itself; or a prospect in Africa or southern Asia that posed maximum temptation. Any of these might strain the peacekeeping machinery to the point of collapsing the system itself if a majority decided over the opposition of a superpower to introduce international forces for purposes of suppression of insurgency. The decision-making process establishing and politically controlling the means of peacekeeping might not in fact work here until some distant stage when the international community possessed such force as to be able to coerce any offender however large or obstinate.

The case of a South African upheaval has deliberately not been placed within any of the three categories. The South African situation, with its predominantly racial flavor and the problems for some European peoples when the question of international intervention arose, might present by far the most difficult challenge to an international peacekeeping system. If the situation deteriorated to the point of a total collapse of law and order and uncontrolled bloodshed, perhaps both white and non-white sectors of the international community would join in applying the only available remedy. If things were not quite that bad, the white government might go a long way in maintaining control, perhaps with the help of white volunteers and mercenaries, while the Africans and other colored peoples appealed to the non-white races — and to the Communists — on grounds of human rights and racial solidarity. These circumstances could be corrosive for the international decision-making process. There is another possible scenario for this tragedy; a majority, abetted by the Communists, seeking to assume political control of the machinery of peacekeeping in order to coerce a South Africa which still had internal conflict under control. The United States, along with West Europeans and perhaps others as well, would doubtless do everything in its power to prevent a UN force from being applied punitively in this fashion, but it could be the decisive crisis for the United Nations or its successor organization.

CONCLUSION

Some of the factors give promise that within limits the international community can use an international force to deal with certain instances of local instability where in an earlier age the great powers once sent in troops to fill the vacuum and restore law and order. But we have also suggested that the job cannot always be done by an international force. Vacuums will always exist, and the need for stability requires that they be filled in acceptable ways. But it is a long road historically from the Boxer Rebellion to Luanda or Johannesburg — or Berlin. The road becomes positively tortuous at those points where the great powers, singly or in pairs, are themselves the creators, controllers, or abettors of the particular disorder, or if they are divided on "religious" grounds about its desired outcome.

It is evident that the first category — the major powers in essential agreement — is the one in which political control is the least complicated or difficult. The decision to use a force, the definition of its mission, and the instructions to the Secretary-General about its deployment are all well within the range of the possible. Political control is thus established, and it remains only to make the operation a success in fulfilling its mission. (As the Congo showed, this may not be so easy.)

The second category — the great powers in some disagreement, but not necessarily willing to risk all, particularly if we postulate their increasing dependence on international security mechanisms in a disarming world — is not very different except in detail. When the chips are down, it is likely that the required political consensus will develop, particularly if the convenient escape hatch of abstention is still available. The involved great power will find it expedient to turn back, disassociating itself from its protégé or proxy. At the least, while continuing its grand strategy it will adjust its tactics in order not to run risks so high as to break up the system. This sort of situation will complicate tremendously the problem of political control at the administrative level of the Secretary-General, who will be given the task of carrying out what is likely to be an ambiguous directive, accompanied by contradictory instructions and under conditions of sporadic and uncertain support by members. (The Congo came to involve all these qualities.)

The final category — one or more great powers irrevocably in opposition to international action because of their stake in the local situation — is the most difficult for the system to master, and action taken in the face of it will at the worst destroy the system, at best supply impossibly controversial political directives to a force. The exact degree of difficulty depends on multiple factors: the exact stage of disarmament, the evolution of international machinery able to coerce great powers, the growth and use of adjudicatory organs and attendant enforcement measures, the existence of provisions for genuine peaceful change, the actual mechanics of decision-making under the proposed system (whether in terms of weighted voting, qualified [three-quarters, four-fifths, etc.] majorities, or other special features), and whether there exists a fall-back arrangement comparable to Article 51 or the "Uniting for Peace" procedure which even under disarming conditions might ensure that the law-abiding faction of the comunity could assert its will for peace and order.

Before drawing conclusions about the way we ought to think about world order and world force, it is illuminating to look briefly at the attitudes adopted by the Soviet Union on this range of issues.

Four

THE SOVIET VIEW

OF INTERNATIONAL FORCE

The Soviet Union's conduct in the United Nations has consistently reflected its persistent suspicion of "supra-national" armies.[1] All attempts to endow international institutions with any real power, such as the negotiations for Article 43 forces to be put at the disposal of the Security Council, as well as the Uniting for Peace Resolution in 1950 and subsequent efforts to field UN troops, have invariably met with Russian insistence on the right to veto so long as the Soviet Union is in a minority position. The Congo experience simply brought to a head the tendencies which had already long since been evident.

Thus in dealing with specific decisions to mount UN field operations during the postwar years the Soviets have always — or almost always — tied their position to their broader insistence on using the Security Council, where the minority position of a great power can be protected. Alternatively, they have proposed arrangements for the operation of international agencies, such as the so-called Troika Principle, which even without the power of veto in the Security Council would serve to protect Soviet interests against the feared coalition of the non-Communist powers. The Soviet Union abstained in the vote establishing the UN Emergency Force in Egypt in November 1956 on the ground that only the Security Council could approve the creation of any UN armed forces. The Soviets also abstained on the resolution

[1] Alexander Dallin, *The Soviet Union at the United Nations* (New York: Praeger, 1962).

setting up the UN Observation Group in Lebanon in the summer of 1958, and in the same period they opposed the advanced planning tentatively proposed by the Secretary General with a view to making contingents more readily available.

The Soviet Union did vote in the Security Council in favor of ONUC in July 1960, but doubtless, as with its temporary absence from the Security Council when the Council put the United Nations into the Korean fight ten years before, it soon came to regret its impetuousness. In June 1963, with regard to the decision to send a 200-man observer corps to Yemen, the Soviets insisted that it should be dealt with by the Security Council and not by the Secretary General.

Behind the superficial manifestations of this policy lies a profound cleavage between Communist and Western views about the very nature of international organization.

By any authentic interpretation of Communist doctrine a powerful non-Communist supranational organization at this stage of history can only mean a plot by the capitalist powers to check Communism's forward momentum and destroy its hard-won gains. By this interpretation existing international organizations such as the United Nations must be checked when they go beyond a purely servicing function. If they cannot be checked, the Communists prefer that they be eliminated. Moreover, unlike the West, the Soviets do not accept a necessary relationship between disarmament and world government. Thus, whether or not the Soviets really want some significant disarmament, they tend to view with profound suspicion any attempt to impose a new and, by definition, anti-Communist international order which under the guise of disarmament controls would frustrate their movement. It is not even a question of degree. At the level of minimum arms control the issue is still that of penetration into Soviet society by a necessarily hostile power. And when one goes up the scale of disarmament measures toward truly comprehensive programs, the conflict sharpens acutely; the Soviets determinedly oppose both the Western assertion that supranational institutions are required and the equally conventional Western thesis that the necessary amount of inspection, political authority, and the like increases with the degree of disarmament.

When it comes to the notion of world peace forces to take the place of national armies under general and complete disarmament, the

Soviet position has been a curious one, apparently shifting in the course of the late 1950's and early 1960's, but perhaps not really shifting at all in any fundamental sense of the political relationships at stake.

In October 1959 Premier Khrushchev addressed the Supreme Soviet on the subject of disarmament, making it clear that the international forces gambit on the part of the West was doubtless a ruse about which right-thinking Communists should be highly suspicious:

> The discussions on disarmament have hardly begun, and the skeptics have raised the question of what international forces should be created in place of the national forces. . . . When all countries disarm and all armies have no arms, then nobody will be able to start a war. The question arises: For what purpose, then, are supranational armed forces necessary?[2]

Secretary of State Herter's February 18, 1960 speech to the National Press Club, quoted earlier, which set the tone for the Western official line regarding international forces and disarmament, set in motion a series of Soviet responses. The first one came in the form of a relatively lengthy analysis of the problem by S. Vladimirov in the Soviet journal *International Affairs* in April of that spring. In that article Mr. Vladimirov laid out with clarity the underlying Communist view of the Western line. His first point was that disarmament and international armed forces were incompatible concepts since disarmament would remove the need for any such peacekeeping activities:

> Disarmament will remove mutual suspicion, mistrust and fear of cataclysmic war; these feelings will give way to trust, mutual understanding, and businesslike co-operation. The only sensible policy, the policy of peaceful co-existence and economic competition between the two social and political systems, will reign supreme in international relations.

Heaping scorn on the notion that international armies would have anything to do, Mr. Vladimirov took a look at the potential threat from such national forces as would remain:

> The "possible threat" to peace on the part of the national police or militia is likewise a poor argument. Even with a runaway imagination

[2] *Pravda,* November 1, 1959, p. 3.

it is hard to picture that these contingents will be a threat to other countries in a disarmed world with all-embracing international controls and an atmosphere of mutual trust, considering that they will be small numerically, equipped only with light arms, and dispersed over the home territory.

And in the event of some state "complicating the international situation by its actions," even though this should not happen, given the pitiful capabilities of remaining national forces, "there will always remain the possibility of applying moral pressure as well as economic and political sanctions provided for in international agreements."

If this unexpected faith in moral pressure did not suffice as an argument, there was the further reassuring belief in the inevitability of ideological progress:

> It should be specifically emphasized that the forces of peace, already a powerful deterrent to imperialist war moves, will multiply immeasurably in a world completely disarmed. Their impact on the development of international relations, which is growing from day to day, will become even more pronounced when, in a disarmed world, the bellicose imperialist circles are deprived of the material means of starting war. The forces of peace will not allow anyone to return to the old practices of the arms race and international gambles.

As a result of all of these factors, "a disarmed world does not need an international police force."

Having thus disposed of the logic of the problem, Vladimirov then turned to the real issue: the villainous hidden purposes of those who were making such preposterous suggestions. The real motive in setting up an international gendarmerie corps, he said, was "to turn it into an instrument of a certain group of Western Powers . . . the West as before is striving for an international military instrument which, officially an organ of the United Nations, would in practice be at the beck and call of a certain group of powers. And the purpose? What the Western powers want most is to use the UN flag to secure privileges to promote their selfish interests."

Specifically the Western powers were seen by Mr. Vladimirov as planning to use international forces for the following purposes:

> First, to fight the national-liberation movement in the colonies and dependencies.

Second, to crush any action by the democratic forces within the capitalist countries.

Third, the plans for such a police force are spearheaded against the peoples of the small countries.

Fourth, some people in the West plan to use the international police force to exert military and political pressure on the disarmed Socialist countries.

In other words, the present campaign in the West for an international police force sets itself tasks which are not merely foreign to peace and universal security but clash with them.

That fall Mr. Khrushchev again spoke before the UN General Assembly. At some time in the interval preceding this speech the Soviet Union apparently decided to accept, at least verbally, the principle that some kind of international military force should be a concomitant of disarmament. For according to Premier Khrushchev the Soviet Union had prepared a position for the disarmament discussions in June 1960 along these lines:

> After our proposals were submitted in September last year, the question was raised of how to ensure the maintenance of international law and order under conditions of general and complete disarmament. . . . We carefully studied these considerations and drew the conclusion that the only realistic possibility in present conditions would be, in accordance with the United Nations Charter, to place, when necessary, police (militia) detachments at the disposal of the Security Council to ensure keeping the peace.[3]

As Alexander Dallin wrote, "the change was significant if one contemplates that it required overcoming a deeply ingrained hostility and ceasing the intense campaign just waged in opposition to such a plan. Once reached, the decision became part of the Soviet disarmament scheme."[4] Thus in his several addresses to the General Assembly in September and early October 1960 Premier Khrushchev said the Soviets agreed in principle to the idea of international forces:

> An identical point of view has materialized in our proposals, as well as in those of the countries making up the NATO military alignment, regarding the necessity to follow up agreement on disarmament with the creation of armed forces of all countries under international con-

[3] *New York Times,* June 4, 1960.
[4] *Op. cit.,* p. 139.

trol, to be used by the United Nations as decided by the Security Council.

But he insisted on linking agreement in principle with the Troika solution, ridiculing the idea that such forces could be under the command of the Secretary General.[5] The Soviet delegation tabled a draft disarmament resolution calling upon states "to make available to the Security Council, where necessary, units from the contingents of police (militia) retained by states for maintaining internal order."[6]

The die appeared cast for a policy of public acceptance of the Western world government corollary, but this was illusory. The notion of a world force at the disposal of a majority appeared to the Soviets — as it probably also appears to the US Senate, the French and British governments, and many others when they are being fairly honest with themselves — to be full of potential dangers and injustices. The ambivalence of the Soviet attitude was revealed by Mr. Korovin in an article in February 1961, in which the logic of the Soviet line seemingly conceded the need for international forces after general and complete disarmament, but for rhetorical and polemical purposes only. The existence of an international force after disarmament was completed was, according to Korovin, quite unnecessary. But for such a force to be constructed *before* the world was totally disarmed would compound the dangers that make the same proposal in a disarmed world dangerous and unnecessary too. Thus the circle was closed.

> The formation of an international army before general and complete disarmament is effected would lead in practice either to the rise of unprecedented "supermilitarism," if the international armed force were stronger than the armies of the Soviet Union and the United States, or to the perpetuation of extreme inequality in international relations if the international force were employed only against small and weak countries.[7]

If the Soviet planners believe as deeply as they have appeared to in the potential dangers for the Soviet Union in a world in which the Red

---

[5] *Documents on Disarmament, 1960*, Department of State Publication 7172, p. 276.

[6] UN Document A/C.1/L 249, October 13, 1960.

[7] Y. Korovin, "Disarmament and Security," *International Affairs* (USSR) February, 1961, p. 57.

Army was demobilized and Moscow's rockets destroyed, and in which justice would be administered by a majority still susceptible to Western control, they nonetheless somehow have been able to continue publicly to swallow their profound doubts in order to accept formulae for a negotiated agreement with the West. The most striking of the formulae is that of the Joint Statement of Agreed Principles for Disarmament Negotiations agreed to between the United States and the Soviet Union on September 20, 1961, quoted earlier.

The Soviet draft treaty for general and complete disarmament was originally submitted by the Soviets to the General Assembly on September 23, 1960, was circulated at the request of the Soviet delegation to the United Nations on November 8, 1961, and has been reiterated at intervals since. In it there is no provision for an international military force in the first or second stage of the proposed treaty arrangements except for the following:

> In the second stage joint studies will be undertaken of the following measures to be implemented in the third stage: (a) measures to ensure observance of the treaty on general and complete disarmament after the implementation of all the measures provided for by that treaty; (b) measures to maintain peace and security in accordance with the United Nations Charter under conditions of general and complete disarmament.

But in the third stage, in the very last numbered item in the Soviet draft treaty we have the following:

> Measures for preserving peace and security in accordance with the Charter of the United Nations will be put into effect. States will undertake, where necessary, to place at the disposal of the Security Council units from the contingents of the police (militia) remaining at their disposal.[8]

One is forced to conclude, on the evidence before us at the present time in history, that the Soviet Union has no intention of voluntarily relinquishing to a majority of non-Communist states the effective control of power in the world, specifically the capacity to enforce on the Soviet Union the will of that non-Communist majority. At the same time, the Soviet Union for its own reasons has accepted Western in-

[8] UN Document A/4505, September 23, 1960.

sistence on the international forces corollary, but it has been careful at all times to keep this explicitly within the framework of the great-power veto. In the Soviet draft treaty the reference to the Security Council is in truth a reference back to the world of 1945 in which under Article 43 such forces were to be placed at the disposal of the Security Council, where the great-power veto obtains.

One might even conclude that the Soviet leadership is more aware of the power implications of the general and complete disarmament program and its world government corollary than the planners in the West appear to be. For there is consistency between the Soviet view of power relationships in the present world and its view of such relationships under disarmament. Since this consistency takes a form which is in important ways destructive of progress in the attainment of a more satisfactory world order, Western policy must do all in its power to substitute for the Soviet vision of the future one which reflects real harmony and trust among nations organized efficiently to keep the peace. This in truth is the paramount task before us.

But the one virtue of Soviet consistency is to convey an unmistakable message to us in the West as to the prospects for any genuine transformations in the international system so long as Communist leadership retains its hostile and mutually exclusive outlook and philosophy. It could be, as some increasingly believe, that the fundamental quality of hostility and exclusiveness is eroding under the tides of change and progress in Soviet society itself. It may be that the continued infection of its global outlook with some of the rigid dogmatic Communist positions of the past is a transient phenomenon the end of which we can now dimly foresee. But Western policy cannot count on this. It can only continue to assert what it believes to be right and feasible, to probe for agreements, and to influence the process of moderation in every possible way.

There is one conceivable change in the arrangements for organizing international forces that could have a serious effect on the present Communist view of their utility and propriety. That would be the acceptance of units from Communist states in international military forces in the present world, or indeed any other kind of world. One can envisage certain future circumstances in which forces from the Soviet bloc would find their way into an international UN expedition, for example an operation in Southern Africa from which the West was hanging back. In that case one of two things might happen. Either the Communists, who are rarely so inflexible as to fail to exploit a golden opportunity, would use in every way possible an instrument previously denied to them and would make every effort to convert it to an asset; or, as some Westerners apparently believe, the Soviets would accept the overriding purposes and principles of the organization and would forbear to distort their position as part of an international force for narrow national or ideological ends.

Soviet planners are quite clear about which way it would go. Bright new prospects for influence and even control are visible to them as they view a disarmed world through their own private prism. I. Glagolev and V. Larionov wrote in the November 1963 issue of the Soviet journal *International Affairs:*

> Under general and complete disarmament, security will be ensured by the liquidation of the armaments of all countries, international control over disarmament, the remaining security forces and also by international organizations. The economic, political, scientific, and technical might of the countries of the Socialist community will then undoubtedly have been greatly enhanced and will play an even greater part in this.

There is even an ironic echo of the words of Theodore Roosevelt quoted earlier, this time assigning the burden of policing the world in the name of the international community not to reluctant Americans but to eager Russians:

> The Soviet Armed Forces are not designed for attacking other countries or seizing foreign territory. Their main purpose is to defend the freedom and independence of our country and the other Socialist and peaceable countries, the gains of Socialism and democracy, universal peace and international security. This not only makes them a force of national security but also assigns to them the international mission of serving as a reliable guarantee of peace and the security of other Socialist nations, including the Chinese People's Republic, and of all peace-loving nations.

The safest course for world peace at the present would appear to be denial of this temptation to the Communists and the restriction of the composition of UN forces for the foreseeable future to countries not directly affiliated with the superpowers in order that the essential and vital peacekeeping purposes for which these forces are needed would remain paramount, with at least an even chance of succeeding.

Against this stark but indispensable backdrop of political and ideological opposition, matched by an as yet unplumbed reluctance of others including ourselves to accept the full implications of the "world government corollary" of present disarmament plans, what conclusions can we draw?

Five

DISARMAMENT AND FORCE—
SOME CONCLUSIONS

There are two fundamental questions. One is that of reality — will any of this come about? Does it belong within any rational time span as we look ahead? The other is — if the prospects are poor for achieving present disarmament goals, what can be done to improve these prospects, including if necessary revising the goals themselves?

For both comprehensive disarmament and its corollary — limited world government — two difficulties stand out from our analysis as paramount. One is the historic quantum jump implied in centralization of military and political power in the world, a revolutionary concept that we ourselves may not have grasped or accepted any more than has our principal adversary. The other is the presently insurmountable difficulty of bringing into any unified, democratic, world-wide system the Messianic forces of the Communist *imperium* so long as it is on the historic make. The very notion of a politico-military framework superior to both East and West today seems remote, for there has been doctrinal continuity between Litvinov's assertion that only angels can be impartial and Khrushchev's statement that there may be neutral nations but there are no neutral men.

Alongside these dilemmas the details of structure are almost trivial. Defects in those details can hardly account for the likelihood that general and complete disarmament is stalled for present purposes and, barring wholly unforeseen changes in the political and strategic situation, is likely to remain so in its present all-out form.

If a genuine world authority *were* to become politically feasible, there is no dearth of applicable blueprints for its inner detail. There is no theoretical reason, for example, why the present United Nations could not be transformed by Charter amendment into an instrument of effective global power. Alternatively, the process could be a completely new start, in the way the Articles of Confederation were scrapped to write the Constitution. But it is not terribly important which method is used. The paramount issue is not, as some suppose, the difficulty of amending the Charter. It is to reach a political consensus about ground rules in the world. If this came to pass, it would surely be a secondary question whether to incorporate the changes in the present Charter or to write a new one. The overwhelming central fact would be the loss of control of their military power by individual nations. If this became achievable, the details would surely not be insurmountable.

If on the evidence the Communist powers are unlikely to go this route in the present era, it then becomes easy to blame the stalemate on them. And the stalemate assuredly *does* involve a large dose of Soviet intransigency, doctrinal hostility, and sheer wrongheadedness.

At the same time there is increasing evidence that the Soviets, like ourselves, probably sense a deep interest in somehow moderating the arms race but do not really know how to without jeopardizing other vital interests. So to stop with the conclusion that the Soviets are blocking the presently charted road to disarmament has the fatal defect that, while it emotionally satisfies, it does not advance us toward the urgent security goal that we seek, and in fact may be concealing such real opportunities as exist.

On the assumption that the national interests of the states concerned and the common good of mankind require that ways be found to significantly moderate the arms race, one can only conclude that we have painted ourselves into a corner with present GCD plans, which have become the enemy not only of the good but also of the possible. Some are perhaps quite content with the predicament; those who have an intellectual or emotional commitment to predominantly military solutions will no longer support — as some on both sides do now — a disarmament policy when it begins to look even slightly realistic. But if the goal of significantly moderating the arms race has a high priority, political risks must be taken for it.

The most urgent charge on disarmament planners is thus not technical but political. To escape from the present policy prison requires serious and urgent rethinking of the political corollaries to disarmament freed of utopian stereotypes. If serious national interests in realistic arms control and disarmament measures are to be made to converge even moderately, policy must be both believable and attainable. The present proposals for GCD have neither of these qualities. Total disarmament has impressed few responsible people as desirable, or credible. In turn the Western position is made to appear either fatuous or insincere. Neither is worthy of either the problem or the talents available.

What disables GCD planning at root is its "world government corollary," by which significant reductions in armaments can be brought about and controlled only at the price of greatly increased international political authority and military power, to the point where the state system as we know it would be radically transformed. Under present and foreseeable political conditions it is likely that this corollary and therefore the plan as a whole can be implemented only by either defeating the Soviets in war, or in some unspecified way persuading them to surrender without war, and persuading others including ourselves to agree to live with political concomitants that today are safely in the realm of propaganda.

It is here that the question of timing becomes crucial. We can exclude as uninteresting for analytical purposes the imposition of world order by fiat on a basically shattered world (without forgetting that this represents one theoretically possible route). This leaves two other means of achieving the necessary motivation for all-out disarmament.

The path to which a statistician might attach the highest probability on the basis of historic evidence is that of long-term pacific evolution of the Communist world — and our own. Under this process — which, remember, must include China — it is difficult to foresee a limited world government within twenty-five years at the earliest, fifty years more conservatively. Only this path would be likely to embrace the indispensable process of community-building, involving a series of organic stages of consensus, value formation, and the experiences of common enterprise, which must underlie a true international polity.

A second path can be envisaged leading to "crash disarmament." This would involve a grave crisis or limited nuclear exchange sufficient to bring about a sudden transformation in national attitudes through a series of traumatic shocks. Such a set of unnerving trips to or over the brink might happen at any time. It is this contingency that thus has the most relevance for the planner of both disarmament and world order if he is not to substitute wishing for thinking.

Yet it is this contingency that least supports present policies. It is this one that offers least chance of overcoming ingrained political habits. It is this one that least supplies the vital underpinnings of community that give life and durability to a political society. We can say that, perhaps as a consequence of a massive crisis, it may be technically possible to envisage a program whereby all nations scrap their armaments down to the police level, with a reasonable probability of detecting significant evasion or violation through inspection arrangements. But none of this implies that comprehensive disarmament is a political possibility in the foreseeable future even though it is technically feasible, and even though it is not unthinkable strategically (given adequate supranational surrogates for national arms). In the end, a serious attempt to check the arms race and improve international peacekeeping capacities must be governed by Andrew Jackson's classic enjoinder at the Battle of New Orleans to "elevate them guns a little lower."

I conclude that disarmament planning, in order to become more realistic and thus more likely to be feasible, must reduce the connection with a centrally armed world government that the world may not be ready, able, or willing to accept. For many of the same reasons national planning should modify its presently grandiose and politically unimaginable goals that envisage total disarmament down to levels of internal security needs. A more realistic plan for serious reduction of existing military forces to more moderate levels, under suitable — but not excessive — verification, would then carry a corollary that would be not only realistic but also urgently desirable. Existing international institutions for peacekeeping should be strengthened, but not asked to take on impossible and even self-destructive burdens. The pooling of existing military forces to resist major armed aggression would remain for the foreseeable future the function of a constitutional majority at whatever level of delegated sovereignty and reserved powers the political traffic will bear.

What might be labeled "Significant Arms Control Plus a Responsible Capability" must for the foreseeable future connote the ability to carry out the most important national commitments, which means some usable national power. However, it also connotes the ability to deal with what may be the most pervasive problems of a disarming world — local instability. The ultimate goal should be a strategic and political world the West and the Communists have at least a chance of accepting as credible. It could take the form of a new three-stage plan which ends short of general and complete disarmament; it could mean elimination of the present Stage III; or it could be a new "non-stage" plan.

The peacekeeping arm of world organization can develop from the modest proposal outlined later on and eventually provide a stand-by or even standing constabulary-type force, probably of well under 100,000 men, capable of the lower-level actions ranging from observation and patrol to repelling clear cases of aggression across borders by minor states, and even by middle powers, so long as the significant powers agree to intervention. But a form of veto remains as ultimate protection for the great powers and those most closely related to them. However qualified the majority in the Assembly, there can be no pretense in plans made at this stage of history that nations such as the United States and the Soviet Union could be physically coerced by military power in the hands of a numerical majority of states.

The research in which I have been engaged, including political-military simulations referred to earlier, strongly suggests that there may be a significant threshhold, possibly somewhere in Stage II of disarmament as it is now envisaged, which represents a dividing line between the capacity of nations to act responsibly and that nether bank of "the undiscover'd country" of a UN monopoly of military power to whose bourn no traveler may in fact ever go, let alone return. It is possible that the fundamental requirements of minimum deterrence, significant disarmament, and the ensuring of equilibrium in the international system may not have to depend on going all the way to a totally disarmed world, or on having to contemplate living with an undoubtedly unacceptable international political structure.

In practical and specific terms the degree of supranational control is most importantly expressed in a triad of functions including that of forceful action. These are the matters of *inspection, enforcement,* and *international military force.* All three come into focus in terms of international institutions and authority. If one believes that political and social transformation is an essential accompaniment to the kind of disarmament we wish to achieve, one will insist on deep and pervasive inspection and controls, veto-free enforcement, and an unchallengeable international peace force. On the other hand if one believes that a world government is not feasible but that disarmament in *some* form is a necessity, one is forced to modify the position on all three. In a nutshell, a philosophy of "minimum intrusion" consistent with realistic verification and geared to changing technology should be the key to inspection and control requirements;[1] "veto-less enforcement" is, as far as one can look ahead on the road, not the way to any politically acceptable form of disarmament or peacekeeping; and plans for an international military force need to be tailored to the realistic requirements of peacekeeping and conflict management below the level at which the community would need to be equipped automatically to enforce its will on the strongest of the powers.

The structure of a disarmed world can be perceived far more easily than the fundamental building blocks of consensus and community that would have to underlie it, and because of this profound truth we have preoccupied ourselves with the former and neglected the latter. Stage III of GCD would represent an ordering of power, control, and decision-making different from any the world has yet experienced. It might be that, as some have suggested, GCD would bring into existence a world state even if no government were created to go with it. Our historic categories of coalitions, ideologies, and national interests would all be subject to profound modification, and how the world authority would enforce its rulings would become a problem in political mechanics rather than, as now, one of political metaphysics. We can end only by speculating that if such a system ever came into being, through whatever route, it would thenceforth have its own inner

[1] See Lincoln P. Bloomfield, "The Politics of Administering Disarmament," in *Disarmament and Arms Control,* Autumn, 1963.

dynamic. New forces would be set into motion that we cannot now comprehend, leading in the direction of constitutional and organic development that might bear as little resemblance to the planned first stage as the United States in the mid-1960's bears to the thirteen colonies under the Articles of Confederation.

This venture into the realm that links disarmament and international forces, benefiting as it must from our knowledge of the past, leads us not into the future but back into the clamant present. For nothing about the sobering conclusions we have drawn regarding the logic, the feasibility, and the design of world forces under disarmament relieves us of the duty to meet pressing current responsibilities.

Six

THE NEEDS OF THE PRESENT

At two o'clock in the morning, Jerusalem time, on a typically warm mid-July night in 1960, a telephone insistently rang at the bedside of a sleeping general. Grumbling, he reached for the instrument. He came awake instantly when he recognized the precise accents of his fellow Swede. From the 38th floor of the United Nations building in New York Dag Hammarskjöld gave his calm instructions. Major General Carl Carlsson von Horn, then serving as Chief of Staff of the UN Truce Supervisory Organization in Jerusalem, was to leave at once for Leopoldville to take command of the UN force that had just been created by the UN Security Council.

Five days later a badly frustrated force commander arrived at N'Djili airport on the outskirts of Leopoldville, not to receive his first troops but to be received by them. The United Nations, having no aircraft of its own suitable for the long flight, had been required to call for competitive bidding in the chartering of aircraft. While General von Horn sat fuming by his packed kit bag, a succession of chartered planes broke down, crashed, or simply failed to arrive. Finally, in desperation, arrangements were made locally for a United States aircraft to transport the General and the several UNTSO officers assigned with him to help create the Congo force.

But this was only the beginning of General von Horn's — and the United Nations' — troubles in the Congo. The obstacles ranged from the staggering to the ridiculous; all of them are instructive. It will help set the stage for more elevated matters to glimpse a few of them.

There was the lack of advanced planning. After his galling experience in trying to get to the Congo the force commander, once there, knew only days, sometimes only hours in advance what reinforcements would be arriving and by what means. He knew nothing of their organization or equipment except that the latter would be limited to what could be brought by air. (The Irish troops, for example, arrived in winter uniforms.) All the troops had to be deployed immediately, sometimes with a very scanty briefing.

Logistic difficulties were enormous.[1] Within a few days there were between five and six thousand troops of different nationalities spread over thousands of miles of difficult country, without transport except for a few jeeps they had brought with them, without adequate communications to bridge the distances between units, and without food other than four days of hard rations. Such supplies and equipment as were available had to be issued on an emergency basis by the handful of individuals who had to assume administrative responsibility without the benefit of either training or experience. Transport by rail and river was disorganized; air transportation was restricted by the obvious difficulties in establishing an air service *de novo* to supplement the few flights that could be chartered from the Belgian-run Air Congo. Medical services initially were limited to whatever medical officers had come in with the national units, although a small medical planning staff was shortly put together from resources within the Ghanaian brigade. There were no supply or ordnance depots; living accommodations were, to put it mildly, extraordinarily varied; and certainly no attention could be paid to the welfare or morale of the troops. The ONUC force (so-called from the initials of its official name in French) came from many different countries with a variety of languages and customs. But the headquarters staff itself consisted of but twelve officers who had to direct operations, receive and deploy new units, and conduct all negotiations with the local authorities. (When, after that first incredible summer, a somewhat testy complaint was received from New York that a request for a thorough military inventory had gone unfulfilled since the first week of the operation, the force commander, to save his sanity, chose to regard it as a practical joke.)

The deeper one probes into details of that early period of improvisa-

---

[1] Edward H. Bowman and James E. Fanning comprehensively explore the logistical lessons of the Congo operation in their paper in Part Two.

tion the more the men on the ground — and the planners at UN headquarters — deserve our sympathy. The problems seemed to know no limit. For example, if there was one urgent requirement for ONUC it was for an extensive movement-control capability. But it was this very category of essential personnel who were either not available or arrived without proficiency in French (or even English). Good air movement-control personnel was particularly needed. Neither of these needs was adequately filled.

Air operation in general proved a very difficult problem from the outset because of the vast distances to be covered, the inadequate surface transport, and the extreme dispersion of troops. There was no air staff officer among the early arrivals, nor were technical ground personnel available. In fact, two hours before some of the first troop transports were to be arriving at the rate of one every half-hour the sole occupant of the control tower at N'Djili airport was one very drunk Belgian who was discovered collapsed over his instruments mumbling "Je m'en fiche." Canadian Air Force crews were fortuitously at the field, and some at least partially qualified personnel from among them were promptly appropriated to take over in the tower. Almost to the end of the operation the United Nations was still flying fresh vegetables to troops stationed throughout the country while efforts were being made to persuade Congolese drivers that it was safe to take trucks overland over the 500-mile road, for example, from Leopoldville to Luluabourg in Kasai Province.

An acute problem of local relationships was involved in intervening in a country to help restore order. The UN force was in the Congo to furnish the government the "military assistance" required to help it meet its "tasks." But from the beginning of the operation neither the central nor provincial governments functioned effectively. While local authorities were sensitive of their new independence, they were clearly waiting for someone else to take action; indeed, the "Onusiens" were initially welcomed as saviors from the Belgians. Relationships with the Congolese army — the ANC — were complicated by the latter's lack of responsible commanders at any level. But in most instances during that first month the ANC did lay down arms wherever there were UN troops, and ONUC took over custody of the arms, ammunition depots, and arsenals. Local UN commanders used their own judgment as to how to keep the Congolese troops under control, with outstanding success in many areas.

In Equator Province an initial group of only 57 Moroccan paratroopers led by a captain kept the whole province in hand and prevented a secession similar to the one in Katanga. The ANC even provided much-needed services, such as radio equipment and river boats complete with crews. The Tunisian commander in Kasai Province and the Ethiopian commander in Oriental Province were also notably successful in achieving recognition as local military commanders, arranging for the protection of persons, preventing tribal conflicts, keeping the ANC under control, and patrolling remote areas to instill confidence in the local populations.

But during this initial period of cooperation no firm agreement was reached on the status of ONUC forces nor on the responsibilities for the maintenance of law and order — obviously their paramount mission. As calm was restored, and political complexities increased, controlling the ANC became more difficult. And after the decision was taken, for non-military reasons and against the strong advice of the force commander, to return to the ANC their weapons and stores, a climate of suspicion descended. This decision made possible the Congolese military action against Bakwanga and the resulting massacres. The effects of the UN example on such fundamentals as discipline and dress, and the possibility of carrying out effective training, were for a long time lost.

Profound difficulties arose from the special limits on military functions imposed on the force. The most debatable decision was the early directive that UN troops were to use force only in self-defense. In the circumstances it could only be demoralizing for the troops as they had to stand by while atrocities were committed. Even more serious was the encouragement given the Katanga secessionists to believe that the UN Command was ineffective. It is of course hardly surprising that UN troops responded vigorously when attacks were finally directed to their own persons.

The Katanga fighting of 1961, 1962, and 1963 fell under the same restrictions. Despite all the propaganda to the contrary the fighting in Katanga in September and December 1961 occurred only after severe provocation. In this connection the United Nations disserved its own cause by the timidity, ineffectiveness, and even nonexistence of adequate information services, particularly by contrast to the smooth and professional Katangese output. To take only one example, it would probably come as a surprise to those who followed some of the accounts carried at the time in the American press to learn that the United Nations had neither tanks nor bombs during the two rounds of Katanga fighting in 1961, and that the notorious "bombed" hospital was by no means being exclusively used as such.

At a still more serious level was the problem of relationships between civilian and military areas of the United Nations both in New York and on the ground. It is apparent that the division of responsibility between civilian and military components was not defined clearly enough to prevent misunderstandings at headquarters, even resulting in the occasional sending of instructions directly to staff officers and troops without prior reference to the force commander or his immediate staff.

The principle of civilian control was firmly established from the start, and messages to and from New York went directly to and from the Special Representative and his staff. But as the staff grew, coordination became increasingly difficult. The military branch in Leopoldville frequently felt that its views were not sought or else ignored. A crucial example concerned the gathering of intelligence, an obvious necessity which the force commander had instituted at the outset. When radio monitoring was taken over by the civilian branch, however, it was not extended to include the ANC radio "nets"; instructions were then issued that the word "information" was to be substituted for "intelligence," with highly controversial results.

In this same connection, no action was taken during the crucial early period to disseminate information to the troops about their mission or to publicize their tasks and efforts. This did not improve morale, nor did the decision by UN Headquarters not to issue a special ribbon for service in the Congo to distinguish it from the purely observer-type operations of the Middle East and other theatres.

With the sudden and almost facile UN victory over the intransigent, flamboyant, and unsubstantial forces of Moise Tshombe in early 1963 many of these details tended to recede from the foreground. It could be — and has been — said that these examples of improvisation, bureaucratic requirements, inadequate political direction, and insufficient contributions by states of needed components are all inevitable characteristics of emergency military operations undertaken by a multilateral organization under the political direction of quarreling nations. And of course this is true. If at times it seemed to the force commanders that they had no terms of reference and their force no clearly defined mission; if an individual soldier was confused by the fact that he was expected to be unobtrusive and friendly at one time, at another military and assertive; if the public image of the operation in the West was a strange amalgam of hopes and fears, enthusiasm and misgivings, convictions and doubts; one can only say that in the face of the circumstances the real miracle of ONUC, like that of Doctor Johnson's dog walking on its hind legs, was not that it functioned so badly but that it functioned at all.[2]

The Congo crisis confronted the United Nations with the totally novel problem of assembling a politically acceptable international military force and deploying it across the length and breadth of a huge country as quickly as possible in the face of a rapidly deteriorating internal situation. Its mission, as conceived by those responsible, in addition to reorganizing the *Force Publique,* included the maintenance of law and order and the replacement of Belgian troops. The latter *were* replaced at an early date. Confidence was generally restored to the population. In this sense there was no question of the initial success of ONUC. The climax and denouement two and a half years later made it possible to rate the exercise as a whole as successful, contributory to the peace — and responsible for posing questions in the minds of thoughtful people that go well beyond the facts of the Congo operation itself. (The Congo itself typically remains unstable.)

Should the United Nations ever have involved itself in the first place in an internally complex situation of this sort? How could it — or any multilateral military or quasi-military operation — be expected to function in the face of a fundamental great-power conflict of objectives that made it virtually impossible to secure coherent political directives? How could it rely on small states when they themselves began to take sides? What sort of precedents were being set when a nonfighting force

[2] The essays of Herbert Nicholas and Brian E. Urquhart that open Part Two of this volume consider in depth the postwar development of UN forces with particular emphasis on the Suez and Congo operations.

suddenly became a fighting one? And finally, cannot the mechanical side of such an operation be improved to at least the standards of a minimally integrated and efficient national force, including training, earmarking of reserves, logistical planning, and improved execution when actually put to use?

It is important to develop objective answers to these questions, for nothing could be less safe than to assume that the Congo represented the last such operation. The disorders of our age have by no means come to an end. The hasty abdication of a colonial power, leaving behind it a dangerous vacuum that tempts international trouble-makers, has doubtless not happened for the last time. The competing interests and ambitions of great powers — possibly between Communist great powers — could once again pose to the world as the preferable alternative to great-power intervention the not very tidy or efficient notion of international force. Racial conflict and border wars also lie ahead in Africa, as well as internal chaos in the unformed nations.

Thus we find ourselves forced to look ahead to situations in which once again we might be offered the options of 1956 in Suez and 1960 in the Congo. Given those options, once again the common sense of statesmen may choose as the preferable alternative intervention in the name, as Harlan Cleveland has provocatively put it, of non-intervention.

For despite the inherent difficulties and the controversial by-products of UN policing operations, from the standpoint of mankind's most challenging problem — preventing a major war — the most important function of the United Nations in this period may well be that of an executive power. This does not necessarily mean a superstrong international secretariat. It does imply an agency capable of carrying out in detail the general will of the constitutional majorities in the United Nations within the limits of the powers granted to the organization in its Charter. Barring a wholly unexpected South African or Rhodesian or Portuguese reversal of policy, there will be more Congos; and next time they may be in multiracial societies, with complication and reverberations which may make the Congo seem simple by comparison. It is predictable that the same sorts of issues as arose in July 1960 in the Congo will recur and pose comparable dilemmas. They must be met.

Nations concerned with keeping the peace have a profound interest in the executive capacity of the United Nations to intervene in situations like that of the Congo, in which any alternative appears even less desirable or acceptable. The only real alternatives[3] tend to be overlooked in criticisms of the United Nations Congo action. They were — and may again be — three: intervention by the former colonial power, intervention by the United States, or intervention by the Soviet Union. If the colonial country intervenes, the likelihood is a racial war of continental dimensions, benefiting only Communism. If the United States or the Soviet Union intervenes, there may be a great-power war with all the dangers of escalating to a thermonuclear general war. The United Nations, with all its difficulties, complexities, imperfections, lack of consistency, and lack of uniform support, is probably the only acceptable means unless a regional organization is able to do the job.

The option of UN intervention is most clearly desirable in conflicts, disorders, and vacuums that at the outset do not directly involve the great military alliances. The simple and compelling rationale for choosing the UN option so far has been that in the judgment of responsible decision makers it has seemed to carry with it the least likelihood of direct great-power confrontation, military escalation, and that one outcome — general war — that no one wants. All that happened in the UN Congo operation constituted the price paid for avoiding something even more undesirable. By any rational standard the difficulties in the Congo should have been accepted as the virtually inevitable logical consequences of such intervention.

The surprisingly effective Suez and Congo operations seemed to many to be the precursor of a vigorous and on-going pattern of international action which would damp down conflicts before they spread further, interpose between angry combatants rational enough to be willing to disengage, and buy time for peaceful settlements or alterations in the rules that would end the given injustice or grievance. It was reasonable to believe that there was at hand an unanticipated capability of the imperfectly organized world society, a capability that might have profound significance for keeping the peace primarily by furnishing a substitute for great-power intervention.

In short, one would have thought that with the experience of UNEF

---

[3] The apparent urge of, e.g., the African states to operate an "All-African" force in the name of the United Nations is highly unrealistic on financial, logistical, and political grounds at the present, although this may change in a relatively short time.

in Egypt and ONUC in the Congo the responsible states, large and small, would have sought to make far more substantial any future capacity of the United Nations to handle such problems. For the preconditions exist today to make significant improvements in a whole gamut of techniques for training and earmarking UN "police," for better methods of deployment and command, even for a nucleus of a wholly international constabulary. Alongside these are greatly needed improvements in political and institutional means of dispute-settling and peaceful change, without which plans for policing the world scene today or tomorrow remain mechanistic, crude, and irrelevant to the real problems.

But to some critics, Western as well as Communist, the same pattern boded no good. It portended the possible intervention of a military force wearing a UN label arguably in violation of the domestic jurisdiction clause of the Charter — whether in Pretoria, Luanda, Jackson, Paris, Salisbury, or East Berlin. Nightmares are conjured up of such a force voted in by the Afro-Asian states against the futile opposition of the great powers, firing live ammunition and dropping bombs on those who pay the bills, all of this without any of the foundation of legitimacy, consensus, or at any rate custom that traditionally gives such rights to individual states. To make it still worse, the costs would be at least on the order of ten million dollars a month, as in the Congo, to pay for which only a few states seem either willing or able.

Instead, then, of congratulating themselves about the good fortune the United Nations had surprisingly bestowed, however imperfectly or even ineptly, a large number of nations made difficulties about the relatively trivial costs. What was more serious was that responsible people began to draw back from the United Nations in some alarm as they projected into other hypothetical situations its newly demonstrated ability to intervene. The savage reaction of Soviet policy to the United Nations' frustration of its ambitions in the Congo should rationally have been matched by a major exploitation by the loyal majority of the United Nation's capacity to keep the peace in such sticky situations. Instead the Soviet reaction was mirrored in parts of the West by extreme caution and conservatism, even apart from the egregious and atavistic stands of such nations as France. Those who officially or otherwise advocate an overwhelmingly powerful world authority as an accompaniment for any substantial disarmament agreement might well ask themselves how real their hopes can be in the face of the inability so far to make any real progress in institutionalizing the United Nations' modest capabilities based on present powers.

One natural ally of those who oppose such institutionalizing is the very nature of international military action. If the natural habitat of the fish is water, so historically the natural habitat of a soldier is his national army under his national flag. Deracination of the soldier represents an even greater wrench than that of the bureaucrat.[4] It is commonly supposed that mixing up one's own troops with "foreign" soldiers diminishes military efficiency. In an earlier multi-national sortie into Katanga a 19th-Century mercenary concluded that "on the whole . . . such enterprises are less likely to succeed than those conducted on more homogeneous lines. Political considerations naturally cause a company thus constituted to adopt a somewhat flabby and vacillating policy."[5]

Such sentiments are echoed in more than one mid-twentieth century defense establishment, particularly when all other criticisms fail. For there is always the plausible and even moving argument of the military man whose experience discourages experiments with polylingual commands, multiple logistical requirements, mixed calibres of ammunition, queer diets, and the just-plain-cussedness of the foreigner. General Montgomery summed up the soldiers' complaint with his customary bluntness (but ignoring, e.g., the splendid "Danor" unit in Gaza):

> You must keep people together in national units under national control. The politicians don't understand these things. They never fought or commanded troops in battle. I did, I know. You can't mix different people up in the same box of tricks.[6]

[4] This question is developed in Dr. Henry V. Dicks' chapter in Part Two on the psychology of the individual soldier.

[5] Joseph A. Moloney, *With Captain Stairs to Katanga* (1893) quoted by Conor Cruise O'Brien in *To Katanga and Back* (New York: Simon and Schuster, 1962).

[6] Interview by C. L. Sulzberger of Viscount Montgomery: *Boston Herald*, March 31, 1963. Elaborating on this theme, Rear Admiral G. T. S. Gray, R.N., scorned the concept of a mixed-manned NATO fleet by arguing differences in "language, pay, discipline, career structures, recruiting of personnel, assignment to duty, national

(Continued on page 74)

The Eisenhower or Burns or Gyani whose more sophisticated balance sheet takes into account the sometimes great political benefits of multinational commands, however trying they may be administratively, are rare. Even rarer is the acknowledgement that given decent directives and leadership it is possible on the historical record to achieve high motivation and morale in joint or mixed expeditions.

Another real difficulty in making progress in planning in advance for a policy in troubled areas of the future is that the examples are few. Moreover, since each so far has required a method hand-tailored to the situation, it is usually concluded, particularly by UN Secretariat officials well aware of the hostility of the Communist countries as well as some others toward the very idea of UN forces, that forward planning is not really possible and each case should be handled *ad hoc*. Again, there is a half-truth here. The "population" of crises to be studied is small — fortunately — and general rules are applicable only *mutatis mutandis*. But it would be better to have them, to make them flexible and to be ready to apply them when needed, than to leave undone even the modest preparations that are so urgently called for.

What are some of the general rules that one can abstract from the experience so far, rules that fix the present limits to UN military intervention (always excepting Korea as a special and unlikely-to-recur case)?

First, there must be agreement, however tacit, among the superpowers that they are not going to intervene. Second, the operation should be composed of units from non-great powers, preferably countries not involved in the local dispute. (The *partis pris* attitude of some of the African countries with troops in ONUC undermined this rule, diminished their usefulness, and contributed to the troubles of the operation.) Third, the very fiction on which the United Nations rests — that of the sovereign equality of states — underlies the principle that a UN force goes in only with the consent of the "host," however

---

differences in food, religion, habits, and outlook. . . ." Apparently on the principle of *in vino veritas*, he clinched his case with the following: "British sailors by tradition are entitled to a daily rum ration; French are not. French sailors receive a daily allowance of wine; Germans do not. German sailors are allowed to purchase schnapps and whiskey in their ships; Italians are not . . ." "A NATO European Navy: How Practical," in *Naval Review*, 1964 (Annapolis: United States Naval Institute, 1963), pp. 90, 92.

flat on his back the "host" may be (as Egypt was in early November 1956 and the Republic of the Congo in July 1960). The corollary of the third principle is the fourth, and here the Congo episode represented a change from the past: the continued presence of the United Nations within a national territory is in major ways subject to the will of the "host." (In the Congo Hammarskjöld said that the Security Council and General Assembly would have to be parties to any withdrawal desired by the host.) A fifth limiting principle established in UNEF was that the "host" had a veto over the composition of the force. (In the Congo this was modified to qualify the unilateral veto power of the host.) Sixth, the military units are contributed *ad hoc* by member governments on a voluntary basis in the form of homogeneous units, preferably of at least battalion size. And seventh, the mission for forces constructed within the ground rules is characteristically one of policing rather than military combat.[7]

Under present conditions, to try to alter any one of these limiting principles would represent a major political leap. For instance, inclusion of great-power elements would undermine the basic rationale of limiting the chances for involvement and escalation. Moving in without the consent of the "host" would undermine the principle of equal sovereignty on which the international organization itself rests. To recruit a truly international force rather than using homogeneous, nationally recruited units would step across the boundary that keeps the United Nations a service organization rather than a quasi-government, and thus tolerated by national governments.

The very notion of a deliberately designed fighting force transforms the essentially innocuous — and thus generally acceptable — image of the United Nations into one that is anathema to many states which believe the United Nations has no business developing an explicit combat capability, and thus reduces the likelihood that it will be in position to do even the minor chores necessary to the peace. The task

[7] See Ruth B. Russell, "United Nations Experience with Military Forces: Political and Legal Aspects," Research Paper P-27, Institute for Defense Analyses, Washington, D.C., May 1963. An excellent analysis of the UNEF experience is *The United Nations Emergency Force* by Gabriella Rosner (New York: Columbia University, 1963). Details of the Congo operation based on published reports are found in Arthur Lee Burns and Nina Heathcote, *Peace-Keeping by U.N. Forces — From Suez to the Congo* (New York: Praeger, 1963)

for policy then is to make progress with a stand-by UN policing capability but to understand that it might involve shooting. When UN soldiers fired back in self-defense in the Congo, it was clear that a threshold had been crossed in the perceptions many people held of the organization and its place in the political scheme of things. When eventually the UN force quickly and almost bloodlessly disposed of the Katanga mercenaries, Secretary General U Thant was quoted as saying, one surmises a bit defensively, "For a peace force, even a little fighting is too much, and only a few casualties are too many." [8]

Politically, Mr. Thant was speaking wisdom. But practical pressures might change the theory. As Andrew Boyd wrote:

> The idea that a UN soldier should need no weapon more lethal than a blue flag on a pole is an attractive one. To *hope* that duty will never require such a soldier to kill, even in defensive action, one does not need to be an idealizer. To *assume* this, however, is something else. [9]

The truth was that the Hammarskjöld strategy of UN neutrality between "internal factions" had not worked. The principle of nonintervention gave way in the Congo to an enlarged mandate including the use of force, not just as a "last resort" but in order to apprehend the foreign mercenaries. This "sliding UN mandate" may have incurred disapproval; but its greater significance was that it previsioned comparable situations in which the UN intervention might become the only feasible alternative — as was true in the Congo — but where, once committed, new capabilities have to be generated to perform the mandate.

Some governments seem both to grasp the significance of the development of UN policing abilities and to be able to act on the insight. But the majority has not appeared to accept the need or the desirability of advance planning. Indeed, one of the most unpromising aspects of the picture is the unwillingness of member states to make advance commitments of forces to be volunteered when needed. If an organization depends on such offers because it is not developed enough to maintain a standing police force of its own, then the prospects seem

---

[8] Secretary General's Report on the Congo dated February 4, 1963 reported in *UN Review*, February, 1963, p. 7.

[9] *United Nations: Piety, Myth, and Truth* (Middlesex: Penguin, 1962) p. 21.

dim indeed for making notable improvements. It will be recalled that in the spring of 1951 the Collective Measures Committee circularized the membership asking for the earmarking of national units. The only relatively unconditional offers of national contingents were from Thailand, Greece, Norway, and Denmark for a total of 6,000 plus two destroyer escorts offered by Uruguay. Bearishness was already setting in when the Secretary General in 1958-59 chose to poll as to their attitude toward stand-by arrangements only the 23 states which contributed to UNEF and the UN Observation Group in Lebanon.

Many nations supply rhetoric on the subject; the Foreign Minister of Iran, for example, dramatically called in 1962 for a permanent United Nations force, "however small in number and embryonic in concept." [10] But few responded in concrete terms to the Secretariat's invitation. Standing almost alone were the three faithful international-minded Scandinavian governments which in April 1963 announced the formation of a 3,000-man international "fire-brigade" to be placed at the disposal of the United Nations for emergency actions, consisting of 2,000 Swedish infantrymen and 1,000 Danish and Norwegian military experts, engineering troops, emergency field hospital personnel, and helicopter crews.[11] Canada, which under Lester Pearson had stood in the forefront of creative leadership and contribution to UN forces, announced to the 1963 General Assembly that Canada "now maintains forces, trained and equipped for the purpose, which can be placed at the disposal of the United Nations on short notice anywhere in the world." [12] Canada (which incidentally has become almost the sole provider of signals units to the various UN field operations) had already formally earmarked a battalion; Finland offered troops; the Netherlands promised 300 Marines, and the United States promised supplies and transportation. But for most of the approximately 100 other members of the United Nations the attitude has been one of indifference or hostility.

It might of course be argued that since the job must be done when new crises and new dangers arise, it must be the few responsible parties who will carry the load for the rest — a not uncommon phenomenon

[10] Abbas Aram, *New York Times*, September 25, 1962.
[11] *New York Times*, April 24, 1963.
[12] Lester Pearson, *New York Times*, September 20, 1963.

in any walk of life. Unfortunately the peacekeeping job at the level we are discussing depends on the many. If it did not, they could be safely ignored and the few responsible states would act as needed in crises. And unfortunately, Scandinavians and Canadians are the wrong color and race to be politically appropriate in UN presences in some likely kinds of future operations. Because the operation is useful only to the extent it appears to be "neutral," there still seems no alternative to the use of personnel from the smaller countries, concentrating on the sorts of duties experience in the recent past has shown to be most useful.

The implication of all this is that something is needed which the United Nations does not now have. But it is also that the nature and scope of any improvements in UN peacekeeping must be modest rather than bold. We are driven to this conclusion by the climate of international relations, in which the rational needs of an international community struggling to be born are resisted or ignored by the majority. We are driven to them by the overpowering danger to the world if the great powers directly collide, a contingency that not only gives point to the urgent need for "third-party forces" but also severely limits the cooperation necessary to support such forces. We are driven to them by the intense doctrinal hostility of the Soviet Union to the very notion of international forces that by definition are not controlled by Communists. And finally we are driven to modest conclusions by the past knowledge of overambitious schemes that failed and by the conviction that successful politics here can only be the art of the possible.

In the light of all this I am emboldened to make a new proposal which hopefully mediates between the equal dangers of excessive caution and overambitiousness.

Seven

A PROPOSAL

Let me advance a concrete proposal which will synthesize the points I have been making and which is geared to the conclusions reached as to what the traffic today might bear — but only might.

THE GOAL

It helps first to restate the goal. The goal is to improve the capabilities of the United Nations for peacekeeping action with the limits of political reality but beyond the confines of excessive inertia, caution, or timidity. In order to meet this standard a proposal should address itself to the present and immediate future rather than to the long-range or even middle-range future. It should build on the lessons of UNEF and ONUC. It should pay appropriate — but not hypnotized — attention to the political hostility of the Communists and others. It should be sobered — but not paralyzed — by the financial crisis produced by the Congo operation. These constraints favor something other than a standing military body, the need for which is in any event not proven. They also rule out that other form of international police force — the individually recruited UN constabulary whose members lose their national uniform and identity as national soldiers. But a proposal bounded by these restraints would nonetheless go beyond the existing situation.

I would therefore propose the creation of a modest *stand-by force of* the proper sort, trained and equipped for the proper jobs, and in an appropriate condition of readiness and availability when needed. The ultimate size of the stand-by reserve force would be 25,000 men plus

several specialized units. It would be built up to full strength over a
five-year period, after which the annual training of new contingents
would offset attrition. It would be subject to the appropriate organs of
the United Nations, following precisely the same constitutional procedures as at present and with the same authority and safeguards *against*
authority. Thus for the first time one could count on the availability
and readiness of a reasonable number of trained personnel for peace-
keeping assignments at a modest level, on as good a geographic distribution basis as the UN membership itself, and able to get to trouble spots
in the necessary strength in the necessary time and with logistical support for a suitable period. The trained units would constitute a cadre
which could be supplemented as needed.

ORGANIZATION

My proposal is based on the assumption that battalion-strength units
represent probably the most appropriate basis today for contributions.
The battalion is a unit of a size likely to be maintained by smaller countries. It ensures some homogeneity in terms of morale, customary diet,
religious practices, and the rest. At the same time it permits relatively
low-level integration of units within regiments, different-sized task
groups, brigade groups, even divisions. From the standpoint of simple
arithmetic an eventual stand-by force of 25,000 can be made up of
single understrength battalions of approximately 500 men each from
50 countries, or of overstrength battalions of 1,000 men from 25 countries, without the participation of the great powers or of the predictable number of smaller powers which would not take part because
they have no armed forces, disapprove of the policies a substantial
United Nations majority is likely to favor, or object to UN police
forces in principle. The total adds up to a modest stand-by force which
is potentially organizable into five brigades or two small divisions; it is
more likely that battalions would be made up into a tailored force, such
as UNEF and ONUC, not necessarily corresponding to any conventional military formation.

The image of the proposed stand-by UN force should be that of
police rather than army, and preferably that of constabulary rather
than police. Whatever label is used should denote primarily the roles
of observation, patrol, and civil-pacifying functions rather than en-

forcement, punitive, or typically combat functions. At the same time the force should be equipped — as UNEF and ONUC were in fact — to defend itself and to hold off equivalent-sized military formations until it could be reinforced.

It is here that the experiences so far go a long way to supply the details of this proposal. The action in the Congo showed the special need for training in sophisticated riot control and civil government, in troop and vehicle movement control, in helicopter operations, and in signals (communications). These are of course the skills likely to be in the shortest supply in the very countries most suitable politically to do the job. It therefore seems as sensible today as it did when first proposed that the United Nations vote to organize a modest UN training program at reasonable cost, rotating battalion-size units in and out for special peacekeeping training purposes, and, when they are trained, returning them to their home forces, where they would be kept in special and hopefully honorific reserve status until called on by appropriate vote of the Security Council or Assembly.[1]

As was suggested then, the force could be trained at a facility made available by a neutral country such as India. Approximately 2,500 men would train at any given time, that is to say five 500-man battalions for a period of 6 months. This would result in training 5,000 men a year, or a total of 25,000 in 5 years, about the maximum time for ensuring that at least a substantial cadre of trainees would be available at the end of the cycle. The men would be regulars, or at any rate volunteers and not short-term draftees. For one thing, the former are demonstrably far more successful in the difficult assignments involved; for another, they will stay in the service and remain available longer.

THE TRAINING PROGRAM

The personnel requirements for such a training facility might vary within certain broad limits, depending on the extent to which the trainee units might bring their own support personnel, the extensiveness of the training, the condition of base facilities, and so on. A care-

---

[1] See Lincoln P. Bloomfield, "The UN and National Security," *Foreign Affairs,* July 1958, and *The United Nations and U.S. Foreign Policy,* (Boston: Little, Brown and Company, 1960). A most valuable early analysis with recommendations is *A United Nations Peace Force* by William R. Frye (New York: Oceana, 1957).

ful analysis of probable needs to accomplish the precise mission envisaged here suggests that the training facility would have a permanent base unit of 802 men organized as indicated in the following table, with an alternative column based on a reduced strength of 3,000 trainees annually.[2] The instructing staff could well be drawn from the military officers and non-coms in more than 30 countries that have now served in UN operations. The new UN Institute might be the over-all "employers."

Estimated Personnel Requirements for a UN Training Base

	Facility Operation and Maintenance	Training Function (for 5000 Trainees per Year)	(Alternate Figures for 3000 Trainees per Year)
Personnel and Administration	20	20	10
Intelligence and Security	20*	20	10
Operations	10	80	60
Supply and Maintenance	50**	50	30
Food Service and Rations	40***	5	5
Plans	20	20	15
Construction and Engineering	100**	50	20
Accounting and Finance	10	—	—
Communications	100**	60	30
Public Information	5	20	10
Chaplain	2	5	5
Inspector General (Safety and Standardization)	—	10	10
Surgeon	40	30	20
Judge Advocate	5	10	8
	422	380	233

TOTAL   802 (655)

*Base security only; i.e. military police.

**Initial preparation or modification of the facility will require additional personnel. Figures listed would be required to replenish consumables; repair vehicles; maintain light aircraft; maintain grounds, buildings, and training areas; maintain communications facilities and training equipment; etc.

***If units being trained do not bring their own field-messing facilities and food-service personnel, this figure will have to be increased proportionately. More unification and *esprit*, as well as better health, probably would be attained by having the base supply all food service.

[2] For the staffing out of this proposal, as well as other helpful advice, I am most indebted to Colonel David L. Evans, USAF, who at the time of this writing was Air Force Research Associate at the MIT Center for International Studies.

The curriculum for a six-month intensive training course would be pointed to those skills and functions that are unique to the sort of police or constabulary job actually needed. A major part of the course would be elementary grounding in language. A basic familiarity with English or French as a second language would be most important in terms of obeying military orders and acknowledging communications. Second would be a standard signals procedure for communication between units and up and down the chain of command. Third would be observation and patrol duties, including special military and civil-police type of training, crowd handling, maintenance of law and order in small units in isolation, enforcing discipline, observing ceasefires and the violations thereof, making accurate vehicle and head counts at checkpoints, surveillance and reporting techniques, and so on. There should be a training unit in intelligence functions that, under whatever name, are indispensable to any UN field operation.

It should be possible to experiment with a minimum common diet for mixed troops in the field. It might be desirable to experiment with mixing the units below the battalion level, possibly building on the "buddy" system successfully developed in Korea between American and Republic of Korea forces.

The curriculum should include at least one actual field exercise, in which, for example, one battalion would simulate a mob, or a disaffected populace, or refugees. Such "police games" could build profitably on both the experience in political-military simulation developed in the past few years and the more traditional war-gaming employed in military training the world over.

It may be argued that the financial problem implied by the proposal I have outlined is so overwhelming that this sort of training should be limited to commissioned and non-commissioned officers. Certainly that would be better than what we have now. But training of actual troops has important values that go well beyond those of the more modest proposal for training officers. The principal reason lies in the small resources that even at best would be available to perform police or constabulary tasks of the sort in mind here. The more ready a group of men is to take on the responsibilities and duties which at best cannot be precisely anticipated, in an alien area that cannot be predicted, and under conditions foreign to their normal military environment, the more efficient a job the United Nations can do with small resources. Five-hundred trained men can do the job of 5,000 untrained men, as was demonstrated positively by the unique abilities of the Nigerian military police in the Congo, and negatively by the difficulties that arose there with relatively untrained and unsophisticated units. An unrelated but vital reason why the new African countries urgently need cadres of disciplined, police-trained troops was vividly illustrated in early 1964, when 30 Cuban-trained guerrillas took over, and subsequently in Tanganyika, Kenya, and Uganda.

Another reason for preferring the training of enlisted men as well as officers is that, as an incidental benefit, the program could begin to produce from neutral nations some manpower trained in at least some of the special skills that will be required to verify compliance with arms-control and disarmament agreements that may be reached. One of the political-military simulations mentioned earlier unexpectedly brought out the potential usefulness of disarmament inspectors as a source of ready-trained observers in a crisis. It could work quite the other way around, with great potential benefit, if and when an arms-limitation agreement is reached that suddenly imposes a demand for appropriately trained neutrals. In fact, an "elective" subject for those men already possessing the required language skill could well be training in disarmament and arms-control verification techniques.

Experience indicates that it is equally important to have a suitable advance plan for the logistical movement and support of any UN force that is to be moved unpredictably to some unforeseeable location. I can only repeat recommendations for advance and highly specific ear-marking of airlift and sealift facilities so that improvisation will not be quite so frantic next time, so that they can be called on virtually automatically by those charged with moving a force almost overnight, (and so that, in the absence of other alternatives, it would not be necessary to accept Soviet offers of air transport — with, as in the Congo, the accompanying influx of Soviet *agents provocateurs*). In this connection it must simply be faced that there is no real equality among the nations, and that, as Calvocoressi writes:[3]

[3] Peter Calvocoressi, *World Order and New States*, (New York: Praeger, 1962) p. 94.

At present the UN is dependent on countries great and small for the launching of any operation except a minor observation task. However large the majority in favour of despatching a UN force, no action will follow unless the UN can borrow enough transport aircraft, and it is almost true to say that this requirement alone gives the United States a veto undreamt of by the framers of the Charter. Even a less powerful state like India can be all but indispensable, for the Indian army is the only army in the world which is both large enough to supply a whole range of combat and service units without being gutted and is also accepted as uncommitted in the cold war.

For some time to come the United States may remain the only power fully equipped to respond to such a call even on an improvised basis. But the capabilities of others are growing, specifically in the wide distribution of jet transport craft, which are now the status symbol of the smallest non-Western countries. From a political standpoint it will be highly desirable to have on earmarked reserve transport craft not belonging to the great powers as soon as it is possible to integrate these efficiently into a planning system.

In addition to the basic constabulary type of training described above, there should also be a technical assistance program aimed at preparing specialized units from the underdeveloped countries for service along the lines we have indicated. At present it is virtually impossible on short notice to recruit a signals unit from any but the most advanced Western countries. This may be true for a period of time, but technical assistance can shorten the wait for the various specialties such as transportation units, troop and vehicle movement control units, and helicopter service personnel that proved to be in such short supply in the Congo operation. The technical capabilities of some of the middle-tier countries are advancing sufficiently so that they should be able to contribute specialized units of this sort if additional training of a uniform nature can be furnished.

I proposed several years ago that the United States take a fresh look at its Military Assistance Programs with a view to their far more pointed utilization to develop units for UN police purposes — a purpose clearly spelled out in the original MAP legislation but ignored in practice. The retrograde succession of military coups in Latin America,

doubtless to be emulated elsewhere, gives special point to the suggestion.[4] As a bonus, troops could be trained at least in part for "civic
action."

FINANCING

To return to resources, the issue of financing, often said to be the
dominant difficulty in seeking to improve the United Nations' readiness for peacekeeping operations, discourages any really major advance
planning for the future despite our intuition that there are bound to
be new situations where a UN force may become the best available
option. In another perspective the financial opposition merely symbol-
izes the political opposition. For in any relative terms the costs involved
are so small in proportion to the defense expenditures or gross national
product of the advanced countries as to make UN forces a bargain by
any reasonable standard. (All United States contributions to all UN
programs from 1958 through 1962 equaled less than one-third of one
per cent of the current annual budget for the US Department of Defense; the total of all UN expenditures to date is less than one month's
advertising budget for radio and television; over a 17-year period the
total of all annual UN costs to the United States averages only seventy-
five cents for every man, woman, and child in the country.) Never, in
this perspective, has so much fuss been made over so little where such
large values were at stake.

Yet policy must consider both perspectives as representing valid
forms of political reality, and so it might help to consider two points
not commonly made. The first is that, despite all of the difficulties encountered in the later financing of the UN Congo operation, there still
is no instance on record of any responsible person asking at 3 o'clock
in the morning, when the guns are firing and a UN mission is urgently
needed, where the money was going to come from. It thus seems reasonable to expect that in a future crisis the financial problem will not
occur to anyone till either there is a falling out among the sponsors of
the operation — which was the principal reason for the financial crisis
in the Congo — or financial stringencies for one reason or other come
to seem as important as the crisis itself.

[4] See footnote 1 of this chapter. Cf. President Eisenhower's speech to UN
General Assembly, Sept. 22, 1960.

The second point is more important. It is that when all is said and done, it is not reasonable to believe that those whose ambitions have been frustrated by a UN operation will cheerfully pay for it. The United States has happily been in the majority and had its way in all the UN peacekeeping enterprises from start to present; and there is every reason to think this will continue to be the case unless the United States drastically alters its policy, loses its perspective, or defaults on its leadership. We are then entitled to hope that the United Nations will act as we think it should in future peacekeeping interventions that are in our interests even when opposed by the Soviets. I would say that even if the Soviet bloc, or others who feel themselves the victims of the operation, will not pay up, the cost to us for this kind of political victory is minimal if it is limited to dollars and does not call for the shedding of blood, including American blood.[5]

We should agree among ourselves that we do not really expect enemies of improved peacekeeping capacity to pay their fair assessment while publicly continuing to demand that they meet their share. In the same way we should also continue to demand token payments from the poorest countries, payments which are meaningless financially but significant politically for their self-respect and stake in the international order. The General Assembly in the spring of 1963 identified only 26 countries as the developed countries of the world.[6] In fact, whatever the fictions, these must be the ones to pay for UN peacekeeping activities or there will not be any. If we consider it to be in the American national interest, the Western interest, and the global interest to have such peacekeeping activities in order to avoid great-power confrontation, escalation, chaos, savagery, and all the rest, this will be the reality.

Having considered these two points, there remains the practical problem of financing the force proposed here. Some other studies indicate

---

5 (An indication of how the United States might react if the United Nations ever did take a serious operational action that displeased us was furnished by the Congressional threat to the entire American contribution to the UN Special Fund in 1963 as a result of a relatively small project of assistance to Cuba. In fact the United States has approved of 287 out of 288 projects developed by the Special Fund — an enviable record for any great power).

6 General Assembly Resolution 1875 (S-IV), June 27, 1963.

the range we are seeking. For example, the Clark-Sohn Plan for a World Peace Force calls for the annual expenditure of $9 billion.[7] William Frye's more modest proposal in 1957 for a standing peace force of 7,000 men was estimated then to cost $65 million for the base, $1 million a year to maintain it, and $25 million a year to operate and sustain the force on the most economical basis.[8]

I am going to assume here that a training base can be secured for the purpose without a major capital outlay, as a contribution in kind by, for example, India, Sweden, Pakistan, or the Philippines. (If it had to be financed, the cost of the base, including permanent barracks, classroom facilities, hospital, warehouses, runway, vehicle repair facilities, electric power, roadways, water and sewage, senior staff quarters, recreation facilities, training and maneuver areas, etc. would total at least $50,000,000 — an unacceptably high figure.)

Even the $26 million figure of Frye exceeds the perspective we are limiting ourselves to here. The projected operating costs for the training command proposed here would be in the neighborhood of $10 million annually, wholly apart from the training facility itself, the base pay and allowances for the trainees, and their transportation to and from their home country. This is less than the cost of supporting ONUC for one month during the Congo operation.

The figure of $10 million is arrived at as shown on page 89, with alternative figures showing the estimated cost if the annual intake of trainees were 3,000 instead of 5,000.[9]

This figure may be compared with a total of $8.3 million arrived at on the basis of an earlier formula of $8 to $10 per day per man for such a training facility — $7.3 million for 2500 men at a time on the lower rate — plus $1 million for base maintenance.[10] To both these would

---

[7] *World Peace Through World Law,* 2nd ed. (Cambridge: Harvard University, 1960), p. 320.

[8] Frye, *op. cit.,* pp. 75-78.

[9] I am indebted to Colonel David L. Evans, USAF, for this table and the subsequent one on headquarters staff. The figures used for personnel costs assume officers at the average rank of major, and a preponderance of non-coms among the enlisted personnel. It would be important to be able to select and pay superior personnel as instructors.

[10] "Military Aspects of a Permanent UN Force" by Lt. Cols. Charles A. Cannon, Jr., and A. A. Jordan, in Frye, *op. cit.,* p. 167.

be added the approximately $1.5 million for the augmented head-
quarters planning staff discussed below. Both total approximately $10
million.

Annual Base Operating Costs	$1,000,000
Cost of Base Support and Training Personnel	
350 @ $6,000 plus 452 @ $4,000	3,908,000
(300 @ $6,000 plus 355 @ $4,000)	(3,220,000)
Rations for Trainees	
2500 @ 1.07 per day	946,400
(1500 @ 1.07 per day)	(585,800)
Cost of Training per Trainee	
2500 @ 2.50 per day	2,281,250
(1500 @ 2.50 per day)	(1,386,750)
Total Yearly Training Costs	
for 2500 men	8,165,650
(for 1500 men)	(6,174,550)

The alternative figures are based on reducing the program to an
ultimate total of 15,000 men trained over a five-year period, 3,000 per
year, 1,500 at any one time. The base and training staff would be reduced proportionately. (The ratio of trainees to instructing staff under
the larger scheme is 6.57 to 1, and under the more modest one, 6.43 to 1;
this compares with approximately 10 to 1 in United States military
training, but it is justified by the special circumstances.) The over-all
annual cost would be somewhere around $7.5 million. It would seem
that the larger program would be considerably more economical.

The total annual cost of $10 million depends on cutting the costs
in every way possible. One means suggested earlier that would reduce
the budgeted assessed costs of the operation would be a maximum of
contributions in kind. As indicated, the training facility could be a
contribution without cost to the UN; the instructors could be
loaned from the advanced military powers on a similarly credited basis;
the troops could be lifted for training on planes or ships of powers, including ourselves, who might consider it a useful training exercise in
transport of non-American forces in an emergency. (It would also represent the start of the earmarking arrangement.) The rations could
be contributed on the same basis. All these, as suggested, would stand
as credits against future assessments for UN field operations.

It may well be that some who oppose the strengthening of international institutions would refuse to pay their share of this item in the regular budget, along the line pioneered by the Soviet Union when it announced in May 1963 its intention to deduct selectively from its regular contribution the Soviet share of those detailed items to which the Soviets object. Here too the debts of the defaulters should be carried on the books. The United Nations should continue to dun them. But their failure to pay should not be permitted to erode and eventually destroy programs we want and need, producing a victory for the Soviets they neither deserve nor really expect.

For the longer run, it has become increasingly clear that the present method of financing the United Nations is an imperfect one, and may be no longer suitable or adequate to the needs. The bond issue has been a stop-gap, not a permanent solution. Suggestions have been made for increasing the sources of independent revenue for the organization, and one that may be promising — but is a relatively far distance in the future, both technically and politically — is for the United Nations to receive the revenues from potentially fertile sources such as the waters of the high seas, the sub-sea bed, the moon and planets. Perhaps these are worth investigating further.

But the financial problem is political in its roots. There is no dearth of money to do the job if states are willing to supply it. Indeed, the United States could handily do it all, except that it would probably be fatal to the health of the organization and to American support for it. The fundamental issue of sovereignty in all its contemporary ambiguity underlies the financial problem; the latter cannot be solved by somehow assuming a solution to the former.

The practical problem is not just paying for the UNEF and Congo forces. The problem is what to do about the next crisis requiring that the United Nations mount a field operation, and the next. Suggestions have been made to buy time in which such vital operations can be fielded, by establishing a security fund on the basis of a long-term, interest-free loan. This kind of proposal now takes the more modest form of a bond issue, colloquially summed up as "Fight Now, Pay Later." But this remedy is only a temporary one. Moreover, it still requires repayment by the very countries now refusing to pay.

The United Nations is simply going to have to have resources of its own to enable it to do a job which is in the interest even of those who are seeking to sabotage it by withholding their financial support. My own suggestion has been for an Endowment: a capital fund sufficient to provide annual income that will enable the United Nations to carry out at least a significant part of the task the nations charge it to do but without always following up with the financial wherewithal. No increase in international powers is involved; simply the knowledge that means exist to back up a decision made by exactly the same political process as today.

No one can foretell the reaction to such a proposal. It may be wildly optimistic to guess that a world-wide appeal for, say, a one-billion dollar endowment fund for the United Nations would be oversubscribed by individuals, foundations, governments, and private corporations. Already there have been a number of efforts on the part of American citizens to supply private funds to the United Nations. Some Quaker groups in the United States have made a practice of "tithing the tithe" for the United Nations as for a church. Some communities in this country recently have sent to the United Nations money which they would have spent on fall-out shelters. These gestures are idealistic, and, because of their small size, quixotic, although well meant.

What is now needed is an effort on a world-wide scale to supply funds by tapping a wellspring of good will, hope, idealism, and the urge to make a personal contribution to a meaningful cause; who can say how deep this spring runs? I can envisage a general fund-raising drive that might give the whole enterprise precisely the shot in the arm it so badly needs. Contributions should of course be tax-exempt. With a growing reserve of funds, the organization can go ahead and do its job without depending either on its enemies to pay their share — an unrealistic hope — or putting the US government in the position of appearing wholly to subsidize it.[11]

The various proposals outlined above should not be taken as a quantum jump from the existing realities to some novel kind of world force.

[11] Lincoln P. Bloomfield, "The United Nations in Crisis," *Daedalus*, Fall, 1962. See Norman J. Padelford, "Financial Crisis and the Future of the United Nations," *World Politics*, July, 1963. For a comprehensive analysis of the whole financing problem see John G. Stoessinger, *Financing the United Nations System* (Washington: Brookings Institution, 1964).

They should be presented as a modest series of measures that build on past experience in the light of anticipated needs of the future. Those who oppose the growth of constructive and stabilizing peacekeeping capacities for the United Nations will predictably continue to oppose even these modest steps — although in some likely circumstances they will once again find it to be in their own interest, and it would not be the first time those who lead have had to interpret the interests of others for them. Above all, the proposal should not be tied to the utopian vision of peace forces, international armies, or world police under general and complete disarmament. The degree to which any of the great powers see it as a potential major threat to their security would thus be minimized. The proposed force would be employed under the same constitutional majorities in the Security Council and General Assembly as today in terms of actually fielding an operation. The substantial difference would be in readiness and efficiency.

OTHER MEASURES

This proposal need not stand in the way of the equally urgent list of lesser measures deriving from the lessons of UNEF and the Congo. The chief one is an augmented headquarters staff of officers assigned to study past experience and prepare the necessary manuals and aids that would make the operation smoother next time. Ample proposals exist today for strengthening the staff of the Military Adviser to the Secretary General to achieve these results without its having to be extensively debated as a new program. Indeed, that staff is already considerably larger than it was formerly. The experiences of the Egyptian, Lebanese, and Congo operations have been studied by it, and hopefully some of the promised manuals of operations are in preparation. One experienced official suggests a staff of 25,[12] but if the training command outlined above is created along the lines suggested, then the headquarters staff would probably have to include closer to 100 in order to give general supervision to the training program and oversee the special logistical problems it involves. One professional estimate of the requirements would look like the following:

[12] Andrew W. Cordier, "The Rule of Law in the World Community," *University of Pennsylvania Law Review*, May, 1963, p. 901.

Estimated Personnel Requirements for Headquarters Planning Staff

Personnel and Administration	5	Accounting and Finance	15
Intelligence and Security	10	Communications	20
Operations and Training	15	Public Information	2
Logistics	20	Surgeon	5
Plans	20	Judge Advocate	5
Engineering	5	TOTAL	122

A further refinement is the recommendation by Col. R. B. Tackaberry, C.D. of Canada that the headquarters include a nucleus field headquarters on a permanent basis. Alternatively, with some economies, seconding of staff to this group from UN departments and so on, the figure might be shaved down to one even less formidable, particularly by making use of the new UN Training and Research Institute.

The reference to logistics points to an area of complexity and needful improvement virtually from top to bottom.

(1) First of all it is desirable to add to the expanded headquarters staff a capability the lack of which has plagued previous UN operations in the field. A modest logistical unit in the military component of UN headquarters would represent an improvement from the standpoint of UN field forces that in the past have relied on the various civilian supply sections.

(2) It would not be impossible to purchase, rent, or have donated as a credit against future peacekeeping assessments several warehouses located in different parts of the world and stockpiled with supplies adequate, say, for 30 days in a variety of climates. These supplies could be similarly donated for subsequent credit, from surplus stocks of rations, field tents and kitchens, basic medical supplies, and the like. The progress that the U.S. Army Quartermaster Corps, for example, has made in the irradiation of foods to preserve them could be drawn upon here.

(3) It would have made life far simpler in the Congo if the 129 different vehicle types had been standardized. In the proposed warehouses or in nearby motor pools could be spotted a modest stock of standard vehicles (jeeps or land-rovers, half-ton trucks, etc.) with standardized spare parts. Thus at least the initial elements in a UN field operation would not be dependent on a wide and hopelessly unstandardized variety of vehicles which would later have to be replaced (as UNEF finally did with the aim of standardization). Here again,

contributions of such vehicles could be the special activity of an appropriate country which would receive a credit against future field-operation assessments.

(4) One of the most interesting aspects of the makeshift peace-keeping operations of the recent past has been the unique role played by the UN Truce Supervision Organization for Palestine in acting in effect as a training area, replacement depot, and stockpile of key personnel for other UN operations. UNEF in 1956, UNOGIL in Lebanon in 1958, the Congo operation in 1960, the UN Security Force in New Guinea, and the Yemen observation all drew commanders, initial staff, or observers from UNTSO. Had it not existed it would, as is often said of the United Nations itself, have had to be invented. UNTSO is in part a substitute for standing staff or even force. With it there is at least a walking start for new races that must be run without preparation. (Without it, the need for a comparable staff facility becomes even more urgent.)

If the UNTSO is going to be a relatively permanent fixture, the United Nations should consider quietly building up stocks nearby along the lines outlined above. These stocks would include vehicles, rations, tents, field kitchens, blankets, medical supplies, and the rest in a location which could be managed, supervised, and coordinated by UNTSO personnel who in effect would form a cadre for other operations. The supply base could be Cyprus, Malta, Wheelus Field, or Bizerte. One could even consider adding a modest training mission to the UNTSO table of organization, using as the nucleus the staff of the UNTSO officers themselves plus others who have served in UNEF and ONUC.

(5) Other tangible improvements have occurred to many observers. It would doubtless improve efficiency if administrative troops were available at the very outset of a field operation, backed up by the supplies it is suggested be stockpiled in depots that could readily be drawn upon.[13]

(6) In thinking of the first elements of UN forces on the ground, it is essential in future operations that contingents maintain current World Health Organization inoculations in their home countries and

---

[13] See Lt. General E. L. M. Burns, *Between Arab and Israeli*, (N.Y.: Ivan Obolensky, 1962), pp. 212-213.

bring water purification and medical supplies to cover fifteen to thirty days — a further argument for advance earmarking of units.

(7) The diversity of types and calibres of weapons has given rise to many problems. At a minimum it would have been helpful if each government had notified the United Nations of these details at the very beginning and arrangements had been made for an appropriate reserve. If a training scheme is adopted, the pressures will doubtless increase for standard equipage and tactics. In the Congo it would have been useful at the outset to have had tear-gas discharging devices and smoke grenades to enable troops to disengage when conditions proved unfavorable. The Ghanaian battalion used bamboo sticks and shields to excellent advantage in Leopoldville in dealing with mobs. I have mentioned my own specifications for UN research and development, giving highest priority to use of novel and unconventional pacifying devices such as tranquilizer weapons and other psychochemicals. It is time the art of peacekeeping moved technologically out of the age of medieval warfare and into the age of the laboratory.[14]

One more special problem that arose in the UN Congo operation must be dealt with. This is the problem of discipline, including procedures for investigation and either substantiating or disproving charges of breach of discipline. Since a root cause in ONUC lay in the disparities of discipline among troops, a uniform code of military justice has struck many as a crying need for the United Nations. A committee of experts should be attached to the Office of the Military Adviser to the Secretary General for the purpose of exploring the possibility of drawing one up.

But there may be insuperable political difficulties in such a step, growing out of the unprecedentedness of the very notion of international "police" stationed or operating within a country. Injustices that may be committed by the force, by units of the force, or by individuals in it have a very special political meaning and can yield very special political consequences. Ordinary disciplinary action against the individual by his own commanding officer may not begin to deal with these special implications. This is true *a fortiori* if the injustice is committed at the hands of the unit itself, or, as happened so frequently in the

---

[14] One illustrative development is the electrified fence mounted across the front of American tanks in West Berlin for crowd control purposes.

Congo, is ambiguous in its very nature. It has been shown that the general public image of the operation, which determines in good part the political support available to it, can be crippled unless proper procedures exist and allegations of atrocities are not left hanging.

I suggest that the United Nations adopt the Danish device of "ombudsman," a role based on Scandinavian precedents. The ombudsman investigates complaints by the public against government actions where there is no other means of redress. The office of ombudsman was copied from Denmark recently by New Zealand as a check against the rapid concentration of powers in the hands of the state. As a news story described the function:

> Public complaints against the growing grip of bureaucracy on everyday life have increased rapidly in New Zealand in recent years. The Government last year acknowledged that safeguards were needed. For a remedy, it turned to the Scandinavian countries, where an official — known as an ombudsman — exists to investigate public complaints of misuse of state powers. . . . Citizens with a grievance against the Government now can submit their complaint in writing to the ombudsman, with a fee. . . . If he feels that there are genuine grounds for complaint, he can call for Government files on the matter. . . . If the ombudsman believes that wrong rulings have been given — through errors, misjudgments, unreasonable rulings, or for other causes — he makes recommendations to the minister of the department concerned. He cannot change decisions himself, but he can bring strong pressure to bear. If the minister refuses to modify a decision, the ombudsman can take the case to the Prime Minister and eventually to Parliament. At that stage the Government must justify its stand publicly.[15]

The experiment has appeared to prove a success in New Zealand. The creation of such an office for the United Nations, either on a permanent basis or on an *ad hoc* basis when new forces are sent into the field, might go a long way to allaying misgivings about the relative immunity of the United Nations from public accountability for actions committed by troops under its nominal command in the field.

These proposals all presuppose a global organization for peacekeeping as at present. But this is not the only route. A "regionalization" of peacekeeping could one day — but not now — prove a better and safer way. Proposals emphasizing regional forces have been made ever since

[15] *New York Times*, Nov. 4, 1962.

Winston Churchill is reported to have favored a regional rather than global approach to international security during the postwar planning of the early 1940's. Certainly the United States, though Roosevelt opposed Churchill's notion, has at times shown a preference for activity by the Organization of American States, as in recent Caribbean crises. We have noted the preference on the part of some African countries for an all-African force to maintain order in African situations, a view that gained popularity in some African quarters during the Congo operation and even materialized to a modest extent in the Algerian-Moroccan military fray of October-November 1963, when on the agreement of the parties under the auspices of the Organization for African unity officers from Mali and Ethiopia patrolled the disputed frontier.

Some of the thinking that went into the proposals for a multilateral nuclear force for NATO in the early 1960's included many relevant notions. According to one report:

> A joint international force in NATO might very well be a rehearsal or a pattern for some international force that might have to exist in order to police a disarmed world, perhaps under some form of United Nations control over general and complete disarmament. It may be that we will have to learn to control nuclear weapons with our friends before we can safely leave control of nuclear weapons to some worldwide control regime.[16]

Some private proposals have taken the regional tack.

> Perhaps instead of thinking of a centrally controlled police force we ought to think in terms of maintaining a separate regional force for each disturbed region. Each such regional force could then be controlled by a different commission, composed of representatives of between five to seven nations, which would preferably not be drawn from the region itself.

The prolific Leo Szilard, who suggested this informally, envisaged such regional police forces as operating under the auspices of the

[16] "An Authoritative Source" cited by Arthur Krock in the *New York Times*, Oct. 15, 1963. The Institute for Strategic Studies has speculated on the use of such nationally committed NATO forces under disarmament, giving "the appearance of disarmament without for years abandoning the reality of national power", but thus safely creating "the political framework of a disarmed world" that could "through custom and acceptance be relied on increasingly to carry the burden of security." *Disarmament and European Security*. London, August 1963, pp. 70-71.

United Nations, each region's commission to be appointed by a majority vote of the Security Council including the concurring votes of the permanent members. This may be as sound an approach to the problem of international police force in a disarming world as any other, although far more of a jump out of current practices. And it has the virtue of decentralization, pluralism, and balance of power without which the notion of a centrally directed global force with weapons of mass destruction becomes potentially tyrannous. Nonetheless, we had best build on such foundations as now exist. (Some of these are regional, and it might well be preferable for NATO to police its Cypruses.)

The general philosophy adopted here in the matter of UN forces is, then, to strike out in modest ways to enhance essential peacekeeping capabilities while keeping well within the *de facto* ground rules of the nationalistic age, taking the most extraordinary care to preserve the fiction of the sovereign equality of states. Proposals for a standing UN force, for taxing powers to support the force, for direct individual recruitment into a common uniform, or for weighted voting in the assembly are not necessary or relevant to the present system, even reinforced by a modest standby force (although they would all be relevant if and when the General Assembly were ever endowed with genuine legislative powers rather than only the power to recommend). For now, the problem in its essence is to stay within the boundaries of political reality but to get the job done. The most that can be hoped for — and that will be a great deal — is a modest step toward regularizing this international capability so that it does not have to be invented anew and the world organization undergo a political revolution each time the need arises.

One of the cardinal errors of the contemporary peace movement is the notion that steps toward a world community, toward peaceful settlement of disputes, and toward greater tolerance between nations are necessarily habit-forming in the face of overriding ideological, political, or territorial conflict. The inevitability of historic progress toward world order has simply not been proven, however high our persistent hopes and visions. One thing that has been proven to be relatively habit-forming the world over, however, is the "police function." Let us admit at once that anything approaching a genuine police function in the hands of the United Nations is anomalous and even legally inexplicable in the absence of a genuine international political consensus of basic political values that must underlie community and its police powers. But an approach to the problem that is pragmatic and empirical demonstrates both a need and a possibility for an international function that, while neither police nor military, is more the former than the latter.

One might say that this is a case where it is desirable to rise above logic and even legal principle in the name of the higher principle of surviving a period of the world's history when formal institutions are inadequate to the need, when political warfare stands in the way of real consensus, and when only a second-order agreement — not to destroy the world — is the current basis of cooperation among the superpowers.

A genius like Dag Hammarskjöld could perform with virtuosity his political pirouetting along the knife edges of ideological conflict in the name of getting the job done, all without any sound institutional, political, or financial basis. The task that faces the responsible powers is to institutionalize the best of Dag Hammarskjöld's genius so that it does not depend on the presence or availability of such genius. It is to meet as best one can, imaginatively, creatively, but with realism, the day-to-day requirements of a world whose management rests in the hands of simple men with complex problems.

PART TWO

A Symposium
on International Forces

UN FORCES AND LESSONS
OF SUEZ AND CONGO

An Appraisal	*Herbert Nicholas*
A UN Perspective	*Brian E. Urquhart*
Logistics — Experience and Requirements	*Edward H. Bowman and James E. Fanning*

HERBERT NICHOLAS

An Appraisal

I

It is sometimes instructive, as Holmes long ago pointed out to Watson, to begin by asking a few questions about dogs that do not bark in the night. Suez and the Congo are not the only major crises which have disturbed the United Nations. Yet they are the only ones to which it has responded by creating a true United Nations force. Why?

Consider the case of Hungary. Coincident with Suez, it provoked from the General Assembly stronger verbal denunciation. While the Anglo-French attack was described colorlessly as "military operations against Egyptian territory,"[1] the Soviet move in Hungary was denounced initially as "foreign," "armed intervention," and later as a "violation of the political independence of Hungary," a deprivation of "its liberty," and a "violation of the Charter."[2] Yet the employment of a United Nations force of any kind was not even considered; it was left to the Secretary-General to "investigate" and "observe the situation directly through representatives named by him."[3]

Thus, though the United Nations' judgment was unequivocal, its actions were minimal. Vehemence stopped at words because everyone knew that to go further was to involve one's country in an outright clash with a great power in an area which the Soviet Union was obviously going to regard as vital. Nor in this regard was there any difference of degree among the critics of the Soviet Union — all, from

[1] General Assembly Resolution 997 (ES-I), November 2, 1956.
[2] General Assembly Resolution 1131 (XI), December 12, 1956.
[3] General Assembly Resolution 1004 (ES-II), November 4, 1956.

the United States down to the smallest member of the General Assembly, drew back from any action stronger than words. It was not merely the defense of Hungary that was unthinkable; even the admission into the country of the mildest form of United Nations presence, the Secretary-General's representative, could not be insisted upon in the face of Soviet refusal, and was in fact never secured.

Five years after Hungary, India invaded Goa. The issue was brought before the Security Council by Portugal on December 18, 1961, with a request for an immediate cease-fire. A Western-sponsored resolution was not only defeated by a Soviet veto but was also opposed by all three Afro-Asian members of the Council. The "Uniting for Peace" mechanism was not invoked, it is generally understood, because there seemed no prospect of obtaining a two-thirds majority in the General Assembly for any resolution along the lines of that defeated in the Security Council. However, even the defeated resolution gave no hint of the possible employment of a United Nations force; it called only for an immediate cessation of hostilities, a withdrawal of Indian forces, a solution by peaceful means, and the provision of such assistance by the Secretary-General as might be appropriate. India announced the surrender of the Goan forces on the same day that the Security Council met.

In Goa, in contrast to Hungary, no great power was directly involved. Aggression, in most ordinary senses of the term, had clearly been committed. Nevertheless, any realistic observer of the reactions in Turtle Bay to India's action must recognize that, in the present UN context, there is one crime which in certain circumstances may be judged to outweigh the crime of aggression — namely, colonialism. The failure of the United Nations to register even a verbal protest against India's behavior in Goa was basically due to the fact that Portugal had put itself outside the pale by its actions in the same year on Angola. Since the UN can assist only those who at any rate initially can themselves resist, the sheer rapidity of the Indian operation would probably have deprived any United Nations resolution of more than academic effect. But, even if time had permitted the interposition of a UN force between Goa and its attackers, a sufficient number of impartial, small powers would not have been willing to serve on it.

Lastly, let us consider Korea. Here the United Nations came nearest to establishing a fighting force. It did create a United Nations command and requested Members to make forces available to it, but this was a mere anointing of the existing United States Far East command, a sanctification, as it were, of its personnel and its commander, General MacArthur, and of whatever active units Member States might supply and place under his command. In an important sense, the action taken by MacArthur and his forces was United Nations action; this was its status in international law.[4] In terms of international politics and of international organization, however, it fell crucially short of being a real United Nations operation. It was not under the executive control of the United Nations; the Secretariat had no part in its organization or deployment; it was not financed by the United Nations, nor did the United Nations determine in any but the very broadest terms the conditions and objectives of its employment. The response to the appeal to all Member States to furnish assistance was generally poor. One Member, the United States, was the self-appointed Atlas of the operation, without whose broad shoulders all would have failed. By the end of 1950, the only foreign ground troops fighting by the Americans' side were from the United Kingdom, Australia, France, Greece, the Netherlands, the Philippines, Thailand, and Turkey.[5] South Koreans apart, the unified command in Korea consisted of about a quarter of a million Americans compared with only about 36,000 troops from all other Member States combined.

Of the three cases only Korea bears the slightest resemblance to Suez and the Congo in that here the United Nations response to a violation of the Charter took a forceful form. This was due in large part to a series of happy accidents. The fact of aggression could be quickly established, owing to the presence in Korea of the United Nations Commission on Korea. Resistance could be quickly organized, because a great power had its armed forces virtually *in situ* when the fighting broke out (and the other super power behind the aggression had made the mistake of walking out of the Security Council). Supplementary assistance was lent to the United States-United

[4] See Guenter Weissberg, *The International Status of the United Nations* (New York: Oceana, 1961), pp. 78 ff.
[5] In 1951, ground troops were also furnished by Belgium, Canada, Colombia, Ethiopia, Luxembourg, and New Zealand.

Nations command by countries who felt themselves already bound to support American action by virtue of other ties, most obviously by their common North Atlantic Treaty Organization (NATO) membership. And although the Soviet Union was wholly hostile to the United Nations action in Korea, it did not attempt to frustrate it in a manner that might cause a local police action to escalate into a direct clash between two super powers. Indeed, the Korean conflict occurred at a time when the American lead in nuclear weapons made it reasonable to suppose that the United States was, strictly speaking, the only super power.

Soon, however, countervailing considerations made themselves felt. The very predominance of United States strength which made the United Nations operation in Korea possible also diminished its United Nations appeal and reduced the crucial element of universality. This, in fact, accounted for what Mr. Lie called the "disappointing"[6] response to his appeal to Member States for further assistance. More seriously, the open intervention of Communist China transformed the nature of the conflict and greatly heightened the risks of its growing, if not into a conflict of super powers, at least into an interminable and costly war in which military advantages accruing to superior nuclear weapons would be offset by the political impossibility of using the weapon of Hiroshima in the service of the Charter. Support at the United Nations fell away from an operation which previously, however inadequate its United Nations character, was yet felt to serve United Nations objectives.

Subsequently, the emphasis fell increasingly on the search for a Korean settlement, reaching a point indeed where, in the behavior of many Members even outside the communist bloc, the United States and the North Koreans were treated as if both were in equal violation of the Charter and as if each needed in equal measure to be forced to keep the peace. Members differed in their degree of concern over the prolongation and extension of the war, but sooner or later all shared the conviction that to persist in using force, no matter how impeccable its United Nations credentials, was to frustrate the very purpose of the Organization. In this sense, as has frequently been observed, the

6 Trygve Lie, *In the Cause of Peace* (New York: Macmillan, 1954), p. 338.

moral of Korea is not that collective security under United Nations
auspices can be made to work, but that not even United Nations
auspices will persuade Member States to risk military action where no
vital national interest, narrowly construed, is involved, and where
United Nations action may lead to hostilities with a major power.

This brings us to the two clear occasions when the dogs did bark,
and the police did turn out — Suez and the Congo. In neither case can
one explain United Nations action by the operation of a single factor;
in both, several desperate elements combined. Let us take them
in order.

II

In the first place, the complex of military events which it is convenient to call "Suez" occurred in an area long the subject of continuous United Nations concern. At the time of the Israeli attack there
was actually operating at Gaza the United Nations Truce Supervision
Organization (UNTSO) under its Chief of Staff, General Burns. His
presence in the area served something of the same purpose in relation
to the organization of the United Nations Emergency Force (UNEF)
that the United Nations Commission on Korea served in relation to
the alerting of the United Nations in Korea.

Secondly, Suez lay outside the zones of direct great power confrontation. But at the same time it was a key area strategically and econom-
ically which the West could not afford to lose to the Soviet bloc and
which the Soviet bloc was proportionately eager to acquire. Two
permanent members of the Security Council, the United Kingdom
and France, regarded Nasser's nationalization of the Canal as an assault
upon a vital national interest, but they always claimed that their
forceful action to protect this interest was intended only to fill the
void created by United Nations impotence in the face of the Israeli
attack. Whether true or not, the argument made it difficult for them
to refuse a United Nations force when offered, and indeed, in the
case of Britain at least, reflected a profound national schizophrenia on
the propriety of her violent action. Furthermore, the joint strength
of Britain and France, though overwhelming against Egypt, was not
sufficient to put them in the great power class, as became apparent

when pressure was put on them simultaneously by the United States and the Soviet Union. This pressure was strong and potentially irresistible. Yet it was not in the United States' interest to drive her closest allies into too humiliating a retreat, and the Soviet Union's "rocket-rattling" diplomacy certainly worked both ways — stiffening Anglo-French resistance at least as much as it accelerated compliance. Nor did Nasser want to exchange British and French occupation of the Canal for Soviet tutelage. Thus a complex of considerations all led to the acceptance of Lester Pearson's UNEF as a device which would enable all parties to return to the *status quo ante* with maximum speed and minimum loss of face.

It is perhaps true that the UNEF idea owed some of its immediate acceptance to the fact that it was imperfectly understood: Britain and France in particular hoped to see the force act as the agent of the United Nations in implementing the six-point recommendations on a Canal settlement announced by Mr. Hammarskjöld on October 12, 1956, while Israel hoped to see it remedy her grievances about transit through the Canal and the Gulf of Aqaba. If true, however, this remains a marginal consideration. UNEF was created basically because no interested power could impose a solution alone, and all powers, great and small alike, preferred an internationally contrived and controlled solution to a conflict which could develop dangerously into a wider war. Negative considerations pointed the same way; neither of the two alliances, the Warsaw Pact or NATO, felt their vital interests threatened (however much, briefly, Britain and France may have), and neither Israel nor Egypt, on reflection, wanted a fight *à outrance* then and there.

To see these as the underlying factors that made UNEF possible is not to depreciate the efforts of Lester Pearson and the other representatives who came to be known at the United Nations as the "fire brigade," or the role of the Secretary-General and the Secretariat. "Factors" by themselves do not stop wars; they have to be assessed and manipulated by human beings. If courage, perseverance, diplomatic skill, imagination, and personal prestige had not existed in the right quarters at the right moment in 1956, the resulting drift and confusion would have required more than a UNEF to remedy them.

The celebrated conditions of UNEF laid down by the Secretary-General in his two reports of November 4 and 6, 1956,[7] were the necessary preconditions of its existence and also set the limits to what it might achieve. No one except the Soviet bloc states and the convicted trio of Britain, France, and Israel was willing to enlist in a United Nations force with coercive powers; no one was willing to fight Egypt or Israel, or possibly both simultaneously, in order to impose a just settlement — whatever that would have been — on these old combatants. Once this was recognized, it followed inevitably that the United Nations force could have only the function of facilitating the invaders' withdrawal, of maintaining a minimum of order in the transitional phase from war to armistice, and, finally, of keeping the local combatants, Israel and Egypt, at arms' length. The element of force was, strictly speaking, minimal. It was military only in being composed of soldiers; its functions were fewer even than those of a normal civilian police corps. Police exist to prevent crime and enforce the law as well as to preserve the peace, but UNEF has no powers to prevent anything save the most blatant frontier violations. Its role is pacific and passive. It is essential interpository in character, a moral United Nations presence given physical embodiment on a scale sufficiently extensive to guarantee that neither side can aim the slightest blow at the other without involving itself by that very act in larger, international consequences. Ever since the cease-fire and withdrawals were effected, UNEF has been in fact a larger and more physically impenetrable UNTSO.

In this capacity its success is undoubted. It has not only achieved its immediate objectives; it has also kept the peace between Egypt and Israel ever since, both in the large and obvious sense and in that of reducing to a previously unknown level the number of incidents along the border. This has been due to many factors besides the efficiency and

---

[7] UN Documents A/3289 and A/3302. The conditions were later codified in Document A/3943. In summary, these principles were:
(i) No permanent member of the Security Council or any "interested" government should contribute contingents.
(ii) The force should not be used to affect the military or political outcome of the dispute.
(iii) Its arms should only be used in self-defense.
(iv) It should not be stationed on a state's territory except with that state's consent.

loyalty of the force. Though the basic local antagonisms remain, nothing has occurred to provoke another 1956 flare-up, while the great power outsiders have all for various reasons been tolerably content not to stoke up the fires of Egyptian-Israeli animosity.[8] Then again there has been a simplicity, a straightforwardness about UNEF's role, rare in international affairs, which has helped it greatly. Its task is only to patrol a strip of desert, for the most part totally uninhabited, where it can exercise its simple function with a minimum risk of offending the susceptibilities of its host country or of anyone else. To adapt Tacitus, "Because it is a solitude, they can keep it at peace." The boundary it patrols is ideal for its purpose — open to view, clearly demarcated, uncomplicated by the presence of any human or economic factors more portentous than the occasional Bedouin herdsman and his flock.

Finally, the Arab-Israeli rivalry for all its intensity is basically parochial in scale. Outside the Moslem world few countries feel themselves deeply committed to one side or the other. This has made it comparatively easy to recruit for the force contingents whose nationality does not involve them in any serious risk of partisanship or even in accusations of partisanship. The Americas, Scandinavia, India — from this core it was not too difficult to construct a force which satisfied the criteria of geographical representativeness and detachment from local and great power conflicts.

In consequence, the difficulties of the force have been virtually confined to the familiar problems of finance. These, of course, reflect the fact that what was originally welcomed as a solution to an emergency has now become an apparent permanency. The fireman has turned into the lodger. The respite which UNEF provided for solving the Middle East problem has turned out to be the solution itself. It might even be argued that the existence of UNEF has relieved all the parties concerned of the need to find some other more lasting solution, but this argument would carry more force if anyone could suggest what such a solution might be. As it is, the forces of world politics and the circumstances of Middle East geography have made it possible to provide inveterate antagonisms with a mutually tolerable insulation. In so

---

[8] Some would list the protective blanket of the Eisenhower Doctrine among the dampening influences on the Middle East, though this seems to me more disputable.

doing they have created a precedent and left a legacy of practical experience in the organizing and operating of a United Nations force.

When this legacy was drawn on in the Congo, it was in circumstances that soon made one wonder how far UNEF could properly be regarded as a precedent for the United Nations operation in the Congo (ONUC).[9] To take the simplest factor first, in place of the sealing off of a desert peninsula as in Suez, the Congo crisis required the insulation of an almost land-locked subcontinent, as well as the internal policing of that same huge area. Similarly, whereas UNEF had only to keep two organized and accountable states apart, ONUC had the double task of excluding outside intervention and creating internal viability. While UNEF could operate in an area physically free from complicating interests or inhabitants, no United Nations operation in the Congo could possibly avoid contact with Congolese life at every point — and in circumstances where any contact (or indeed no contact) inevitably involved interference. Finally, whereas it was relatively easy to construct a UNEF out of the contributions of disinterested states, disinterestedness was a much harder quality to command where the Congo was concerned. (What is more, for reasons of incipient Pan-Africanism and color consciousness it was, when discovered, by no means so obviously welcome.) At the very outset all these complications presented a formidable challenge to ONUC; before it had been long in operation, others, and worse, arose for which there was no precedent in the annals of international organization or in the records of international law.

Paradoxically — and the whole Congo operation was a jungle of paradoxes — it was easier to get ONUC established than UNEF. The whole United Nations was intensely "Africa-conscious"; the Secretary-General, then at the height of his prestige, had already established a United Nations presence in Leopoldville in the person of Dr. Bunche; and the fact that, at least in one aspect, ONUC could be viewed as a technical aid operation made its initial acceptance easier. Again, the need for the force did not immediately proceed from any actual clash of major powers which might try to bargain and prevaricate before

---

[9] In the interests of convenience I have used "ONUC" throughout to refer to the United Nations military force in the Congo, although strictly speaking, of course, it applies to the important civilian operation as well.

making way for it; only one power with modern armaments was involved, Belgium, and even it did not oppose the force in principle. The prize of the Congo was indeed a rich one, but no one in July 1960 was willing to be labeled a colonialist in order to win it, not even the Soviet Union. The United States in particular was content to see a neutral Congo established. The now classic rules of super-power diplomacy operated: neither side wanted to see the other gain control of the territory, but equally, neither wished to see a Congo civil war escalate into something more general. Each side no doubt gave different weight to different considerations, but initially the result was the same — a Security Council vote in which the United States and the Soviet Union voted on the same side and France, Britain, and Belgium abstained, ostensibly only because of reservations about the wording of the paragraph asking for Belgian troop withdrawals.

There was from the beginning an ambiguity about the authority and objectives of ONUC which reflected the anomalous position of the Congo itself, a state so newly independent that the *Loi Fondamentale* designed to authorize its constitution had not yet been ratified by the body appointed to do so, the Congolese parliament. In part, ONUC was a routine response to a routine request from a new state for technical assistance; what was novel was that it was for *military* assistance, a category hitherto unknown in United Nations technical aid circles. Simultaneously, however, it was an appeal for United Nations protection against the reintroduction of Belgian troops into the territory of an ex-colony now independent and also, from the United Nations point of view, a necessary safeguard against unilateral assistance pouring in from rival sides in the Cold War. ONUC's role from the outset was consequently a dual one — the provision of both internal and external security. Though the words "international peace and security" do not appear in the Security Council resolution[10] passed at its first meeting concerning the Congo on July 14, 1960, the Secretary-General later [11] stated that his authority to summon the meeting came from

10 UN Document S/4387.
11 Security Council *Official Records* (15th year), 884th meeting, August 8, 1960, p. 5.

Article 99 of the Charter,[12] and any such verbal deficiency was quickly made good in the following resolution of July 22.[13] Thus the force had a role closely analogous to that of UNEF — to facilitate and accelerate the withdrawal of foreign troops and to remove by its presence the justification for any other powers' interference; but it could not assume, as UNEF did, that the host country would look after internal security. Indeed ONUC's ability to restore internal security was a practical (if not a legal) condition of the successful discharge of its obligations toward international peace and security.

Nevertheless the Secretary-General took the view that the principles which he had laid down for the UNEF were equally valid for ONUC. As he told the Security Council on July 13, 1960,

> The United Nations Force would not be authorized to action beyond self-defence[14]. . . . They may not take any action which would make them a party to internal conflicts. . . . The selection of personnel should be such as to avoid complications because of the nationalities used. . . . This does not . . . exclude the use of units from African States, while . . . it does exclude . . . troops from any of the permanent members of the Security Council.[15]

In saying this, the Secretary-General could hardly have been unaware, even at this early stage of the operation, that the problems presented by the Congo were vastly different from those of Suez. His emphasis on UNEF principles in the Congo context must therefore have re-

[12] To "bring to the attention of the Security Council any matter which in his opinion may threaten the maintenance of international security."

[13] UN Document S/4405.

[14] How strictly this was originally interpreted can be seen in the wording of the leaflet distributed by Dr. Bunche and General von Horn to all members of ONUC on their arrival in the Congo:

"You serve as members of an international force. It is a peace force, not a fighting force.

The United Nations has asked you to come here in response to an appeal from the Government of the Republic of the Congo. Your task is to help in restoring order and calm in this country which has been so troubled recently. You are to be friendly to all the people of this country. Protection against acts of violence is to be given to *all* the people, white and black.

You carry arms, but they are to be used *only* in self-defence. You are in the Congo to help *everyone*, to harm no one."

[15] Security Council *Official Records* (15th year), 873rd meeting, July 13, 1960, p. 5.

flected, as was surely right, a concern for the context of international politics within which the problems of the Congo would have to find their solution, if at all.

As every UN debate from the July 13 Security Council meeting on-wards showed, the gravest differences of opinion existed among Member States as to what kind of settlement, what kind of Congo indeed, should be aimed at — differences, moreover, not merely between the Soviet bloc and the West but also within the West, within the Afro-Asian group, and even within the ranks of the Africans themselves. Even before Katanga's secession or the outright clash between Kasa-vubu and Lumumba, these differences were violent enough to guarantee that, if the United Nations attempted to formulate a positive policy for ONUC, it would not merely provoke a clash of opposites; it would reveal the lack of *any* clear majority consensus. (This was precisely what did happen in December 1960.) The only way to avert such a clash was to insist on the principle of non-interference and its corollary of no initiative in the use of force and to hope and work for conditions in which the empty formalism of the first and the acute frustrations of the second did not become too evident or impose too great a strain on those who had to apply them. Nor is it relevant to say that such a policy could not succeed unless it can be shown what other course of action would have been more successful.

Certainly, if a proving-ground for the Secretary-General's principles were desired, no more exacting one could be devised than the Congo. As might be expected, having regard to the conditions which provoked ONUC's presence, the first principle to come under strain was the ban on the use of armed force. In a country where the government was little more than an expression and where the army had no officers and was mutinous, any peace force was bound to find itself in a self-contradictory position. In Suez and Gaza there were always local police forces to whom UNEF could turn over any violators of the peace who came its way. In the Congo such entities hardly existed, yet ONUC itself had no powers to arrest or even disarm the mutineering elements of the *Force Publique.* Such a power eventually was given, and critics have argued that the biggest error of the whole Congo operation was not to have given it at the very beginning. This may be so, but two things have to be remembered. First, in a continent hypersensitive about "neo-colonialist" interference and in a country teetering on the edge of mass hysteria, it was important for the United Nations' long-term mission to preserve the image of itself as a pacific agent seeking only to help Africans to help themselves. Secondly, although some states that contributed to the force, e.g., Ghana, were willing, even eager to have their troops employed forcefully, others would have refused contributions to a force which was involved in the killing of Africans even in the best causes and even at the hands of other Africans. When, later on, resolute measures were taken, certain states did seek to withdraw in protest.

But, of course, more was involved than clashes with *Force Publique*. The issue of force or no force merged into the issue of interference or non-interference. Non-interference was even less possible in practice than abstention from force, because the mere presence of ONUC was interference. Non-interference, however, was also a more indispensable principle because there was no agreed alternative to put in its place. Even after the passage of the Security Council resolution of February 21, 1961,[16] authorizing "the use of force, if necessary, in the last resort," it was still the United Nations' position that it was not going to become a party to any internal conflict in the Congo. Similarly, when in September 1961 open fighting developed between ONUC and the Katangese forces, the United Nations' objectives (*pace* Mr. Conor C. O'Brien) were only the expulsion of "foreign mercenaries," the prevention of civil war, and the defense of its own positions. When finally, by the Security Council resolution of November 24, 1961,[17] the Secretary-General's authority was broadened to include "vigorous action, including the use of requisite measure of force if necessary," the object of this was still said to be the exclusion of foreign intruders.

It was also true that the United Nations accepted the unity of the Congo as axiomatic and secessionist activities as illegal. It explicitly rejected Katanga's claim to independence. Nevertheless, it never laid on ONUC the task of enforcing Congolese unity or ending Katangese independence. These objectives were to be secured by conciliation, moral pressure, or, at most and not until very late in the day, economic

16 UN Document S/4741.
17 UN Document S/5002.

and financial sanctions. Moreover, since ONUC had a positive obligation to prevent civil war, it was as opposed to the central government's
forcible occupation of Katanga as to Katanga's forcible secession.

In all these senses the United Nations was impartial. Within the
framework of Congolese unity it was for the Congolese to decide who
should rule and how. But in almost all the actual power contests of
Congo politics the United Nations could not avoid taking decisions
which favored one side or the other. Seizing the radio station and closing the airports was a logical application of ONUC's duty to stop civil
war and external interference, but it was also inescapably an act which,
at the moment it was taken, tilted the scales in favor of Kasavubu and
against Lumumba. The fact that this occurred in the Alice in Wonder-
land situation when the President claimed to have dismissed his prime
minister and the prime minister claimed to have dismissed his President provided a further legal justification for the United Nations
action but left its practical consequences unchanged.

In its external role as the United Nations' agent for relieving the
Congo of Belgian interference and protecting it against all other non-
UN intrusions, ONUC ran into comparable difficulties. Its early claims
of success in effecting Belgian withdrawal turned out to be premature
since Katanga remained a center of foreign influence and activity,
hostile alike to the UN and to the central government, while ONUC's
inability to restore order even in the rest of the Congo provided Belgium with an excuse for retaining or reintroducing her forces. This in
turn aggravated Congolese impatience and encouraged factional leaders to seek extra-UN assistance of a kind which was only too readily
available, with the result that a month or so after ONUC had come
into operation massive Soviet aid was placed at the disposal of
Lumumba.

The Soviet assistance came by air and, to be countered, necessitated
the closure by United Nations forces of all Congolese airports. No
doubt this action hampered Soviet plans for further intervention,
though its legal justification and its immediate purpose were to prevent
Lumumba from using the troop-carrying Ilyushin planes to launch his
forces against Kasai province. Nevertheless, it is almost certainly true
to say that it was Mobutu's seizure of power and his ensuing expulsion
of all Soviet bloc representatives rather than any direct ONUC action

which put a stop to Soviet intervention. It was on this account that no direct on-the-spot clash between the Soviet interlopers and the ONUC command occurred. No doubt the Soviet Union, in the interests of its relations with the African powers, was glad not have any such show-down. On the evidence available, however, it cannot be said that the mere presence of ONUC was adequate, as many hoped it would be, to deter great-power intervention. It is one thing to violate a clearly held United Nations patrol line; it is another thing to fly "volunteers" into a civilian airport with little or no show of military might. ONUC's experience here is a reminder that the third dimension of the air can make nonsense of the attractive concept of a United Nations buffer force whose mere physical presence on the ground serves as an adequate moral trip-wire or plate glass window.

The cross-currents set up by factional fighting inside the Congo and intervention from outside complicated the Congo operation in two other respects. In getting on to a decade of operation UNEF has had little difficulty in holding its national contingents together or in maintaining equable relations with its host government. ONUC speedily ran into trouble on both fronts. Dag Hammarskjöld's decision to make ONUC a predominantly African force was certainly a right one; no other course would have secured the indispensable moral backing in Africa or the African votes in the United Nations. But it was impossible for a force so composed to be completely disinterested. Each contributing state had strong views on every Congo issue, and every decision that ONUC had to make imposed a strain on its loyalties. Looking back over the fiercely troubled course of the Congo since July 1960 one is truly impressed to see how well in such circumstances the conglomerate ONUC held together. Nonetheless, it is instructive to notice how and where the bonds of loyalty chafed.

Thus in September 1960 ONUC's denial to Lumumba of the use of the radio station and airports provoked Guinea, Ghana, and the United Arab Republic to threaten a withdrawal of their troops and claim a right to place them at Lumumba's disposal. This led the Secretary-General to elaborate the basic principles on which a composite UN force operated, as follows:

> Were a national contingent to leave the United Nations Force, they would have to be regarded as foreign troops introduced into the

Congo, and the Security Council would have to consider their continued presence in the Congo, as well as its consequences for the United Nations operation, in this light.[18]

This important circumscription of the conditions under which withdrawal could take place was further sharpened the following January when Morocco ordered its brigade to "cease to perform its functions" while remaining in the Congo. The Secretary-General insisted that it could remain only "as an integral part of the United Nations Force" and that any other position would be "untenable."[19] Morocco agreed to its troops remaining under the United Nations flag until repatriation could be arranged, "but if called upon to act against their conscience" they would feel bound not to accept any decision contrary to the interests of the Congo and of legality."[20] The Secretary-General's own inimitable blend of legal argument, moral authority, and diplomacy in fact prevented most of these threatening checks ever being presented for actual payment, but even so he could not eliminate the enervating effect which they had on the United Nations operation. Whereas UNEF was a force united in a common acceptance of a clearcut task, ONUC for long periods at a time lacked any agreed purpose, indeed at certain periods was sharply divided within itself. Even if the disagreements of participating governments were not fully reflected in the behavior of their contingents, they could not but impair their full cooperation.

To speak of a "host government" in the context of the anarchy which prevailed for most of 1960 and 1961 in the Congo is to bring out how remote were the realities of the United Nations operation from the language of law and diplomacy in which it had to be clothed. Repeatedly ONUC found itself not merely at odds but actually at blows with the agents of the government whom it was to "assist" and "consult with," to quote the language of repeated United Nations resolutions. Most of these incidents belong to that level of UN-Congolese relations which had more to do with bizarre bargaining and gang warfare than diplomacy, but some of them raised issues not only

---

[18] Security Council *Official Records* (15th year), 896th meeting, September 9, 1960, p. 20.

[19] UN Document S/4668.

[20] *Ibid.*

important at the time but having possible future significance for United Nations procedure and international law. This was conspicuously true of Kasavubu's attempts to impose impossible conditions on ONUC, particularly in connection with the use of the port of Matadi in March 1961. These led the Secretary-General to issue the following interpretation of their relations:

> The relation between the United Nations and the Government of the Republic of the Congo is not merely a contractual relationship in which the Republic can impose its conditions as host State and thereby determine the circumstances under which the United Nations operates. It is rather a relationship governed by mandatory decisions of the Security Council. . . . Only the Security Council can decide on the discontinuance of the operation and . . . therefore conditions which, by their effect on the operation, would deprive it of its necessary basis, would require direct consideration of the Security Council. . . .[21]

Here, obviously, we have a potentially far-reaching modification of the 1956 doctrine requiring the consent of the host state as a necessary precondition of the presence of a United Nations force. Partly this reflects the shift in the source of the mandate from the General Assembly to the Security Council; partly it reflects the distinctive role of a United Nations force called in to provide internal aid as well as external protection. Yet even so, a word of caution must be added. It is in the Congo context that the Secretary-General is speaking — i.e., in a political hall of mirrors, where the reality and its reflections become swiftly indistinguishable and nothing is quite what it seems. For if one seeks to establish what sanctions the Secretary-General employed to secure the cooperation of the Congolese authorities or at least to curb their obstructiveness, one finds that they amounted to nothing more or less than the threat to withdraw the presence which offends. It was in these terms that Dag Hammarskjöld wrote to Kasavubu on December 21, 1960, warning him against behavior which would lead on to civil war:

> I sincerely trust that no situation will develop which would give me no choice but to recommend to the Security Council that it authorize the withdrawal of the United Nations Force . . . thus throwing on the

21 UN Document S/4389/Add.5.

authorities of the Congo the full responsibility of maintaining law and order.[22]

We are back, not for the first time, in the world of the nursery where authority and prudence alike reinforce the wisdom of Hilaire Belloc's advice:

> And always keep a hold of Nurse
> For fear of finding something worse.

III

Any lessons which one may draw from these events while the Congo operation is so recent must be tentative. Even so, something can be said.

First a *caveat*. It is often said that the Congo is *sui generis*. It certainly differs from any situation the United Nations has had to tackle before, but is it so different from what may arise in the future? As long as underdeveloped countries are in ferment and communist (or other) powers prefer subversion to open aggression, variations on the Congo theme are practically bound to occur. No doubt also it is true that the United Nations is not designed to cope with such situations; as an international organization it is built on the assumption that viable states are the entities with which it has to deal. This palliates failure, but it cannot excuse inaction. Future Congos cannot be ignored simply because they were not dreamed of in the philosophy of San Francisco. This is not to say that the United Nations ought to get into every situation where internal breakdowns occur; if such crises can be settled without such intervention, so much the better. But if they threaten international peace and security, the United Nations cannot side-step them on any narrowly legalistic ground.

But it is also probable in any foreseeable future that the balance of world politics, in particular the near-deadlock rivalries of East and West and the persistent floating votes of the nonaligned, will remain much as before. If so, Suez and the Congo suggest that there are limits to what any United Nations force can, at present, achieve. UNEF represents about as successful a buffer operation between states as can be imagined — in about as propitious a set of circumstances. Happy

[22] UN Document S/4606.

the UNEF of the future which has as easy a task. In the more likely case, however, in which external clashes are accompanied by internal breakdown, some if not all the problems of ONUC seem likely to recur. There may be fewer difficulties on the ground — there could hardly be more — but there are likely to be just as many in the council chambers of the United Nations. If this is so, it seems idle to press for a United Nations force which would discard the three principles of "force only in self-defense," "non-interference," and "entry only with the consent of the host country." Of course these principles are not adequate (whatever that may mean); they are merely in the present state of the world indispensable. They may be stretched, modified, even conceivably bypassed; they cannot within the framework of the present United Nations be replaced by any positive alternatives.

If this is true, it does not follow that no improvements on ONUC are possible or that no advance planning, even perhaps advance organization, for a United Nations force, can be contemplated. On the contrary, the peculiar strains which such a role imposes on a United Nations force and its leaders make it the more desirable that everything which is politically possible should be done to train it for the discharge of its very distinctive functions. It lies outside the scope of this paper to consider how this could be best be done, but that it should be done is certainly in accordance with our conclusions.

Certain other conclusions also follow. If one asks why, despite all its difficulties, ONUC was able to function as well as it did, or — to concede everything to its critics — to function at all, the answers are three-fold. First, because the West, and in particular the United States, has been willing to foot the financial bill. No doubt it is wrong — in terms of the Charter — that this burden should fall as unevenly as it does. But if, like Britain, any Member State is inclined to feel self-righteous when it pays its share or, like France, self-justified when it does not, let it pause to ask whether its national interest would be better served if the Soviet Union paid the whole. Piper-paying and tune-calling are not interchangeable terms in the United Nations — otherwise what would the Charter be for? — but they are connected. Certainly, no future ONUC can operate unless it has funds, and if it is to operate with higher efficiency than the present Congo force, it will need larger funds. These can only come from the well-to-do West — unless they are to come from the Soviet Union.

The second reason for ONUC's survival is the general willingness of most of the states variously described as "nonaligned," "neutralist," or the "fire brigades," to support the operation by their votes and often by their contributions. In this the role of the Afro-Asians has been crucial not only because of their numbers but also because of their position on the spectrum of United Nations politics. They alone could supply the disinterestedness which comes from their relative impotence and the loyalty which reflects their own dependence upon the Organization.

This dependence has often seemed to be personified in their support of the Secretary-General and has even been ascribed to a personal confidence in Dag Hammarskjöld. But to see it entirely in these terms is to mistake the man for the institution. It is not by an accident of personality that the creation and functioning of UNEF and ONUC have been linked so closely with the office of the Secretary-General. It is because any sustained executive functions, however limited, can only be discharged in an organization like the United Nations by its Secretariat, a body which the Secretary-General at once leads and personifies. Only the Council and the Assembly are capable of authorizing a United Nations force, but if the history of Suez and the Congo demonstrates anything, it is that they are utterly incapable of running it. In this more than in anything else that the Secretary-General is called upon to do, the now familiar concept of "filling a vacuum of authority" manifests and justifies itself.

There is a logical connection between the Soviet opposition to ONUC and its advocacy of the "troika." An equivalent logic dictates that no future United Nations force is conceivable for which executive authority is not delegated to a Secretary-General willing and able to act when his "parliamentary" overlords are deadlocked. An advisory committee may abate his loneliness; it cannot relieve him of his responsibility and should not seek to curb his authority. If the office seems dangerously potent, as so developed by Dag Hammarskjöld and as apparently now operated by U Thant, the weapons of negation and · frustration are at hand in the Security Council, the General Assembly and, behind both, in the financial deliberations of the Fifth Committee. Those who wish to use them, however, should do so with a full awareness of the consequences. Nothing in the experience of Suez and the Congo suggests than an international force is exempt from the workings of the inexorable rule that he who wills the end must will the means as well.

BRIAN E. URQUHART

A UN Perspective

At its founding one of the UN's most publicized advantages over its predecessor, the League of Nations, was the fact that it was a peace organization "with teeth." This somewhat unattractive phrase referred to Chapter VII of the Charter and the possibility of military force being put at the disposal of the Security Council. In fact this provision of the Charter was one of the first victims of East-West disagreement, and, although the Military Staff Committee met regularly for many years and in the early years held voluminous discussions, the actual military arrangements foreseen in Chapter VII never became a reality. The assumption of the continuing unanimity of the great powers, which particularly affected this part of the Charter, proved to be illusory almost at once, while the idea that the Organization could not and should not take collective action against one of the great powers has continued, with the partial exception of Korea, to be respected. Thus it has become increasingly clear that the United Nations can neither deal with an aggression arising from a great-power conflict nor use the military resources of the great powers directly in dealing with other breaches of the peace, since such a use might all too easily project the great-power struggle onto the situation being dealt with. The development of new forms of peace-keeping machinery have in part been the response of the Organization to this dilemma.

The difference between the present reality of great-power relationships, at least in the context of the United Nations, and what was foreseen at San Francisco has made new developments in the United Nations not only possible, but desirable. In 1945 the great powers were the victors over Germany and Japan, the custodians of peace in an exhausted world, the arbiters of destiny; and on this image some vital parts of the Charter were based. Very soon, however, their own virulent rivalry and the development of weapons of mass destruction by both sides in the East-West conflict showed this image to be a hollow one. What was to have been the leadership and inspiration of the reconstructed world turned out to be a vacuum, in which the most powerful countries of the world tended to be increasingly immobilized by rivalry, suspicion, and fear. For some years this vacuum persisted, and it seemed likely that because of it the United Nations might be doomed to play at best a peripheral role in an essentially hopeless situation.

But with the growth of the membership of the Organization and the emergence of new forces and alignments, it now seems possible that the United Nations and the vast majority of its members are in the process of establishing a collective influence and authority in the affairs of the world — an influence and authority which they might never have achieved if the great powers had behaved as was foreseen by the authors of the Charter. No one would deny that the persistence of East-West rivalry, the inability to reach agreement on disarmament, and the failure to bridge ideological differences still rank as dominating problems in the world, and that so far the United Nations as such seems to have been able to make little progress with them. But other activities have shown a very promising potential in the Organization and a solidarity, as well as a vitality, which bodes well for its future growth. It is perhaps of some significance that those on the extreme right and left who used to criticize the United Nations for its ineffectiveness in the days of great power domination now tend to complain more of its new vitality and activity in peace-keeping operations.

The Korean action in 1950 gave rise to a temporary enthusiasm for and renewed belief in the possibility of the classical type of collective action against aggression. It was also realized that the freak conditions which had allowed the Security Council to take action on the Korean question without a veto were unlikely ever to recur. The result was the adoption by the General Assembly in 1950 of the "Uniting for Peace" resolution, which has had a fundamental effect on the capacity of the Organization for taking action in dangerous situations. The object of the resolution was, in President Truman's words, to prepare the United

Nations "for quick and effective action in any future case of aggression." The original hopes of the authors of the resolution, however, were never fully realized, nor did the new enthusiasm for collective security survive the disillusionments and confusions of the latter part of the Korean operation. Regional pacts thus came more than ever to be regarded as the maximum practical basis for collective action, and the Collective Measures Committee and the Peace Observation Commission set up by the resolution have had little or no practical impact on events.

Nevertheless, the other main feature of the resolution, which provides for the General Assembly to move quickly into a critical situation if the Security Council is paralyzed by the veto, has had extremely important consequences — even if they are not precisely the ones envisaged by the original authors. It has been the basis upon which the consideration of matters affecting peace and security have come within the purview of the whole membership of the United Nations and upon which quite new methods of resolving crises, such as the extension of the role of the United Nations as mediator and the use of the United Nations' peace-keeping forces, have been built up.

While this part of the "Uniting for Peace" resolution provides a quasi-constitutional device for liberating questions of peace and security from the dead hand of the unanimity rule in the Security Council, other practices and precedents have grown up which have, over a period of sixteen years, extended the capacity of the United Nations to deal with emergencies and have evoked from the Organization a practical response to such situations very different from that envisaged in the Charter. The demands of dangerous situations, and the obvious need for some effective method of dealing with them without involving them in the ultimate stresses and strains of the East-West struggle, have been one motivating force in this process. Another and very important factor was certainly the leadership, diplomacy, and political imagination of the late Secretary-General, Dag Hammarskjöld. A third has been, in spite of criticism and occasional disillusion, an increasing reliance on the United Nations in situations of real emergency, especially by the smaller powers, and, resulting from this, their firm support of its efforts. A corollary of this last development has been the tendency of the great powers to neutralize each other in situations of emergency through fear of getting involved to the extent of atomic war, thus leaving a certain freedom of action for the smaller powers and the international Secretariat. In fact, in certain situations of intolerable stress the United Nations has become a way out both for the great powers and the small from the ultimate consequences of a great-power clash.

In the early years of the United Nations, before its membership was more than doubled by the advent of new nations, there was a tendency among the major powers toward extreme distrust of any initiative on the part of the Secretariat. Some overtly and others tacitly made it clear that the Secretariat was basically a servicing staff which, except in very unusual circumstances, had little or no freedom of action of its own. Even the smallest show of initiative or independence on the part of the Secretariat tended to be greeted with raised eyebrows or letters of protest. When one thinks back to the first four or five years of the United Nations, a most significant development is the change in this attitude. Before the Secretary-Generalship of Dag Hammarskjöld it was very unusual for a Secretariat official to enjoy executive powers. Such powers were very occasionally delegated to someone of distinction and known reliability, as, for example, Count Bernadotte or Dr. Bunche in the Middle East, but normally situations were handled, or were supposed to be handled, by intergovernmental commissions set up by one of the organs of the United Nations and serviced by members of the Secretariat. When in doubt delegations tended to invoke the name of Sir Eric Drummond and the League of Nations Secretariat as the ideal of discreet Secretariat behavior.

In these early years, while the use of military personnel on a large scale and under the exact terms of the Charter was being discussed with diminishing prospect of agreement in the Military Staff Committee, methods of using military personnel productively on a far smaller scale evolved almost by accident. In Greece the military attachés of the members of the United Nations Commission proved themselves invaluable as an observer group in checking on infiltration into Greece from her northern neighbors. In Kashmir an observer group of military officers was formally set up by the Security Council and is still operating, its success being vouched for perhaps most eloquently by the fact that one scarcely ever hears about it.

The first truce agreements in the Palestine war in July 1948 were enforced on the ground by some 700 United Nations military observers working under the United Nations Mediator and Chief of Staff. This team developed into the United Nations Truce Supervision Organization (UNTSO) after the armistice agreements between Israel and her Arab neighbors were concluded in the period from February to July 1949. This organization of officers from many countries has played a vital role in keeping peace in the Middle East, in umpiring frontier incidents, and in giving time for tempers, grievances, and historic disagreements to cool off.

Such ventures have resulted in the gradual creation of an officer cadre in many countries with international experience of peace-keeping operations; to that extent, the armies of many countries are being indoctrinated in the peace-keeping process. In a turbulent world it is pleasant to reflect that the professional soldiers of Brazil, Canada, Denmark, Ethiopia, Ghana, India, Indonesia, Ireland, Malaya, Morocco, Nigeria, Norway, Pakistan, Sierra Leone, Sweden, Tunisia, and Yugoslavia — to name only a few — have recently been daily performing the functions of controlling and mitigating frictions in several regions, and by example creating a new role for military discipline and common sense.

The Suez situation of 1956 was complicated by the heavy involvement of two great powers and by the ominous threats of a third. It was a situation in which traditional alliances fell apart and where everyone seemed to have been caught unawares by an action as ill-advised as it was ill-planned. Even if the surprised indignation generated by the Suez action had not demanded recourse to the United Nations, the UN was undoubtedly the only place left in which there was a hope of sorting out such a confusion with the minimum loss of life and face. Almost everyone concerned was to some extent in a state of shock, and the gravity of the situation called forth a completely new form of international institution, the United Nations Emergency Force (UNEF) in the Middle East. That such an institution could come into being so fast in a situation in which two great powers were directly involved was a token both of the baffled anxiety of the world community and of the then almost universal confidence in Hammarskjöld. Even five years before, it would have been inconceivable that one of the great powers would meekly accept a cease-fire and a face-saving device of such an entirely novel kind. It would also have been inconceivable for the General Assembly to ask the Secretary-General to write his own plan for such a novel venture and entrust him completely with the negotiations and executive action required. Now, on the contrary, the Assembly did this with enthusiasm, while many of its members also volunteered troops and all sorts of assistance in the most expeditious and informal way. This was not a force designed actively to counter aggression. Rather, it was a security force designed to allow common sense to prevail and the armies of the parties concerned to disengage and return to their own soil.

The force was assembled in a few days, and United States aircraft flew them to a staging point at the Capodicino airport at Naples (made available by the Italian government), whence Swiss aircraft would take them into Egypt as soon as agreement for their arrival was received from the Egyptian government. An agreement with the Egyptian government was negotiated by the Secretary-General, which was based very much on the concept of "good faith" and which has not been subjected to a serious breach or disagreement for over six year. The Israelis, British, and French, once they had agreed to being replaced on the soil of Egypt by the international force, also cooperated, sometimes almost with enthusiasm. The British, for example, made over the United Nations vehicles and supplies for the use of UNEF in Egypt.

It is idle to speculate whether such an experiment could have succeeded as well as it did without the skill and indefatigability of Hammarskjöld. In the growth of an institution the genius of a great man is one very important factor among many factors, a thread in history which, combined with other threads, can produce great developments or, if it is missing at a crucial time, great disasters. Personality, skill, and the inspiration of confidence are likely to be more important initially in the creation of historical precedents and in dealing with crises of a new order of complexity than in conscious institutional development.

It was not only the creation of UNEF that liquidated the Suez crisis. Under Hammarskjöld's executive planning and direction, the clearance of the Canal was negotiated and completed. He thus silenced those critics in France and England who had originally greeted with derision his acceptance of responsibility for this vital operation, which their own misjudgment had largely made necessary.

For eight years UNEF has watched over the borders of Israel with the United Arab Republic in the Gaza Strip and through Sinai. Ships now pass freely through the narrows at Sharm-el-Sheik to the port of Elath, and in Gaza the crops grow right down to the border from both sides, and the area has never been so prosperous. UNEF has not been in the news for years, nor have the provocative actions of extremists, which used to make that frontier a permanent trouble spot. UNEF provides politicians on both sides a reason for resisting extreme counsels and avoiding useless mischief, just as it initially provided a useful face-saver for the British and French. The one serious problem it poses is how to terminate its existence without generating new and dangerous instabilities.

When the problems of an international force are discussed in theory, numerous problems are raised which often prove in the event to be illusory. It used to be said, for example, that problems of language, diversified equipment, and differences in training and tradition would make an international force very difficult to operate. In UNEF such problems have turned out to be minor, negligible, or, in the case of different customs and traditions, a positive advantage. Such differences provide an interest during the long dull terms of duty in the desert, and on Christmas Day the Indians take over duty from the Christian contingents, who reciprocate during Indian festivals.

But, as in most affairs, the unexpected problems are the hardest. They must be met as they appear, unless a sufficiently all-embracing international military establishment can be founded and supported to meet every conceivable contingency. Such an establishment is obviously impossible in the present complex state of world affairs and the present stage of development of the United Nations. For this basic reason the late Secretary-General was lukewarm to the idea of establishing a permanent international force at so early a stage in the practical development of the idea. In 1958 he summarized the lessons learned from the UNEF operation[1] and concluded that the special circumstances surrounding UNEF did not justify the projection in detail of its organization onto unknown situations in the future, as had

[1] UN Document A/3943.

already been shown by the differing requirements of the situations in 1958 in Lebanon and Jordan. He therefore proposed that stand-by arrangements for future action should for the time being be limited to the approval of certain general principles, which would provide a framework for mounting future operations without delay and in accordance with the demands of the actual situation. These principles were later to provide the basis for Hammarskjöld's proposals on the Congo force.

By the autumn of 1958 the United Nations had been involved in another crisis of another kind in the Middle East. In Lebanon a domestic political struggle in the 1958 election campaign had become the basis for accusations of foreign infiltration and interference which had been taken up in earnest by interested powers. The Security Council set up a three-man observer group and left the Secretary-General considerable latitude in the arrangements to make this group effective. A mobile team of 600 officers was quickly organized to police the frontier of Lebanon by road and air against the possibility of infiltration across the border, while the scene was set for the necessary negotiations and discussions to reduce the temperature and resolve the crisis. Although the United States landed a division of marines in Beirut, and the British at another juncture sent a parachute brigade to the airfield of Amman, the storm finally blew out and both of these forces were withdrawn, the latter with the assistance of the United Nations officers in Lebanon and Jerusalem. The United Nations observer group was also withdrawn by the end of 1958. There was some pressure at the height of the crisis for sending another UNEF to Lebanon and, had a standing international force existed, the pressure might well have succeeded and involved the United Nations most embarrassingly in a conflict that was very largely domestic.

The emergence of the new African countries and the twilight of colonialism in Africa became a dominating feature of the United Nations after 1959. The Organization, as well as stimulating this development, has provided, and still provides, it with a place where the leaders and officials of these new countries can get a quick education in the ways of world politics, learn for themselves what motives and what realities lie behind the policies of other states, and establish their own views on the world situation as it affects them. Not least important, the United Nations allows them to see themselves and each other more sharply within the context of world affairs. The new nations of Africa were destined very soon to play an important part, notably by the provision of troops, in the most critical and unprecedented United Nations peace-keeping operation.

Although the United Nations was already much concerned with the emergence of Africa and with the help to be given to the new countries, it was in 1960 suddenly confronted with the problem in a form so ugly and urgent as also to involve its ultimate responsibilities for the maintenance of peace and security. This emergency arose from the chaotic events immediately following the independence of the former Belgian Congo on June 30, 1960.

No one realized better than Hammarskjöld what a tremendous risk the Congo operation represented for the Organization and for himself as Secretary-General. But he also realized vividly the intense danger of the Congo situation — the imminent possibility of great power interventions and clashes, the exacerbation of rivalries among African states, and the explosive mixture of big money, tribalism, adventurism, inexperience, and susceptibility within the Congo itself. Weighing the relative risks and foreseeing all too clearly the appalling difficulty of the task ahead, he knowingly accepted the danger to the Organization and to himself rather than countenance the consequences which would almost certainly ensue from inaction.

Both external and internal factors added to the extraordinary complication of the Congo affair, and even without them it would have been difficult to deal with the basic situation resulting from the total unpreparedness and lack of experience of the Congolese government. The position of the United Nations itself was also of necessity a very delicate one. It was present in the Congo at the request of the central government (a government, incidentally, which was not legally constituted for almost a year from September 1960 to August 1961), and also because in the judgment of the Secretary-General and the Security Council the situation was a potential threat to international peace and security. It was there to assist the government in all ways, including the maintenance of law and order, until the government could fully exercise its functions itself. It was precluded from interfering in the internal political dissensions of the country, and yet it was held responsible for the protection of life and property and the maintenance of normal services. It had a force (18,000 strong in the fall of 1962) which was in fact the mainstay of order in the country, but whose right to use force was limited by directives of the Security Council to self-defense, to the prevention of civil war, and, in the last resort, to the apprehension of foreign military personnel. Because the Congolese National Army (now about 30,000 strong) tends to be split among the rival factions and was until very recently on terms of active hostility with the Katangese *Gendarmerie* (about 20,000 strong but with a slightly superior military performance), the work of the United Nations force was anything but easy. It was further complicated by the facts that large sections of public opinion in the world held the United Nations responsible for almost everything that happened or did not happen in the Congo, and that different political factions in the Congo each had their passionate supporters in the world outside.

In 1960 and early 1961 opinion at the United Nations itself was divided on almost diametrically opposed lines as to the correct course of action in the Congo, and this division made the lives of officials dealing with critical situations on the spot very difficult indeed. One school of thought, which had supporters among the governments furnishing essential logistical and financial support, was averse to anything which might be interpreted as a forceful solution. Both sides had their own decided views as to the acceptability or non-acceptability of certain Congolese leaders, and the murder of Patrice Lumumba added to the already overheated situation a tragic and violent element. Perhaps fortunately, the remarkable illogic and inconsistency of the internal Congolese situation blurred these lines of disagreement, and there began to be recognition that the situation could not be judged by normal standards and had to be dealt with more at its own level within a broad interpretation of the principles underlying the United Nations action. This does not mean that the task of the United Nations in the Congo was any easier, only that its difficulties were more generally recognized.

In its stay in the Congo, the United Nations force, predominantly composed of soldiers from African and Asian states, was confronted with a series of situations more varied and eccentric than anything the armies of the old colonial powers had to face, and it did not have any of the freedom of action which those armies used to enjoy in meeting emergencies. It was put together overnight and precluded from using, except for transport and supply outside the Congo, the military resources of those great powers whose military establishments were the only ones in the world designed for such far-flung operations; it was deployed with bewildering speed into obscure and totally unpredictable situations, while being constantly restrained by political directives which made a mockery of established military principles. Nonetheless, it met its responsibilities in such a way that the situation it left was far calmer and more promising than that which it found in July of 1960. In so doing, it suffered numerous casualties as well as occasional humiliations and failures. It was the target of both ill-informed and malicious criticism and propaganda from the left and the right, criticism which was often curiously similar in its terms and clichés. It received very little gratitude or appreciation from those — and there are many — who abuse the United Nations in good weather and are the first to run to it for protection when a storm blows up. It not only had to moderate the consequences of Congolese political and tribal rivalries but also to keep calm in a situation where secessionist movements, especially that of Katanga, produced incessant threats of civil war and were supported by a bewildering variety of outside interests and adventurers.

Few peacetime military tasks can be less enviable than the one to which the Members of the United Nations committed the officers and men of the UN force in the Congo. The necessity for calm under provocation, insult, and violence; the need to comply with political directives which must inevitably often be incomprehensible to the soldier on the spot; the variety of other tasks, including assistance to refugees, civilian protection, and all sorts of assistance to the civil authorities; the prevailing attitude of resentment, especially by the European population, except when protection or help are needed; and the interminable machinations of a raffish crew of military and civilian adventures in pursuit of money are not the conditions which an ordinary national army would accept. The high morale of the soldiers, their enthusiasm, and their astonishingly few complaints (for an army) could only result from a job that was challenging and responsible and which the soldiers thought was worth doing. Those armchair critics of international organizations who said that the UN people, military and civilian, were in the Congo for the money or the power should have viewed for themselves the conditions of service there, or studied the fate of the Ghanaians at Port Francqui, the Irish at Niemba, the Sudanese at Matadi, the Italians at Kindu, or the Indians manning a roadblock in Elisabethville, and then tried to make an honest reappraisal. The thousands of soldiers from some twenty countries who accepted this challenge in the Congo began to learn to apply the arts of war to the infinitely subtle and difficult problem of maintaining the peace — this may be a development of more lasting importance than what eventually happened in the Congo itself.

The involvement of United Nations troops in three episodes of actual fighting in Katanga raised in many quarters the question of the appropriateness of the use of force by a peace-keeping international force. The question was obscured and inflated by a great deal of misrepresentation both deliberate and unintentional.

The conditions under which a resort to force by the United Nations force in the Congo was permitted by the Security Council were three: ultimate self-defense, the prevention of civil war, and, in the last resort, the apprehension of foreign military personnel. In September 1961 the United Nations force in Elisabethville came under attack when it tried, on September 13, to continue the rounding up of the mercenaries which had started peacefully with the cooperation of Mr. Tshombe on August 28 and had then been suspended at the request of various consuls, who undertook to carry out the task themselves but proved unable to do so. The fighting, by any normal military standard, was on a very small scale and the casualties were light. This did not stop various people and groups, with various motives, from alleging that the September 1961 episode was an effort to suppress the secession of Katanga by force. This was neither the intention nor the result. Had it been the intention, which it could not have been under the Security Council mandate, the preparations and arrangements would have been very different and the military and civilian action of an entirely different kind.

In December 1961 the Katangese *Gendarmerie* was under the control of a group of former Secret Army Organization (OAS) officers who

conceived the notion of eliminating the United Nations force in Elisabethville at a time when it was at its weakest due to the rotation of
units. A prelude of this operation, in which a number of European
civilians were also involved, was a series of incitements to violence,
harassments, kidnappings, and murders of United Nations personnel
in the best OAS style. After a week of intensive effort to persuade Mr.
Tshombe and his ministers to abandon this plan, the United Nations
was compelled to protect the safety of its force and personnel by re-
moving the roadblocks put up by the *Gendarmerie* and by re-establish-
ing its freedom of movement and access to the airport in Elisabethville.
As soon as this was done the action stopped. Once again Katangese
propagandists raised the cry that this was an attempt to end secession
by force. The simple fact is that such a course, including the arrest of
Mr. Tshombe and his ministers, would have been by far the simplest
for the United Nations. It could not and did not take it because it had
no right to take it.

After Mr. Tshombe had signed, on December 21, 1961, the declaration of Kitona, which reaffirmed his intention of cooperating with the
central government, a year passed in intensive talks and negotiations
designed to make this declaration a reality. In December 1962 the
Gendarmerie in Elisabethville again got out of hand and attacked the
United Nations force, which, after accepting attacks for six days without firing back, finally dealt with the Elisabethville *Gendarmerie*.
This precipitated a move which Mr. Tshombe and the world had long
since been warned to expect — namely, the assertion by the United
Nations of its right, under the basic agreement with the government of
the Congo, to freedom of movement throughout the Congo, including
Katanga. This freedom established, all military action ceased. Again
the cry was raised that this was forceful ending of secession, while from
the other side came the counter-cry that the United Nations had failed
to deal with the traitor Tshombe. By the law of most countries there
would be at least an arguable case for accusing Mr. Tshombe of treason,
armed rebellion, murder, sabotage, and genocide against a state which
he himself played an active part in creating and whose territorial integrity the United Nations is pledged to protect. These were internal
questions for the government of the Congo, which granted an amnesty.
Thus Mr. Tshombe continued to be unmolested by the United Na-

tions as long as he conducted himself as provincial president. The complaint of United Nations over-severity therefore seems rather hard to maintain.

It would be silly to pretend that there is nothing in the United Nations operation in the Congo (ONUC) to criticize. If there were not, it would be unique in history. There have, from time to time, been mistakes and failures and errors of judgment at various levels, and the problems were not all solved. But criticisms should be made within the framework of the real and the possible. ONUC was an operation comparable in novelty with the first voyage to the moon. It is a multinational effort to keep the peace, to help an important and large new country get on its feet, and to moderate violence and strife, which had both internal and external origins, so as to keep it from spreading disastrously to the community of nations. The difficulty and novelty of such an effort becomes apparent when one realizes that many of the hundred or so Member States who supported the operation had particular interests in the affair which are by no means always directly served by the United Nations operation, or else, for widely differing reasons, refused to have anything to do with it at all. That ONUC worked and existed at all in these circumstances is something of a miracle in itself.

Institutionally UNEF and ONUC, although involving the service of some 5,000 and 18,000 soldiers respectively, as well as, in the latter case, some 1,200 civilians, were supposedly temporary additions to the Organization rather than new and integrated parts of the structure of the Secretariat. While UNEF virtually runs itself under the general supervision and logistical backing of New York, the Congo operation was politically so complicated and delicate that it was very closely controlled by the Secretary-General, and the original idea that it might become a semi-independent operation was never realized. For different reasons it is hard to envisage a firm date for the final termination of either of these operations, which up to 1964 were by far the most expensive items on the United Nations budget.

The progress and development of the idea of peace-keeping forces has so far been pragmatic rather than institutional. Precedents have been set and experience has been gained, but the structure of the Secretariat largely does not reflect this progress. UNEF and ONUC were essentially emergency operations, although their actual duration may have seemed to make the world "emergency" inappropriate. Although there was a small military staff at United Nations Headquarters to deal with Congo affairs and there is now a permanent military adviser, there is still no permanent military staff to plan in detail for future emergencies or contingencies; nor is there any permanent system of a general kind for the selection of troops for future situations. For both UNEF and ONUC there were advisory committees basically composed of representatives of the countries supplying troops, and these proved an admirable device for bringing governments into the problems which the Secretary-General faced as the executive authority for these two operations. The logistical support of the two forces was a function of the normal civilian services of the Secretariat, temporarily expanded for the purpose. Their other needs — legal advice, public information, etc. — were also supplied by the normal departments of the Secretariat. In fact, apart from the military adviser's small staff and a very small civilian affairs unit, also in the Secretary-General's office in New York, there was no United Nations military or special organization outside the actual areas of operation to backstop the United Nations forces in the Congo, Middle East, and now West New Guinea.

There are undoubtedly strong arguments for some institutional development of a permanent kind. The present system means, in any emergency, a degree of unpreparedness and improvisation which would be considered crazy in a normal army. In both the Middle East and the Congo the initial moves of troops were to a very large extent dependent on the magnificent cooperation of the United States Military Air Transport Service. The logistical apparatus in particular presents vast and expensive problems, especially in the early stages of an operation before a supply pipeline can be established. Transportation of United Nations forces in a large area of operations like the Congo, especially as regards aircraft and suitable vehicles, is an abiding problem under the present improvised system. Since the participation of the permanent members of the Security Council in the actual area of operations is precluded, the aircraft and air organization available for service in the Congo have been anything but ideal for the task.

However excellent their performance, the troops made available, being predominantly infantry, are very often not ideally suited by training to the kind of job they have to do. For example, the value of trained riot police in the Congo, when they have been available to the United Nations, proved to be out of all proportion to their numbers. Nor does the United Nations have the equipment or the men to form highly mobile units for immediate dispatch to critical points. Communications and suitable signals personnel also present a major problem for both language and technical reasons, and planning and execution are complicated by these difficulties. The formation of integrated and experienced military staffs has also proved difficult, while the lack of an intelligence organization, such as is normally available to a national army or police force, has proved at times to be a serious handicap. There was also a serious problem of continuity in a force based on units formed from national armies serving only for short terms in the Congo.

It is a mistake, however, in stating these shortcomings to compare an international peace-keeping force with a national army or police force, just as it is misleading to compare the international Secretariat with a national civil service. The very possibility of objectivity in world affairs on the part of international officials is denied by one group of powers, and, while not denying it in the same categorical way, there are always those in other camps who question it in particular situations. The whole idea of international institutions is in its infancy, an infancy complicated by worldwide political and ideological divisions. At the best of times the development of such institutions would have profound effects on such doctrines as national sovereignty and the rights of nations. The institutional addition at this time of a permanent international police force would in all probability worsen the state of international politics, and it might, by its very existence or through precipitate and inappropriate use, complicate the very situations it was designed to solve. This in itself is a strong argument for the pragmatic approach, whatever its practical disadvantages. There will, of course, be muddling and difficulty, but, on the evidence to date, something at least gets done to avoid the worst disasters, and in the process many people learn a lot and think a lot, which is a good investment for the future.

There is also of course the burning question of money. Although the United Nations, so often piously referred to by statesmen as "the world's best hope for peace," has a budget which is chicken feed by comparison with the defense budgets of a number of powers, the fact is that the Organization is constantly on the brink of bankruptcy, from which only its indispensability and the farsightedness of a few powers somehow usually rescue it. A permanent international force would greatly increase its expenses, an addition which could probably only be accepted by governments after many more years of acclimatization to the idea and the practice of such activities.

Until such a development occurs, some interim measures may be developed to improve the efficiency of the present improvisational system. Various forms of training for international service could probably quite easily be fitted into the normal training programs of national armies. UNEF, ONUC, and the UN Truce Supervision Organization in the Middle East have already provided a long list of officers from many countries with previous experience in and proven suitability to international peace-keeping tasks. On the logistical side too, experience with equipment and supplies can be used to prepare for future emergencies.

In the meanwhile the precedent exists when the emergency is grave enough to demand it, and in spite of the complications under which United Nations forces operate, the performance of their constituent units is encouraging. With virtually no exceptions the soldiers have been admirably loyal to United Nations directives and have remained aloof from politics, either national or local. They have shown themselves to be objective professionals with a considerable capacity for adaptation and improvisation in difficult circumstances, and by their bearing and discipline they have shown how much professional soldiers have to contribute to the keeping of the peace. Any mistake by a United Nations force is of course triumphantly seized on by critics all over the world and magnified out of all proportion. Tragedies have on occasion occurred, and they too are used to give a popular idea of incompetence or worse. This is to be expected in a venture which is both new and extremely difficult.

The Congo operation on its bad days was frequently hailed triumphantly by its detractors as the last time when any country will ever call upon a United Nations force to help in its difficulties. It is therefore interesting that the Dutch and Indonesians agreed to ask for a

United Nations force (a small one, admittedly, and provided by one nation only, Pakistan) to provide security during the interim period in West New Guinea, prior to the Indonesian takeover from the Dutch.

From this rather cursory survey of the theory and practice of UN peace-keeping operations, a number of points emerge. The first and most obvious is that the original plan laid down in the Charter soon proved to be unworkable and is unlikely to prove workable in the foreseeable future. The nature of war and peace have changed too fast for it. Even the secondary plan, the "Uniting for Peace" resolution of 1950, which was produced in the period of enthusiasm for collective security engendered by the Korean War and in the realization that some way round the paralysis of the Security Council had to be found, has been used only in its procedural part for the transfer of issues involving peace and security from the Council to the Assembly.

Instead emergencies have been met in the heat of crisis by developments of a more pragmatic kind and by the gradual evolution of new confidence in and use of the international staff and machinery of the Organization as such. It is not only the leadership and commanding objectivity of Hammarskjöld that pointed the way to and made possible developments which would have been considered revolutionary and dangerous even ten years ago. The very relationship of the great powers to each other in the nuclear age has meant that much responsibility and potential for useful activity in the maintenance of peace has passed to the smaller powers, and the new forms of peace-keeping machinery in the Middle East and the Congo are very largely dependent upon them for their personnel and support. Thus international responsibility has been diversified in an unexpected way, and, with this diversification, support for and understanding of the United Nations has been strengthened and widened. This development is the product of necessity, for there are new situations in which the intervention of any one power or group of powers is too dangerous for anyone to contemplate.

This development has as yet produced no sweeping institutional change. There has, however, been a steady development of thinking and experience and a widening circle throughout the world of military personnel and units with experience of United Nations activities, and this may prove in the long run to be of lasting value. There is also a growing recognition, except in one quarter, that the United Nations in its objective way can, as the mediator of historic change, play a role which can be played by no other agency, and that, despite its manifest imperfections, this role is an irreplaceable one, to which all nations can contribute in good faith and in their own ultimate interest. There is also a growing recognition that the role requires on occasions the use of peace-keeping forces of one kind or another.

The development of an international institution of over 100 members must inevitably be a slow and delicate business. Provided that the United Nations can respond to challenges when they appear — and it has shown already that in many cases it can — it will maintain and enhance its usefulness as an institution and slowly strengthen the basis of confidence on which alone, in the absence of overwhelming material power, it can operate. In the atmosphere of suspicion and rivalry in the world this will be a long and arduous process, but it is already under way and has shown results. If it can be maintained and developed, the necessary institutional changes will come about eventually almost of their own accord, having been already proved and tempered in practice. This pragmatic development, if subject occasionally to muddle and imprecision, has tended historically to produce the strongest and most enduring institutions.

EDWARD H. BOWMAN and JAMES E. FANNING

Logistics – Experience and Requirements

Establishing and maintaining the United Nations Emergency Force in the Middle East (UNEF) and the United Nations operation in the Congo (ONUC) placed a major strain on the logistic support capabilities of the Secretariat. The first sections of this paper review specific logistics problems encountered with UNEF and ONUC. The final section summarizes the military missions' currently most critical operating problems and suggests areas of difficulty that would likely arise if the United Nations had to establish a new military mission today.

The UN Secretariat has many international operations for which it must provide total or partial logistic support. Arrangements and provision must be made for about 500 conferences each year in various parts of the world. Support must be provided for the numerous offices of the Technical Assistance Board. The 35 information centers and the regional offices of the Economic and Social Council all place regular demands for support on the Secretariat. Support has been required for the many special political and peace-keeping missions — to mention a few, the UN Relief and Works Agency for Palestine Refugees, the Korean Reconstruction Agency, the UN Truce Supervisory Organization in Palestine, the UN Military Observer Group in India and Pakistan, and visiting missions to trust territories.[1] The situations in Korea, Suez, and the Congo also fall into this last category, though

---

[1] Walter R. Sharp, *Field Administration in the United Nations System: The Conduct of International Economic and Social Programs* (New York: Praeger, United Nations Studies No. 10, 1961), p. 4, footnote 1.

their difference in scale virtually makes a difference in kind. The Korean conflict will not be discussed here as the UN delegated the command of the UN forces and the entire logistics support (British Commonwealth excepted) to the United States.

The Office of the Secretary-General has been assigned the responsibility of these military missions. The main logistic component of the Secretariat is the Office of General Services. This office provides support for the operations in New York and also for the field operations. The Office of General Services is composed of four services: Communications and Records maintains the worldwide UN radio network, and keeps all UN records; with certain exceptions, Purchasing and Transportation handles all UN purchases of goods and makes all arrangements for chartering transportation, although field missions are occasionally given special authorization to handle purchases out of local headquarters; Buildings Management takes care of the New York facilities; and the Field Operations Service plays a particularly important role in providing logistic support for missions. On most matters regarding logistic support, the Field Operations Service acts as the contact point in the Secretariat for the missions in the field. The field logistic elements for UNEF and ONUC handle most logistic matters directly with the Field Operations Service rather than going through the Office of the Secretary-General. The Field Operations Service has a unit, established in 1949 as the UN Field Service, which provides certain technical services to field missions. Field Service personnel are prepared to handle skilled custodial tasks; for example, installing telephone facilities.

Also, with a view to reducing costs of field communication and protecting itself against interruption of traffic during international crises, the UN operates a telecommunications network of its own, the establishment of which was approved by the General Assembly in 1948. There are now eight major UN transmitters, located in New York, Geneva, Pisa, Gaza, Jerusalem, Karachi, Bangkok, and Seoul; the establishment of each transmitter required the consent of the host government. Messages are relayed by cable to points not covered in the system — for instance, from Seoul to Tokyo. The network is used primarily by the field missions and peacekeeping missions. The savings from the UN network over commercial communication service is estimated at over 50 percent.[2]

The logistic and administrative capabilities of the Secretariat, although adequate for supporting most UN missions, are strained when military missions like UNEF and ONUC are to be initiated. The UN is simply not designed to initiate and sustain large military missions. The Office of the Secretary-General does not contain any single administrative cell for coordinating all of the activities connected with the missions in Gaza (i.e., Suez) and the Congo. The Secretary-General has only one principal military advisor, and this post was established only to aid in dealing with the military problem of the Congo mission. Military missions are thought of by many officials in the UN as "stepchildren," and the organizational structure needed to administer and support the missions is kept to an absolute minimum. In assessing the capacity of the UN to undertake new military missions, one suspects that the lack of administrative superstructure must limit the effectiveness with which such missions can be planned and launched.

Another reason why the UN is ill-suited to undertake military missions is that it has practically no long-range transportation equipment at its immediate disposal. It is disconcerting even to speculate on how the UN would go about establishing a military mission without the aid of the United States Air Force. Perhaps a number of contractual schemes could be arranged with enough nations to assure the UN of adequate transportation for any mission which it might need to undertake, but there is also the problem that the UN maintains no stockpile of supplies and equipment for emergency undertakings.

Nonetheless, even though the UN is ill-suited to sponsor military missions, the fact remains that three such missions have been undertaken (counting Korea) and other military missions may yet be required. For instance, the UN had a minor role to play in both West New Guinea and Cuba, either of which might have called for more extended operations. It is, therefore, not a useless task to investigate ways to improve the effectiveness of UN military missions. As a start in this direction some of the specific logistic problems encountered in the initial stages of UNEF and ONUC are presented here.

[2] *Ibid.*, pp. 231-234.

INITIATING LOGISTIC SUPPORT FOR UNEF AND ONUC[3]

The basic plans for logistic support in both military missions were essentially the same. Each of the national troop contingents was expected to carry from home whatever supplies and equipment would be needed for the first few days of the operation. UNEF contingents were asked to bring along a ten-day supply of rations, their personal sidearms, tents, and essential light equipment. Once a contingent arrived it was expected to operate autonomously for a short time. Both operations had to be launched so rapidly that it was certainly desirable for the UN not to be faced immediately with the problems of providing rations, ammunition, clothing, equipment to handle internal contingent communication, small arms, and all of the other things needed to carry on a military operation.

In the first few days of operations the UN hoped to concern itself mainly with major logistic problems. Air transportation had to be provided for all of the troops and the supplies and equipment which were to accompany them. Provision had to be made for communication facilities between troop contingents and headquarters in the field, not to mention the fact that headquarters itself had to be established. Surface transportation and other heavy equipment had to be acquired for movements within the area of operations. Even if troops brought with them rations for immediate use, this provided only a very temporary solution to the food problem, and it was therefore necessary to establish food supply pipelines rapidly. Not the least of the initial problems was to find trained logistics personnel to handle the many logistics functions: for instance, receiving, storing and dispensing supplies, installing and operating communications facilities, handling both air and surface transportation, and providing medical, postal, housekeeping, and other services.

At the beginning of the Suez crisis in early November 1956, it was

---

[3] Our own research and interviewing has been recent and as such has dealt with the current situation, especially the Congo. For background information on the Suez situation our best source of information by far has been the book by William R. Frye, *A United Nations Peace Force* (New York, Oceana Publications [for the Carnegie Endowment for International Peace], 1957). We draw heavily on this book in the first part of this section, especially from Frye's third chapter, "The Force Emerges," pp. 21—31.

necessary that the initial force consisting of contingents from Canada, Colombia, Norway, Denmark, Sweden, and Finland — about 6,000 men in all — be moved with the utmost speed; the Soviet Union, with its allies, was threatening to flood the area with "volunteers," and their presence could only have served to inflame the crisis. Under the resolution, however, forces could not be moved in until Egypt gave final approval to having the selected contingents on its soil.

Hammarskjöld and his aides thought it unwise to take no action until Egypt gave the "O.K." for entry, and they felt that Nasser might be prodded along toward approval if the force were rallied at some point near Egypt. Thus, one of the first logistics problems faced was to acquire a suitable staging area for the force. The Secretary-General was able to solve this problem with the aid of the Italian government, which volunteered Capodichino, the Naples airport.

The UN was most fortunate in the ease with which a commander-in-chief and a headquarters staff were obtained. When the crisis broke out, Major General E. L. M. Burns, a Canadian, was nearby in Jerusalem as Chief-of-Staff of the United Nations Truce Supervisory Organization in Palestine (UNTSO) with a full staff of officers. He and his staff were dispatched to Capodichino to receive the troop contingents.

After the plan of the Secretary-General was accepted on November 7 and troop contingents were selected on November 8, the Secretary-General was faced with the immense problem of starting from scratch to plan support operations for the mission. The planning task was accomplished by special representatives of the governments sending contingents, personnel of the UN Secretariat, and advisors from the United States.

Three of the major supply problems were acquiring food, surface transport equipment, and some unifying symbol for the force. Establishing in a few days a food supply pipeline for a force the size of UNEF is a virtually impossible task. Hence about the only solution was to tap some already existing pipeline until the UN could establish one of its own. Fortunately the United States was willing to accommodate the UN in this matter. The United States Army maintained a large store of rations at Leghorn, Italy, and at its supply dumps at Metz and

Dreux in France. The UN was sold millions of dollars worth of C-rations from these sources.

In providing surface transport, that is, jeeps and trucks, for the forces there was quite a bit of wasted motion. Many of the national contingents insisted on bringing with them at least some of the vehicles which would be needed for the mobility of their forces. This procedure, as far as it went, would relieve the UN of the immediate problem of having to acquire these vehicles elsewhere. Furthermore, it would seem desirable for the military forces to use equipment to which they were normally accustomed. US flying boxcars were used to transport much of this equipment to Capodichino, but, unfortunately, the equipment got no further in the early stages of the mission. On November 14 Egypt gave the final "O.K." for entry of the UN force, and it then became necessary to move the troops, supplies, and equipment from Capodichino into Egypt. The early transportation from Capodichino, however, was handled by Swissair, which had no flying boxcars. The troops therefore arrived without the surface transport equipment which had been lifted to Capodichino and now sat idle there. However, the ingenuity of the UN in improvising was by no means sapped; procurement people from the Secretariat were sent to Gaza to purchase jeeps and anything else which might be useful from the British. The jeeps were painted white and put to immediate use.

A problem which one might ordinarily think of as being far less difficult than those mentioned so far was that of providing some unifying symbol for the force. When an existing military force is deployed, this problem does not explicitly arise, but in putting together a force of many nationalities it caused the UN no little consternation. The "stir" which accompanied the uniform hunt aptly illustrates the chaos which must have occurred in those first days of UNEF planning.

Food, surface transport, and a unifying symbol represented only three of the major supply problems faced by the UN; there were many more. Since the Sinai desert gets cold at night during November, it was necessary for the troops to have tent stoves. Furthermore, these stoves had to be of the oil-burning variety since the wood supply in the desert is limited. All of the supply problems were not adequately solved, and the first units to arrive were by no means adequately supplied to undertake their functional role. Egyptian former Major General Amin Hilmy II, Nasser's liaison to UNEF, reports that he had to supply the advance units with tents, field kitchens, jeeps, and all sorts of other things. The UN's lack of information — "intelligence" — about the area in which the force would operate was made evident by the fact that most of the troop contingents were ill-equipped for desert operations. Hilmy felt that the Yugoslavian contingent was the only one which arrived fully self-sufficient.[4]

The most critical element of logistic support for the operation was transportation. Airlifting troops and supplies from all over the world was a truly monumental task, and it was handled primarily by the United States. Canada, Switzerland, and Italy also took limited parts in the airlift. The United States handled the job absolutely free at an estimated cost to the country of $2,250,000.[5] By November 14 the United States Air Force and the Military Air Transport Service had flown 649 men and 111 tons of equipment to Capodichino. By the end of November 2,500 men had been transported to duty in Gaza, and by early February 1957 UNEF had been brought to its full strength of 6,000 men and officers from ten Member nations.

Despite the previous experience of the Secretariat in planning and establishing the UNEF operation, logistic support for ONUC in its initial stages was not so well integrated into the over-all scheme as it was for UNEF. One reason for this was certainly the size of the Congo undertaking; there were many troops, and they had to cover a very large geographical area. Moreover, all of the problems of acquiring logistic support personnel, setting up supply pipelines, establishing communications, and providing transportation for men and materials were certainly aggravated by the need for moving swiftly. In his first progress report as the Special Representative of the Secretary-General, Mr. Rajeshwar Dayal pointed out some of the difficulties caused by the speed:

> The first units arrived within forty-eight hours of the Security Council decision and were immediately deployed. Such exceptional speed was warranted by the seriousness of the situation, but it also entailed considerable risks and disadvantages. The troops had to be deployed before the headquarters, logistics organization, and signal communica-

---

[4] Conversation with Lincoln P. Bloomfield, Cairo, June 1962.
[5] Frye, *op. cit.*, p. 26.

tions were even formed. Operations in local areas are still being hampered by lack of vehicles. . . . A high degree of improvisation has thus been required at all levels throughout the first stages of the operation.[6]

The Congo operation might have been launched more smoothly if some pre-planning had taken place. The UN had practically no information on the Congo prior to the actual undertaking. The first maps of the Congo, in fact, were obtained from a Belgian shipping company on Wall Street. Lack of information made it particularly difficult to plan support requirements — how, for instance, should ammunition be stored in the Congo climate, what sort of shelter did the troops require, where were airstrips located and which of them were suitable for which types of aircraft? As one professional soldier remarked, "You might just as well have asked the New York Yankees to establish a military force there."

In selecting troop contingents it was the policy of the Secretary-General to favor troops from African nations and then fill out the force with nations which were not vitally involved in the East-West Cold War. This policy caused him some difficulties in finding capable logistic staff personnel as many of the African nations and the neutrals did not have trained people available for logistics specialties. Medical personnel, pilots for aircraft operating within the Congo, supply personnel, communications operators, and surface transport personnel were all in short supply.The lack of logistic personnel was in part alleviated by moving a large part of the Swedish UNEF battalion to the Congo for temporary service.

SUPPORTING THE FORCE (SOME PARTICULARLY TROUBLESOME ITEMS)

The troops, except for those from Guinea, Malaya, and Indonesia, arrived with only small arms. Initially there was no demand for heavy weapons inasmuch as the ANC did not have access to the depots where their own heavy weapons were stored. With the decision in August 1960 to return to them their weapons, the needs changed. The Malayan battalion and Ghanaian reconnaissance group brought in light armored cars, which were believed to have a noticeable psychological

[6] Security Council *Official Records* (15th year), Supplement for July, August, and September 1960, p. 185.

effect. The diversity of types and calibers of weapons gave rise to many problems. At a minimum it would have been helpful if each government had notified the UN of these details at the very beginning and arrangements had been made for an appropriate reserve.

Medical services were sorely lacking at the outset of the operation. The Ghanaians, however, soon undertook to provide two medical units. Fortunately, no serious epidemic or significant number of casualties occurred before medical services were built up. In obtaining signals personnel a special problem was created by the fact that many bilingual (French-English) operators were needed. The only African nation furnishing pilots during the initial stages of the operation was Ethiopia; most of the sixty pilots were from Argentina, Brazil, India, Norway, Sweden, and Yugoslavia.[7] By mid-August a number of logistic units, as listed in the Secretary-General's report of August 20, 1960, were present in force:

> a supply unit and an air dispatch team from India, an ordnance unit from Pakistan, a bilingual signal unit from Canada, a workshop control and supervisory team from Denmark and Norway, an engineer workshop unit and two movement control teams from Sweden, one movement control team from Liberia, and two hygiene teams from The Netherlands. . . .[8]

The two most acute problems which faced the UN in the initial stages of the Congo operation were communication and transportation. Communications were made difficult not only by the need for bilingual operators but also by the fact that communications equipment of the proper types in sufficient quantities was not available during the earlier stages of the operation.

On July 17, 1960, the communications available to the UN representatives consisted of telephone via a hotel switchboard and commercial telegram. For the first four weeks there were no other communications except for amateur radio "hams," plantation nets, and Air Congo teletype circuits. Because nothing could be transmitted in cipher, native languages were used for security purposes, e.g., Amharic to the Ethiopian brigade, Arabic to the Tunisians, Gaelic to the Irish, and Swedish to the Swedes. Frequently, the only way of communicat-

---

[7] *Ibid.*, pp. 16-29.
[8] *Ibid.*, p. 82.

ing with force headquarters in Leopoldville was to send messages along with aircraft. In his September 30 report Mr. Dayal made the following assessment of the communications situation two months after the first troops arrived:

> Communications of all kinds have hitherto been at a minimum. When a brigade of three battalions is responsible for an area the size of France which is beset by problems ranging from famine to tribal war, the lack of communications aggravates the already exhausting task of the troops. At present radio communications have been established by the Force signals between ONUC headquarters and the majority of the territorial commands. There are, however, still some territorial commands which depend for their link with headquarters on borrowed or public facilities. The situation within the territorial commands is also not completely satisfactory, many of the units being without radio communications between their headquarters and sub-units. . . . With the voluntary departure of European personnel incident to independence, there was virtually no trained staff to supervise the operation of telephone telex and radio transmission installations and these facilities are in operation today only because of the presence of a large U.N.-International Telecommunication Union Team.[9]

In the initial stages of the Congo operation almost all troops and materials had to be moved into the Congo by air. Deliveries from outside the country were made primarily at N'djili, the Leopoldville airport used by the UN. Once the troops and materials reached Leopoldville, however, it was not possible for them to be fanned out by surface transportation. When the crisis began in July, lack of security and supervisory arrangements almost paralyzed all surface transportation; hence, it was necessary for an airlift within the country to be established. The major contributor to the airlift was the United States. By July 20 the United States had completed over 100 flights to the Congo, transporting 2,522 soldiers plus food, equipment, and supplies from Africa, Europe, and the United States. The United States also contributed aircraft to the internal airlift, which was under the direction of General von Horn. The contribution included ten C-47 transports and some light aircraft.[10] A number of other nations contributed to the airlift; Ethiopia and the United Kingdom helped to bring the

[9] *Ibid.*, pp. 185-188.
[10] *Ibid.*, pp. 32-33.

first troops to the Congo, and Canadian, Swiss, and Soviet aircraft participated actively thereafter. A summary of the United States contribution to the end of the year 1961, as presented in a report from the President to the Congress, was as follows:

> During the year [1961], the United States continued to provide the bulk of the logistic support for the U.N. operation in the Congo. By the end of 1961 the U.S.A.F. had flown 1,399 sorties, airlifting over 46,000 troops and 7,800 tons of supplies and equipment to and from the Congo. In addition, from October 1960 to December 1961, approximately 13,000 troops, 4,860 tons [of supplies and equipment], and 612 vehicles were sealifted in or out of the Congo. . . . In terms of total miles traveled U.S. logistical support for ONUC represents the greatest single airlift ever carried out by any country at any time. It is noteworthy that it has been carried out without a single fatal accident.[11]

The intra-Congo airlift posed a number of problems for the ONUC command. Some aircraft were loaned to the UN by Member nations, and the remainder chartered from commercial sources. The borrowed aircraft came from different sources, and so did the pilots. This situation created the need for a costly training program and was not conducive to maximum efficiency of air transport. The commercial charters were unreliable and unsafe, but since nations could not be asked to loan the UN large numbers of aircraft for an indefinite period of time, a system of transport based almost solely on commercial aircraft had ultimately to be phased in.[12]

The difficulties of the air transport force were further complicated by the fact that when the Europeans departed, many of the airstrips in the Congo were left without ground crews; hence, it was necessary for the UN to bring in the required personnel. As of September 21, flights could be serviced only at the N'djili, N'dolo, and Kamina airfields. The air transport force was initially plagued by the fact that there was no weather information available in the Congo. The UN, however, sent in five meteorologists, who dispatched a helicopter once daily to Brazzaville to pick up weather maps.[13]

---

[11] *U.S. Participation in the U.N.*, Report by the President to the Congress for 1961, Department of State Publication 7413, International Organization Conference Series 33, August 1962, p. 87.

[12] Security Council, *op. cit.*, pp. 185-188.

[13] *Ibid.*, p. 188.

From the point of view of the military leadership, inadequate attention was given to the welfare and morale of the ONUC troops. These men were operating under extraordinary difficult conditions, away from their own cultures, frequently on their own in remote areas without adequate communication with superior echelons, serving long hours under a high state of alert, and under verbal and sometimes even physical attack by local populations and later by the ANC. With no newspapers and little mail for many weeks, the majority were without news from home. There were no rest or recreation facilities, no canteens or sergeants' messes, no movies during the first five months except in Leopoldville, and no leave centers largely because of the different nationalities and transportation problems. (UNEF personnel who stay longer than six months have a week in Cairo and another in Lebanon in the course of a year.) Eventually, approval was granted for terminal leave at UN expense, but less than the force commander advocated. The UNEF service allowance equivalent to 43 Congolese francs a day was applied without reference to local conditions. (In 1962 the official rate of exchange was 65 francs to the dollar; on the black market it was 140-150.) This was later increased to 65 francs to enable the troops to purchase items the UN could not supply (civilians, however, drew 300 francs a day).

SYSTEMS FOR CONTINUING SUPPORT

The system for providing logistic support in the field for UNEF is somewhat unusual. Part of the logistic functions are handled by the military staff, but others are carried out by the chief administrative officer (CAO), who is a civilian. The CAO handles all of the financial affairs of the force, and he is also in charge of all procurement. The military staff, however, determines the requirements for military goods and services and submits these in the form of requisitions to the CAO. The CAO, with regard to procurement, is under direct instructions from the Field Operations Service in New York. New York does most of the purchasing for the operation, but on requisitions which amount to less than $5,000, the CAO may use his own discretion and purchase the goods locally if he chooses.

The actual logistic activities — that is, communications, supply, transportation, major medical, maintenance, etc. — are handled by the military staff although some civilian Field Service personnel take part, particularly as radio operators and mechanics. The main concentration of logistic activities for the force is at the maintenance area in Rafah. The UNEF small air unit, which is composed of two Caribou transports (each can carry two jeeps) and a few other aircraft (no helicopters), is based in Rafah. The Rafah base is also the main storage area for supplies, and it is the location of a field hospital unit from Norway. Canadian troops run the Rafah installation and so constitute most of the Force's logistic personnel. A Canadian unit also handles the Headquarters signals. An Indian unit provides postal services. Within each battalion there are support personnel who handle logistics problems internal to the battalion.

About 80 to 90 percent of all UNEF's supplies come in by sea. Some supplies, especially food, are accumulated at a UN storage area in Pisa, Italy, and then flown into Rafah each week on a Canadian charter flight. Supplies arriving by sea are unloaded in Port Said, and from there they must be transported across the desert to the storage area at Rafah. A UNEF transport unit makes daily runs between the port and the storage area with two and one-half ton trucks, many of which are refrigerated. Each week the battalions draw supplies from the main storage area at Rafah. The movement of supplies from Rafah to the various battalion headquarters is not carried out by a single centralized transport unit; each battalion sends its own trucks. To prevent misallocation of supplies and mismanagement of storage facilities, a number of safeguards are in use. Troop contingents file requisitions for supplies issued to them and records of issuance are kept. The chief administrative officer, despite the fact that the warehouses are operated by military staff personnel, is authorized to inspect these facilities.

Supplies for UNEF come from all over the world, the UN procuring its supplies wherever they are cheapest. Beef is purchased in Australia and Argentina; chicken comes from the United States; fish from Norway and Italy. Ammunition and supplies which are for particular types of equipment often come from the source providing the equipment. Swedish rifles, for instance, require Swedish ammunition. Gasoline is procured under contracts with Socony and Shell and is supplied by local contractors. Presently, about 85 percent of all supplies are purchased on the open market. The rest is acquired through assistance arrangements with UN Member governments, UNEF has "assists" arrangements with the United States, Canada, the Scandinavian countries, and India. Of the 85 percent purchased on the open market, 20 percent of these supplies are purchased through local channels, and the remainder is handled through the Field Operations Service in New York. From the day a requisition is sent by the CAO in Gaza to New York, it takes about four to six months for the supplies, traveling by sea, to reach Gaza. The UN, by the way, pays no duty on the goods which it ships.

In addition to handling most of the purchases of supplies, New York also makes all of the arrangements for troop rotation transportation, much of which is furnished by the United States. The frequent rotation of troops is certainly an undesirable aspect of UNEF's operations. In addition to the transportation expense, there are, of course, many other costs associated with releasing one unit and taking on a new one. Losses in efficiency, particularly in logistics tasks, result from having unseasoned men on the job. Newly rotated logistics and supply officers are brought into the base at Rafah for a few days of briefing, before they begin their duties. Most officers feel that very little is lost in the actual efficiency of the troops because of rotation.

Another major difficulty faced by UNEF was the lack of equipment standardization, primarily for transportation equipment, but for other items as well. To reduce both procurement and maintenance costs it is desirable to use standardized supplies and equipment. The multi-national nature of the sources of immediately available goods and the multi-national, multi-custom nature of the users of these goods, however, made standardization difficult to achieve. Rations, for instance, had to be chosen in such a way that the country customs and religious restrictions of the participating troops were not ignored. When the UNEF operation was initiated, because equipment had to be acquired with great speed, the troops brought with them their standard equipment from home. As this equipment began to wear out, the UN was confronted with the problem of repairing and maintaining it, which required large stores of spare parts, and diversity of repair talents. Surface transport equipment presented perhaps the greatest such difficulty. The problem is now being dealt with by replacing all pieces of equipment with standard types as they wear out. Trucks are being replaced by British Bedfords, cars by French Citroëns, and jeeps with the standard American variety. This policy extends to other types of equipment; typewriters, for instance, are being replaced with a standard type made by Olivetti.

In the organization scheme for the ONUC mission, financial power rested with the CAO, who handled all procurement for both the military and civilian activities. Just as for UNEF, major purchases were made in New York, as were transportation arrangements for troop rotation and the shipment of supplies and equipment into the Congo. There were corresponding elements on the military and administrative staffs to facilitate support in each of the major categories.

The organization within the Congo was divided into four territorial commands. Most of the logistic activities were carried out at the force headquarters in Leopoldville, but logistics staffs were attached to each territorial command and are responsible for the support of all UN forces within the territories. Most of the logistic elements at force headquarters were rather large detachments which were specially requested for logistic tasks — for instance, the Canadian signals unit, the Pakistani ordnance unit, the Indian supply unit. They were not essentially integral parts of the brigades or battalions participating in the "primary" activities of the force. The logistics staffs attached to the territorial commands were integral parts of troop contingents. In each of the three territorial commands other than the Leopoldville one, the commanding officer of the territory was also the commanding officer of the large brigade located in the territory. Similarly the logistics staffs of the brigade were used as the staffs for the territories.

Most supplies reached the Congo by sea, arriving at the port of Matadi. Some supplies were also flown into Leopoldville by air. There was a weekly supply flight which brought materials from sources in Europe. Materials for this flight were usually accumulated at Mildon Hall in England, at the UN supply office in Pisa, and at Wheelus Field in Libya near Tripoli. The port of Matadi was operated commercially rather than by the UN. From Matadi supplies travelled by rail to Leopoldville, and from Leopoldville they were flown to supply points within the territorial commands. Supplies for the Luluabourg command were flown only to Luluabourg; supplies for the Elisabethville command were flown to Elisabethville, Albertville, and Kamina; supplies for the Stanleyville command went to Stanleyville and Kindu. Once supplies reached the terminal points they were transported by land to the forces operating within the territories. The UN attempted to keep on hand supplies sufficient for three months of operation within the Congo.[14]

Aircraft within the Congo were basically of two kinds — fighter and transport (there were also a few liaison-type aircraft). The fighter aircraft were under the control of the ONUC air commander; there were three squadrons — one of F-86's, one of Swedish Saabs, and one of Indian Canberras. Air transport within the Congo eventually went on a commercial basis. A number of commercial carriers are under contract to the UN. A movement control section in Leopoldville coordinated all transport activities within the Congo.

The force in the Congo faced most of the standardization and troop rotation problems faced by UNEF. In the Congo these problems existed on an even larger scale, and their solution was less satisfactorily obtained. One major problem encountered in the Congo, but not in Gaza, was air safety, now improved by the presence of United States Federal Aviation Authority inspectors.

UNITED STATES SUPPORT OF UN MILITARY OPERATIONS

The magnitude of the United States contributions to both UN missions at their outsets has already been noted. Provision for the granting of the UN requests is made in the UN Participation Act (Public Law 264, 79th Congress). Some requests made by the UN call for repeated or periodic reshipments of supplies and equipment, while others may request only one particular good or service. The United States presently receives about ten to fifteen requests for routine reshipments and about eight to ten requests for transportation assistance per month.

New or unusual requests for assistance receive close scrutiny from both the State and Defense Departments. Requests for transport are initiated through the Office of the Secretary-General. Requests for supplies reach the United States Mission to the United Nations by way of the Field Operations Service.

The State Department must consider carefully the possible unde-

<hr>

14 *U.S. News and World Report*, March 20, 1961.

sirable consequences which might result from granting any particular UN request. When the Tunisians, for example, were participating in ONUC, they were supplied with American ammunition for use in the Congo. Subsequently, the Tunisians were withdrawn from the force for possible military action against France, and they took the American ammunition home with them. Had the Tunisians used American ammunition against the French, our State Department would have considered this a "most unfortunate turn of events." With regard to ammunition the State Department's position was made particularly uncomfortable by the fact that ONUC did not have an adequate accounting system or effective check-out procedures.

The role of the Defense Department in reviewing requests is to decide, from a military standpoint, whether or not granting a UN request would really improve the effectiveness of the UN operation. When the UN requested tanks for use in the Congo, the appropriate authorities in the Defense Department recommended against granting the request. The UN was advised that tanks would probably not be particularly effective in the Congo. Since crises in the Congo would break out first in one spot then in another many miles distant, the UN forces, by acquiring a few tanks, would only bring upon themselves the unceasing problem of having to airlift the tanks from location to location all over the Congo. The Defense Department suggested that armored cars might better satisfy ONUC's needs.

The United States Air Force was the executive agent for the Department of Defense in matters pertaining to the UN effort in the Congo. Since UNEF does not draw heavily on the United States for support, no special executive agent has been appointed for its operations.

AN ORGANIZATION OF PROBLEM AREAS

United Nations military operations tend in the authors' opinion to be inefficient and overly expensive, and the management of resources in the Gaza and Congo operations measured up far short of present day notions of military efficiency. It is unquestionable that any major power could have handled the logistics support for these forces at a lower cost and in a way that would have facilitated greater effectiveness of the UN troops. But since this obvious means of providing logistics support — that is, contracting with some efficient major power to manage the task in its entirety — is almost certain to be unfeasible, it is important for the United Nations to come to grips with many of the factors which limit its effectiveness in handling the job.

Readers who are familiar with the UN military operations will realize that most of the UN's logistics problems can be traced back to political and economic constraints. Hence, the resolution of many logistic difficulties can be affected only in part, if at all, by those managers in the UN who are responsible for the support activities. Large strides toward improved UN logistic effectiveness must stem from developments within the political community.

If we group the problems we have outlined in two major categories — those which are likely to limit effectiveness if the UN were today to launch a new military mission (problems of readiness), and those which limit the effectiveness of logistic support for one of the existing military missions (operating problems) — it appears that the major problems limiting the effectiveness of support for UN missions are as follows:

Readiness problems

1. Insufficient provision for administrative coordination.
2. Insufficient capability for properly planning a large scale military mission.
3. Lack of immediately available supplies, equipment, and transportation.
4. Lack of immediately available logistic personnel.

Operating problems

1. Inadequate administrative coordination and procedures.
2. Insufficiently standardized equipment and supplies.
3. Political staffing considerations.
4. Frequent turnover of personnel.
5. Air transport unreliability.

Readiness problems

1. *Insufficient provision for administrative coordination.* Since logistic support must be based on the activities to be performed by the line organization, it is necessary that at all levels in a military operation

the line activities and the logistic activities are thoroughly coordinated. If line activities never changed, then it should certainly be possible for a once-and-for-all plan to be formulated, thus relieving the coordinator of his responsibilities. If the line activities can be viewed as static above a certain level in the organization, then the need for coordination above this level may be similarly achieved with a once-and-for-all plan. UNEF, for instance, operates in such a way that on the 38th floor of the Secretariat the activities on any one day would appear to be scarcely different from those on another. The Congo force did not present so calm a picture, but certainly the need for coordination of logistics and line activities at a high level in the Secretariat became far less than it was in July of 1960. When the activities of an organization stabilize, it is possible to decentralize the coordination task, delegating it to the lower organizational levels. If the UN, however, must ever launch another military operation, the need for coordination at high levels in the Organization will be acute — just as it was when UNEF and ONUC were launched. There will be few stable activities, and obviously the problems of coordination cannot be passed down to a lower level until one exists.

High-level coordination of the recent military missions is handled within the Office of the Secretary-General. The coordination might most accurately be described as being handled by a team made up of the Secretary-General, the Under-Secretary for Special Political Affairs, the Military Adviser to the Secretary-General, and the Adviser on Civilian Activities in the Congo. With no high-level administrative assistance this team coordinated the activities of the military missions — and of course the Secretary-General and the Under-Secretary must deal with many other activities of the UN. The situation could be likened to that of a large corporation which has a board of directors, some department heads (like the head of the Field Operations Service, the Commander-in-Chief of UNEF, the political officer of ONUC), but no president and vice-presidents. The high-level administrative element is missing.

Even though it is possible to maintain missions without an administrative element, such an element would be vital if high-level coordination of activites were required. Even under the present system an administrative element should smooth out operations and free some valuable time of high-level personnel in the Office of the Secretary-General. Arguments against adding administrative personnel for the military missions usually take one of two tacks. The first is the idealistic point of view: the UN is a peace-loving organization; the military missions are unwanted and undesirable. The United Nations should not incorporate into its structure any more elements for use in military missions than absolutely necessary, since such incorporation might be viewed as acceptance of a military role in world affairs. Others are opposed to improving the effectiveness with which the UN can undertake military activities for fear that the UN might use this improved capability against their interests.

2. *Insufficient capability for large-scale planning.* Sooner or later it is necessary to plan logistic support for any military operation to be undertaken. There is practically no doubt that contingency planning would improve the effectiveness with which the UN could undertake a military operation. Frye says:

> Another time, if such an operation were necessary, it would be greatly facilitated if problems of transportation and logistics could be worked out in advance so that they would not have to be improvised. UNEF was in many ways a major miracle, because so many important details had to be handled on the spur of the moment.[15]

Even if the UN does not undertake contingency planning, the problem of planning support of any military mission does not simply go away. It becomes an even more acute problem the shorter the time in which it must be done.

To carry out planning there must be a staff of sufficient size. The staff must have at hand the information which is needed for planning.

> There shold be experienced men available to the Secretary-General who know answers to the key logistical questions: where air and sea transportation for manpower can be had; where food, uniforms, vehicles, spare parts, weapons, and all other kinds of supplies are available, and how they can be transported where they are needed; where staging areas can be set up quickly; what kind of food troops of various countries want, and what their special needs are; and many

15 Frye, *op. cit.*, p. 27.

other important details. . . . Non-secret maps and data of climatic conditions, for example, could come in handy.[16]

The UN does not have a staff which gathers information (intelligence) and engages in contingency planning (i.e., establishing the possible situations and developing appropriate plans for each); in fact, formally, the UN does not have a single man who does either of these things. Secretary-General Hammarskjöld actually refused to have an intelligence staff. Perhaps he thought that ideally the UN should not have any permanent military organization. In summarizing the UNEF experience, however, he appeared to argue against permanent (military) planning personnel on the grounds that they would not be needed or useful. He said:

> It may be reiterated in passing that the UN Secretariat has by now had extensive experience in establishing and maintaining UN operations involving military personnel and, without improvising or augmenting unduly, can quickly provide operations of that nature with efficient communications service in the field, with headquarters, with transportation and vehicles for local transport, with well-tested administrative and accounting systems and expert personnel to man them, and with effective procurement and security arrangements.[17]

After UNEF was established, was it possible that people in the Secretariat went right along believing they were endowed with the remarkable powers described by Hammarskjöld — that without gathering any advance information, without maintaining any planning staff which had the answers to the key logistic questions, they could suddenly bring to bear whatever logistic support was needed for a UN military operation? The UN experience in establishing support for the force in the Congo, needless to say, should have destroyed any such notion once and for all.

Although the UN formally has no planning staff, the need for undertaking information-gathering and contingency-planning activities has apparently been recognized. The Military Adviser to the Secretary-General presently engages in some such activities. The Military Ad-

[16] *Ibid.*, p. 85.

[17] "UNEF — Summary Study of the Experience Derived from the Establishment and Operation of the Force," Report of the Secretary-General, UN Document A/3943, October 9, 1958, p. 73.

viser feels that a planning staff in his office would improve the effectiveness of the UN in supporting present missions and any new mission
which might need to be established. United States professional soldiers
who work closely with the UN concur with this idea; it was suggested
to us that "the UN must accept the fact that UN military operations
will only be more efficient and effective if a small military planning
staff is incorporated in the Secretariat to improve readiness." Other
proposals for a planning staff were not so modest; a high-ranking officer
in the Congo mission told Lincoln Bloomfield that "in the future, to
avoid a ramshackle, expensive operation, the UN must have an adequate staff in New York to wargame likely area problems with proper
logistic people — 25 to 30 men would do it!"

In any organizational activity, if you start badly it is difficult to
change your ways because of the then established precedent. This
places a premium on adequate intelligence and sensible contingency
plans.

3. *Lack of immediately available supplies, equipment, and transportation.* One of the things which has hampered the UN in establishing military missions is the fact that it does not have its own stockpile
of supplies and equipment which can be immediately tapped for
launching an operation. An even greater problem is that it has no transport force with which to move men, supplies, and equipment to a conflict area. One suggestion for alleviating the supply problem is for the
UN to stockpile supplies at a few points in the world just in case they
are needed. This suggestion meets approval, however, in practically no
quarter. From a political standpoint it would appear certainly doomed.
From an economic standpoint it might be more costly than the present
ad hoc approach. Perhaps a better idea would be for the UN to make
some use of its present supply pipelines to Egypt. When officials in
the Secretariat sense a possible crisis coming up, inventories at Rafah,
Pisa or the like could be increased. If a mission must then be established, the initial wave of supplies could come out of the built-up buffer
inventories. Such a plan would of course be of less value if the mission
were to be established far distant from the supply stores.

There appears to be no easy way to escape the fact that the UN must
depend on nations with massive air capabilities for support. It is conceivable that a sufficient number of contractual agreements could be

arranged with commercial carriers to eliminate the dependence of the UN on the United States or other large nations. Such a scheme, however, would almost certainly result in great inefficiencies. Furthermore, it seems most unlikely that a UN military force would ever be used when it is not backed by some great power which can furnish the necessary transportation. However, at least some preliminary commercial arrangements might increase the flexibility of the UN.

4. *Lack of immediately available logistic personnel.* When nations have contributed battalions or brigades for the existing military missions, the contributed units usually come with logistic personnel to handle support tasks which are internal to the unit. Special requests must usually be made for personnel to handle all the logistic tasks external to the contributed units. In establishing UNEF and ONUC the UN was hampered by the fact that the neutral nations, whose contributions were preferred, often could not make logistic units available. Further complicating the situation was the fact that the UN had little information on which nations had what logistic capabilities.

Because of UNEF and ONUC experience this problem is well on the way to being solved. A number of logistic elements have received training in both forces and then have been replaced in accordance with turnover practices. Records are kept now by the Military Adviser to the Secretary-General on the logistic units which have received training, and also on officers who are familiar with UN operations. Presumably these units and officers could be requested by the UN for service in future military missions. The existence of UNEF and ONUC afforded the further advantage that part of trained units which are on duty in either mission could be used temporarily in establishing new missions. In fact, in periods when a possible crisis is sensed, existing missions could be overstaffed with support personnel.

Activities preliminary to the actual affair can be of great use. A small and effective UN contingent which arrives early in the siutation may be of much greater benefit than a large force later.

Operating problems

1. *Inadequate administrative coordination and procedures.* The importance of adding a high-level administrative element to the Organization has already been indicated. Such an element, although evidently

not essential in the past for administering UNEF and ONUC, should still serve to smooth present operations.

The present UN organization, as regards the military missions, is thought by many informed observers to be entirely too loose. Standard operating procedures (S.O.P.'s) by United States standards were at a very elementary stage of development for the Congo. The procedures for UNEF are probably adequate, but they are below the standards of many national military organizations. ONUC had no regular reporting procedures; Leopoldville did not have to report to the Office of the Secretary-General at any regular intervals and was weak on accounting and records. New York was criticized by some for not issuing clear directives to the force commanders. One informed professional soldier said he doubted that anyone even knows for sure what weapons the national contingents had there. Another professional soldier stated this case against the loose UN organization:

> UN military forces are unprofessional, inefficient, ineffective, and overexpensive. This is not because of the military people involved, but because there is no military organization, no S.O.P.'s, no organization manual. The really overriding problem is the lack of military procedure and information.

The lack of check-up procedures was aptly illustrated by a misunderstanding which arose when an Indian contingent was due to be sent back home on rotation. Refrigerators are scarce and expensive in India, and provide no small amount of satisfaction to the Indians. The Indians appeared at the disembarkation area with as many of ONUC's refrigerators as they could lay hands on and were most disappointed to discover that they were not Indian property and could not be taken along.

A good administrative element at a high level in the Secretariat would certainly serve to tighten up the organization of the military missions. Such a tightening-up would almost certainly require more definitive procedures at all levels of the mission's organizations. The idealistic arguments put forth against improved procedures are of the same "ostrich-with-head-in-sand" variety as those used against the addition of an administrative element or a planning staff.

Many of the people in the field suggest that the UN should have prepared an operations manual, at least for the Congo. They suggest further that operations would be improved if logistic personnel were then trained using the manual before they went on the job. Others even suggest that logistic officers should be sent to staff colleges in the United States or in England.

2. *Insufficiently standardized equipment and supplies.* The standardization problem in Gaza is pretty well solved. Rations are standardized down to four different types; initially there were ten. Transportation equipment, as mentioned earlier, has been standardized. In the Congo, however, resupply and maintenance remained a major problem. Once a force gets started using certain equipment and supplies, it is a very difficult matter to change the situation. Rations, since they are consumed entirely in a short time, are easier to standardize than other things. Food problems in the Congo initially were numerous — Pakistanis had to have their chickens killed in a certain way; Arabs wouldn't eat Israeli jam; Norwegians wouldn't eat Portuguese sardines; and so on. Rations have finally been standardized down to four diets. There were about forty different kinds of vehicles in the Congo, varying ammunition calibres, five different mortar sizes, and three types of fighter aircraft, of which until recently only four Swedish Saabs were operational.

The standardization problem is further complicated by the lack of standard policies, records, and procedures. A prerequisite for standardization is knowing what everyone has. Then it is necessary to have definite policies with regard to which items will be resupplied with standard items by the UN and which items are to be replaced from the original source. Neither of these first steps has been satisfactorily taken.

One informed source comments that the UN does not have the proper focus in supply: "They do not work toward standardization of as many items as possible, but rather attempt to do a better job of supplying non-standard items." A rephrasing of this point is that they try to support different national logistic systems rather than establish a UN system.

3. *Political staffing considerations.* A high-ranking UN official, in discussing the military missions, told us that

the UN had no planned growth scheme for its management organization. People were placed in jobs for which they were not suited. One reason for this is that the UN must distribute jobs to give people a feeling of participation and this breeds inefficiency.

Wide support for both men and materials seems necessary so as not to give the appearance of neo-colonialism.

Many American military men feel that the UN does not take proper advantage of United States experience and know-how. They say that competent United States personnel should be in advisory positions to high officials in the UN where they can do some good. It is not sufficient simply to advise as an outsider because then too much of the advice comes only after the fact. Actually the United States gives the UN quite a lot of advice both formally and informally. In the early stages of the Congo operation the United States sent out a team to investigate the problems connected with the airlift. The team made fourteen recommendations to the UN on handling the airlift, although nothing later came of it. The UN's weak information-gathering capability is in part compensated for by United States sources. The United States military intelligence people in the embassy in Leopoldville, United States officials think, would, if asked, have been able substantially to supplement the intelligence capabilities of the UN in the Congo.

4. *Frequent turnover of personnel.* The nature of the inefficiencies and direct expense caused by the frequent and sometimes unexpected turnover of personnel have already been indicated. With less frequent turnover, the cost of frequent air and sea transport could be reduced, as could the cost of retraining personnel, and the cost related to any loss of effectiveness because of fresh personnel's inexperience. The only apparent solution to the turnover problem is for UN officials to prevail upon governments to extend the periods of service of their troops. From a purely economic point of view, however, it would not seem at all unreasonable for the UN to provide some incentive to governments who would extend the turnover period for their troops. If, for instance, a nation rotated its troops yearly instead of every six months, the cost to the UN of transporting these troops would be halved. From these direct savings in transport expense the UN could offer some form of

economic incentive to the government making the savings possible (e.g., a reduction in its yearly assessment).

5. *Air transport reliability.* The success of the mission in the Congo depended vitally on the operation of the commercial chartered aircraft. Since the aircraft carry not only supplies but also men, their reliability is of particular importance. The death of Mr. Hammarskjöld as a passenger on an ONUC charter plane emphasizes the point.

One high-ranking Secretariat official at one time felt that air transport was the worst problem the UN had there. He told of one flight on a four-motored transport which "scared him half to death." As the plane was taxiing down the runway for take-off, he looked out the window and saw that one of the engines was not operating. With the greatest excitement he told the pilot of their plight. The pilot however, was not all dismayed; he said the situation wasn't unusual — "the fourth one usually catches on take-off." It was also reported that the "Representative of the International Civil Aviation Organization in the Congo would not even travel on the aircraft."

The reliability problem could probably have been best dealt with by establishing strict standards of safety and imposing them without exception on all carriers operating in the Congo.

As should be evident from the foregoing discussion, the problem areas itemized as placing major limits on logistic effectiveness do not exist because of oversights on the part of UN officials. A large share of the difficulties exist because of political or economic costraints or because the UN is not properly designed and endowed to run large military missions. In some cases present readiness or operating effectiveness can be improved before the political-economic barriers are met head on. In the cases of air safety and standardization the constraints are far in the background, and there is reason to believe that time and persistence may gradually alleviate these difficulties.

INTERNATIONAL FORCES

OF THE FUTURE

HANS J. MORGENTHAU

Political Conditions for a Force

I

A police force, domestic or international, must meet two requirements: it must be reliable, and it must be effective. While obviously it cannot be effective if it is not reliable, it can be reliable without being effective, and it is for this reason that the two prerequisites must be distinguished. A police force, in order to be reliable, must be loyal to the political authorities and share their conceptions of law and justice. A police force, in order to be effective, must stand in a certain relation of power to that fraction of the population which is likely to call forth police action by breaking the law.

The police within the state are the instrument of a central authority which is supposed to be endowed with a will culminating in decisions, and it is these decisions that the police are called upon to put into practice. In legal terms the police have the function of enforcing the laws; in political terms they have the function of upholding the authority of the government; in social terms they have the function of protecting a status quo as defined by the laws and expressed in the government's policies. In a well-ordered society the police are but rarely called upon to enforce a change in the status quo; the enforcement of new race relations against groups committed to an outlawed status quo is a case in point in our society. In revolutionary societies, on the other hand, the police force is the main weapon with which a revolutionary minority imposes its will upon a recalcitrant population.

It follows that the police force will be reliable in the performance of its functions only if it has either been forged into so disciplined an instrument of the government's will that it will execute whatever orders it is given regardless of content, or else if its convictions and interests are at the very least not openly at odds with those of the government. Thus the police force, knowingly or without knowing it, is bound to be deeply involved in the political controversies of the society in which it operates.

Lenin maintained correctly against his opponents within the Marxist camp that the dictatorship of the proletariat could not afford to take over the enforcement agencies of its bourgeois predecessor and use them for its own purposes; forged for the purpose of maintaining the rule of an exploiting minority over the exploited majority, they could not be so used. Instead the proletariat had to create its own police, open and secret, appropriate to the special tasks of a new society. During certain periods of violent labor struggles in our society, the police force, regardless of the legal merits of the case, tended to transform itself into a protective guard for the employers, reinforced at times by the latter's private police. The police have at times refused to enforce the law for the protection of members of racial minorities. In certain regions of the United States they have habitually used their power to deprive such members of their rights through positive action. During the crisis at the University of Mississippi in 1962, state and federal police tried to enforce incompatible legal rules and conceptions of justice. Wherever a society is rent by deeply felt controversies, even though they do not lead to open violence, the political preferences of the police are likely to color the performance of its function.

On a lower level of motivation the police, frequently individually and sometimes collectively, have yielded to the temptation of private gain and neglected to enforce the law against certain types of violations, of which traffic, gambling, vice, and housing code violations are outstanding. If this corruption occurs on a massive scale, the police may transfer their loyalty altogether from the legal government to another, private one in the form of a crime syndicate. The police in our society remain a reliable instrument of law enforcement because normally no more than an insignificant number of them will be opposed to the legal order they are called upon to enforce.

The reliable performance of its functions by the police force within the state is thus not a simple technical matter to be expected with mechanical precision. Quite the contrary, it depends upon political, social, and moral conditions which may or may not be present in individual members of the police or the police force as a whole. These conditions must be created and maintained through a continuous effort of the political authorities. In other words, the functioning of a police force depends not only upon its internal technical qualities, but also upon the political, social, and moral climate within which it operates. If the latter is not favorable, the former will avail little.

The effectiveness of a police force is determined, aside from its reliability, by the power relation that exists between itself and the recalcitrant fraction of the population. For the police to be effective, that power relation must meet three prerequisites.

Of all the citizens of a particular society only a very small fraction must be engaged at any one time in breaking the law. If large numbers of citizens simultaneously break the law, as they did with regard to prohibition and rationing and as they are still doing with regard to gambling, the police force, although it meets the standards of reliability, ceases to be an effective agency of law enforcement. Second, however great the differences in power are within a given society, the combined power of law-abiding citizens must be distinctly superior to any combination of even the most powerful lawbreakers. If it is otherwise, as in the case of the medieval feudal lord and his modern counterpart in the form of private concentrations of economic power, the police are bound to be almost as impotent as the citizenry at large. Finally, the police force must be manifestly capable of coping effectively with all foreseeable threats to the legal order. This obvious capability serves to deter attacks upon the legal order that go beyond the piecemeal violations of individual legal rules. In other words, its visible readiness for effective action makes its actual employment in good measure unnecessary.

This quality of unchallengeable superiority, aside from being the result of the reputation for reliability, is a function of the two other prerequisites. In consequence the government is able to rely upon a numerically small and lightly armed police force to maintain law and order. In the absence of these prerequisites the state would need a numerous and heavily armed police force in order to meet frontal attacks upon the legal order itself. That is to say, the state would need an army rather than a police force, and the relations between government and people would be tantamount either to civil war or a military dictatorship.

II

It follows from what has been said thus far that the problems with which an international police force must come to terms are posed by the peculiar character of the international society since that character affects both the reliability and effectiveness of the force.

First of all, an international police force by definition cannot be at the service of a single government to which it gives allegiance and whose orders it executes unquestionably because of that allegiance. An international police force can only be the instrument of an international organization, such as the United Nations. It is this relationship that makes its reliability a continuous problem. In a society of nation-states it is possible for some outstanding individuals to transfer their loyalty from their respective nation-state to an international organization either on a particular issue or even in general. But it is too much to expect that large masses of individual members of different nations could so transfer their loyalties that they would execute reliably and without question whatever orders the international organization might give them. The reliability of an international police force cannot be taken for granted by virtue of the morale and discipline which we have come to expect from the domestic police.

The reliability of an international police force is a function of the legal order and the political status quo it is called upon to uphold. Yet the enforcement of an international legal order and the protection of an international status quo present a police force with problems quite different from those the national police has to solve. Great international conflicts which lead to the violation of international law and conjure up the danger of war and therefore call for the intervention of an international police force are typically the ones in which the survival of the existing legal order and of the political status quo is at stake. The task which the international police force must here perform is not the defense of the legal order and of the political status quo against piecemeal violations, but against an all-out attack. What is at stake here is not the enforcement of a particular legal rule, but the survival of the legal order itself.

One nation or group of nations will be committed to the legal order as it is and to the existing political status quo; another nation or group of nations will be opposed to them; a third will be indifferent. The members of the international police force belong to all of these three types of nations, and their sympathies concerning the issues at stake are bound to vary with the preferences of their respective nations. The members of an international police force will be a reliable instrument of an international organization only in the measure that their legal preferences and political sympathies happen to coincide with the policies of the international organization they are called upon to support.

In consequence the international organization commanding a police force will have to cope with three different contingencies with which national political authorities do not have to deal under normal circumstances. If the challenge to the legal order and the political status quo emanates from or is supported by a great power, the police action reverts to the traditional pattern of a coalition war. That is to say, an army composed of contingents of the nations supporting the legal order and the political status quo will be opposed by contingents of the nation or nations opposed to the legal and political status quo, with the contingents of neutral nations tending to one or the other side. This was the pattern of the Korean War. That this war was called a police action by the supporters of the status quo did not affect the nature of the operation. At best it made it easier for certain nations, which otherwise might have been inclined toward neutrality or a half-hearted effort, to join the defense of the status quo or to commit themselves more fully to it.

If the status quo is challenged by a nation of the second or third rank which has a vital stake in changing it, the sympathies and interests of many other nations are likely to be actively engaged on one or the other side. This contingency will confront an international police force with choices that are bound to be detrimental to its reliability or efficiency or both. If the international police force is composed of national contingents assembled in advance of and without regard to this particular conflict, those of its national contingents which are out of sympathy with the status quo may not be relied upon to defend it. If the international police force is being assembled *ad hoc* in view of this particular conflict and hence is being composed only of reliable national contingents, it faces the risk of being too small to provide an effective defense of the status quo against the forces opposing it.

Even if an international police force appears at the beginning of a conflict to be a reliable and effective instrument of an international organization, it is still faced with an ever present threat to its reliability and effectiveness. An international police force may be politically cohesive at the beginning of a conflict on the basis of a community of sympathy and interests on the part of the nations to which its individual members belong. Yet it is a moot question whether and to what extent such a community of sympathy and interests can survive the initial stages of the conflict. New interests may replace or modify the initial ones; new opportunities may present themselves for the pursuit of old ones. As the interests of the nations concerned change, so will the reliability of the respective contingents of the international police force to defend a status quo which may run counter to those interests. A multinational military force, be it called an international police force or an army, is thus always threatened with partial or total disintegration. Its survival as a reliable and effective force depends upon the persistence of the national interests on which it rests.

What distinguishes an international police force from a national one is, then, the lack of an automatic commitment to a particular legal order and political status quo. Such a commitment can be taken for granted, at least normally and except for piecemeal or marginal deviations, in a national police force. It cannot be taken for granted in an international one, but must there be created and re-created and maintained for each issue. The task an international organization faces in fashioning a police force for a particular issue parallels that of a group of nations seeking political and military support for a particular status quo. The international police forces which have been organized by the United Nations have reflected both the composition and the political and military character of the two-thirds majorities of the General Assembly to which they owed their existence. That is to say, no nation which did not support the police action by its vote in the Security Council or General Assembly supplied contingents for the police force, and of those who so supported it only a small minority supplied contingents. The contributions of these nations were a manifestation of their political interests and military capabilities.

Thus, of the then sixty members of the United Nations only sixteen provided in 1950 armed forces of any kind against North Korea, and of these only the United States, Canada, Great Britain, and Turkey can be said to have contributed more than token forces. South Korea and the United States provided about 90 percent of the armed forces that fought in Korea on the side of the United Nations. For the United Nations Emergency Force stationed along the Egypt-Israel armistice demarcation line, the international frontier south of the Gaza Strip, and at the Gulf of Aqaba the following nations provided troops: Brazil, Canada, Colombia, Denmark, Finland, India, Indonesia, Norway, Sweden, and Yugoslavia. The United Nations force in the Congo was originally composed of contingents from Ethiopia, Ghana, Guinea, Morocco, Tunisia, Sweden, and Ireland. The composition of that force subsequently changed according to changes in the policies of some of the participating nations. However, what remained as the distinctive feature of the United Nations force in the Congo was the numerical predominance of contingents from African nations, which had a special interest in the pacification of the Congo without the intervention of non-African nations. What this United Nations force had in common with that of the Middle East was the absence of great-power contingents, pointing to the policy of the United Nations to use its armed forces for the purpose of isolating the territorial issues from great-power intervention.

The tenuous character of an international police force reflects the tenuous character of the commitment of a number of sovereign nations to a particular legal order and political status quo. The deficiencies of an international police force are the deficiencies of the international order revealed in the perspective of a particular task. In a world of sovereign nations the idea of a reliable and effective international police force, after the model of the national police, is a contradiction in terms. An international police force, by dint of being international rather than national or supranational, cannot be more reliable and efficient than the political interests and military capabilities of the nations supporting it allow it to be.

This situation would not be materially affected by arms control or limited disarmament. As best the control and limitation of national armaments might increase the effectiveness of an international police force in conflicts among major powers, provided that the stabilization and decrease of national armed forces were to go hand in hand with a corresponding increase in the strength of the international police force. Without the latter proviso, arms control and disarmament might well have an adverse effect upon the effectiveness of an international police force; for they might adversely affect the ability and willingness of national governments to put armed forces at the disposal of an international organization. The best that can be expected from arms control and limited disarmament is a change in the distribution of armed strength between national forces and the international police force in favor of the latter. But the basic political issue bearing upon the reliability of an international police force will continue to make itself felt even in a partially disarmed world; for such a world would still be a world of sovereign nations.

The situation would be radically different in a totally disarmed world. Total disarmament can no more be envisaged in isolation from the over-all structure of international relations that can an international police force. Total disarmament requires as its corollary the existence of a supranational authority capable of committing organized force to the defense of the legal order and the political status quo. In other words, total disarmament and world government go hand in hand; they complement each other. In a totally disarmed world the problem of an international police force ceases to exist and reappears in the form — new in its dimensions and old in its substance — of the police of a world government.

III

A historic example will serve to illustrate the dependence of an international police force upon the political purposes which it is intended to support. The illustration is provided by the armed action of the Holy Roman Empire against Frederick II of Prussia during the Seven Years' War. It is surprising that to the best of my knowledge nobody has analyzed the Holy Roman Empire as it existed from the Peace of Westphalia of 1648 to its dissolution in 1806 as the prototype of an international organization which shows revealing similarities with its

20th century successors — the League of Nations and the United Nations.

The medieval emperor of the Holy Roman Empire was supposed to perform the peace-preserving and law-enforcing functions for the sake of which modern international organization has also been established. In the words of James Bryce:

He was therefore above all things, claiming indeed to be upon earth the representative of the Prince of Peace, bound to listen to complaints, and to redress the injuries inflicted by sovereigns or peoples upon each other; to punish offenders against the public order of Christendom; to maintain through the world, looking down as from a serene height upon the schemes and quarrels of meaner potentates, that supreme good without which neither arts nor letters, nor the gentler virtues of life can rise and flourish. The mediaeval Empire was in its essence what its modern imitators have sometimes professed themselves: the Empire was Peace: the oldest and noblest title of its head was "Imperator pacificus." And that he might be the peacemaker, he must be the expounder of justice and the author of its concrete embodiment, positive law. . . .[1]

Originally the emperor was supposed to perform these functions as the head of a universal empire, that is, as the highest secular authority within the Empire's territory. The Treaty of Westphalia reduced these functions to international ones by recognizing the territorial sovereignty of the princes and cities subject to the emperor. The emperor was in consequence precluded from interfering directly with the administration of any territory belonging to the Empire. All major political decisions concerning the Empire, such as the making of war and peace, levying contributions, raising troops, building fortresses, passing or interpreting laws, were the exclusive competence of the imperial Diet. Yet the Diet, in the words of James Bryce,

originally an assembly of the whole people, and thereafter of the feudal tenants-in-chief, meeting from time to time like our early English Parliaments, became in A.D. 1654 a permanent body, at which the electors, princes, and cities were represented by their envoys. In other

---

[1] James Bryce, *The Holy Roman Empire* (New York: The Macmillan Company, 1923), p. 259.

words, it was not so much a national Parliament as an international congress of diplomatists.[2]

The Diet had the authority to protect the legal order and the political status quo of 1648 by summoning the members of the Empire to collective military action. In addition France and Sweden, which were not members of the Empire, had in 1648 been made guarantors of the order of 1648 and hence had received the right to intervene in the affairs of the Empire on behalf of that order. But the Diet, similar to the United Nations, could only request member states to put money and armed contingents at the disposal of the Empire, taking what the member states were willing to give; it could no longer, as it once did, enforce the "matricula" specifying the quota of contingents each state was obligated to furnish to the imperial army.[3] Thus the Holy Roman Empire developed in a way which is the reverse of the development many expect the United Nations to take: starting as a supranational organization, it ended as a federation of sovereign states.

After Frederick II of Prussia invaded Saxony in August 1756, the Elector of Saxony appealed against this breach of the peace to the Emperor and the imperial Diet. After the Emperor had exhausted the peace-preserving and law-enforcing measures with which the imperial constitution empowered him (the so-called *Dehortatoria*, addressed to the King of Prussia; the *Avocatoria*, ordering the Prussian armed forces to leave the seditious service of their king; and the *Monitoria*, the *Excitatoria*, and the *Inhibitoria*, addressed to the imperial territories in order to prevent Prussian enlistments) the council of princes of the Diet decided on January 17, 1757, by a vote of 60 to 26 to declare in the name of the Empire war against Prussia and to employ the military resources of the Empire for the purpose of restoring the Elector of Saxony to his throne. Pursuant to this resolution a special tax was levied on all the states of the Empire, and an imperial army was raised.[4] The composition of that army, the factors determining its

2 *Ibid.*, p. 396.
3 *Ibid.*, p. 394.
4 F. C. Schlosser, *Geschichte des Achtzehnten Iahrhunderts* (Heidelberg: J. C. B. Mohr, 1837), Vol. II, p. 319; Reinhold Koser, *König Friedrich der Grosse* (Stuttgart and Berlin: J. G. Cotta, 1903), Vol. II, p. 47 ff.

composition, and its fate shed a significant light upon the problems facing an international police force.

The states of the Empire split according to their religious and political preferences. All the Catholic states took the side of Austria; the majority of the Protestant ones, that of Prussia. The Protestant princes of Hanover, Brunswick, Lippe, Waldeck, Hesse, and Gotha protested against the resolution of the Diet; they were allied with Great Britain, which in turn supported Prussia. On the other hand, the King of France as guarantor of the Treaty of Westphalia — which guaranty had originally been aimed at Austria — declared his support for Austria in its struggle with Prussia, and it was especially due to his efforts that the imperial army was assembled. In other words, it was not so much the resolution of the Diet but special political relations between France and individual German states which induced the latter to provide contingents for the imperial army. Thus the King of France requested the electors of Cologne and the Palatinate to provide the number of troops promised him in previous treaties. He concluded new treaties with the Elector of Bavaria and the Duke of Wurtemberg in which he promised them subsidies as compensation for a number of regiments to be provided. He made similar agreements with a great number of minor German princes. As a result of these efforts an imperial army numbering 32,000 men was assembled. They marched into Thuringia in September 1757 to join a French army numbering 24,000 men.

When 9,500 of this "Combined Army," as it was officially called, encountered 1,900 Prussians on a reconnoitering expedition, they were put to flight. As the *Cambridge Modern History* put it:

> Here the extraordinary deficiencies from which the combined army suffered for the first time made themselves evident. . . . The army of the Empire was composed in motley fashion of contingents supplied by numerous small dynasts. This had not hindered Marlborough and Eugene from winning partly by means of the army of the Empire the battle of Höchstädt; but in their day English and Dutch subsidies had helped to establish that army on a satisfactory footing. At present, in consequence of lack of money, such intolerable conditions prevailed among the Imperial troops that Hildburghausen [the commanding general] despaired of being able to keep his forces together for long, and therefore impatiently sought a decision by battle.[5]

[5] *Cambridge Modern History*, Vol. VI: *The Eighteenth Century* (New York: The Macmillan Company, 1909), pp. 265, 267.

On November 5, 1757, the day of the battle of Rossbach, the imperial army had shrunk to 11,000 men. Of these, 7,000 were disbanded at the beginning of the battle. Those who remained were put to flight. The Bavarian and Franconian infantry drew their rifles away while the Prussians were still in the distance. The precipitous and disorderly retreat of the run-away army at the beginning of the battle became in the eighteenth century a by-word for cowardice and disorganization.[6]

The battle of Rossbach signified the end of the imperial army. According to Ranke, the very name disappeared.[7] The reasons for this catastrophe must be sought in the unreliability of the imperial army, which was the result both of religious and political factors. The appearance of France in Germany as the ally of Austria against Prussia could not fail to be considered as a Catholic alliance against the foremost Protestant power in Germany. Thus the Protestant elements of the imperial army quite openly sympathized with Frederick II. The disintegrating effects of the religious preference were reinforced by divergent political sympathies. This became obvious at the battle of Leuthen, following the battle of Rossbach by a month. The Austrian commanders could not trust ten Bavarian battalions because of the political conflicts which then existed between Bavaria and Austria; the same was true of fourteen battalions of Wurtembergers who hated their tyrannical ruler and admired the victor of Rossbach as the champion of German Protestantism. The Austrian commander placed those contingents on the left wing where he did not expect the Prussian attack. Frederick attacked exactly at this point with the result that eleven out of the fourteen battalions of Wurtembergers fled immediately, leaving behind only a few killed and wounded.[8]

[6] Koser, *op. cit.*, pp. 132, 135.
[7] Leopold von Ranke, *Sammtliche Werke*, Vol. XXX: *Zur Geschichte von Österreich und Preussen zwischen den Friedensschlüssen zu Aachen und Hubertusburg* (Leipzig: Duncker and Humboldt, 1875), p. 312.
[8] Schlosser, *op. cit.*, p. 335; *Cambridge Modern History, op. cit.*, p. 275.

STANLEY HOFFMANN

Erewhon or Lilliput? —
A Critical View of the Problem

The predictive power of the social sciences is poor. That of the science of international relations is particularly mediocre, since it deals with a type of social action — the conduct of foreign policy — that is pervaded by uncertainty and in which even the most carefully calculated actions partake of gambling. Therefore, to try to forecast the chances of "international military force" in general during the years to come would be an exercise in futility. There are, however, two tasks which a political scientist can begin to perform. One consists of making the necessary distinctions; they may appear tiresome to the general reader and trifling to the impatient reformer, but both those gentlemen ought to remember that the opposite of distinctions is confusion. The second task consists of examining what kinds of international forces appear to be compatible with the international system in which we live.

I

Our experiences with international forces begin to be impressive. In addition to the United Nations experiments, discussed elsewhere in this volume, we should keep in mind not only such precedents as the Boxer expedition and the temporary international administration of Crete after 1897 but also those military alliances that have, in war or in peacetime, united a very large number of states against their enemies. Attempts at devising other international forces either through negotiations or in the literature of international reform provide us with more types. Consequently, even if we limit our discussion to armed forces that are supposed to intervene (violently or not) in order to prevent, to restrain, or to repress the use of force by nations in conflict, and thus do not consider here the kinds of surveillance forces or inspection systems that arms control or disarmament agreements may entail,[1] we discover that the expression "international force" covers a large number of possibilities. I would like to list the main questions which ought to be asked apropos of each such force.

1. A first group of questions deals with the *political context*.

A. What is the situation of national forces, i.e., what might be called the *arms context?* Does international force operate in a world in which each nation remains fully armed and free to arm, or does it play its role in a disarmed world, or in a disarming world—and in the latter case, at what stage of the process? Carrying out any of the missions that will be listed below would present different problems in each of these cases. We are familiar with the conflicts to be expected in an armed world; the circumstances may be full of surprises, but the types of clashes are quite well classified. A totally disarmed world is something we know nothing about, since it is difficult to imagine an international system without a hierarchy of nations, or to think of a hierarchy in which the scale of military might would play no part. Furthermore, such a world may well be an impossibility (for national police or constabulary force might play the same role after "disarmament" as the previous armies). A disarming world may combine the disadvantages and the dangers of an armed system and of a disarmed one—i.e., suffer from all the traditional conflicts as well as from the incidents and suspicions of the disarmament process.

It is interesting to note that the statesmen's ideas about the relation of international force to the arms context have come full circle. In the days of Versailles and the League Covenant, it was deemed essential for collective security to operate in a world in which national armaments would have been reduced to a minimum. After World War II the Charter of the UN reversed the order of precedence: the machinery of Chapter VII was to be put into effect first, and the Charter is remarkably discreet about disarmament. The dangers of the arms race and the

---

1 The United States proposals for general and complete disarmament of 1962 distinguish also between the functions of the International Disarmament Organization and those of the UN peace force.

failure of collective security in an armed world have brought the super powers back to schemes that would seem depressingly familiar to Léon Bourgeois; this is especially true of the recent United States "Outline of Basic Provisions of a Treaty on General and Complete Disarmament in a Peaceful World." Whether this cyclical turn of recent history is a vicious circle or not remains to be seen.

B. What is the *basic structure* of the international system? Does the force operate in a system of competing units, or as the secular arm of a world state? All known international systems are variations on one or the other of those models. Obviously, each one can appear in a variety of forms. A federal world state would differ from an imposed empire, and the medieval *Civitas Christiana* was something else again. World arrangements in which sovereign units are the essential actors include balance of power systems and revolutionary ones; systems in which the units compete without institutionalized efforts at cooperation and systems in which international organizations try to regulate and mitigate the competition; and systems in which the autonomy of the sovereign unit is real and systems in which military, economic, and ideological developments have resulted in a considerable amount of "integration," i.e., a devaluation of national borders unaccompanied by anything like a world state.

Despite those variations, I would maintain that there are essential differences between the two models. Any scheme which aims not at abolishing national armies but at moderating the amount of violence to which states can resort is based explicitly or implicitly on the assumption that there can be no sudden mutation in world politics and that the state, despite academic indictments or burials, is here to stay. Any scheme which aims at disarming states and at setting up an international authority (political and military) that would settle disputes and maintain order establishes in fact, if not in words or in intention, the beginning of a world government.

C. What is the nature of the relationship (or relationships) of *major tension* in the system? Let us assume that we are still in a world of competing units, fully or partially armed. As long as there is no world government, even if the units have only "police forces" at their disposal, and even if some international forces exist to prevent the units from resorting to violence, the risk of interstate war—the distinguishing mark of international relations—will persist. Consequently, two questions are important, both concerning the relations between the big powers. Are we dealing with a bipolar or with a multipolar world? (Despite all the analyses that stress the changes from the simpler calculations of power of the present,[2] the traditional distinction, which takes military might as the chief criterion of the great power, remains valid.)[3] In the case of a multipolar system, are the tensions between the major powers of a shifting or of a more permanent character? In other words, what is the degree of rigidity of the alignments in the system?

It is difficult to describe what effect the existence and spread of nuclear weapons will have on the traditional dynamics of world politics —and consequently on the chances of an international force. Some of the prophets of a world government endowed with a world police display what Raymond Aron, when discussing Marx, termed catastrophic optimism. According to these prophets, only if the nations of the world have reached the very brink of thermonuclear war or have already gotten a taste of doomsday will they be wise enough to put an end to a game they keep playing out of habit and mutual distrust, even though it has become insane since it is now capable of annihilating the players; and the more nuclear players there are, the more this tragic moment of truth becomes likely.[4] If one believes on the contrary that statesmen will succeed in the effort to have their cake and eat it too—i.e., stick to the game but play it with enough self-restraint to avoid the catastrophe of nuclear war and the cure of a world leviathan—then the lessons of the recent past become more applicable. A serious crisis between the major powers will bring about not the leviathan but the kind of turbulence with which Berlin and Cuba have acquainted us, and in which international force seems to have the choice between no role at all and

[2] As examples of these analyses, see George Liska, *International Equilibrium* (Cambridge: Harvard University Press, 1957) and Glenn H. Snyder, *Deterrence and Defense* (Princeton: Princeton University Press, 1961), who distinguishes a strategic balance of terror and a tactical balance of power.

[3] Military might itself depends, of course, on industrial potential, population, space, etc., and the use of this might, now that it includes nuclear weapons, poses problems and suffers limits that will be mentioned below.

[4] This seems to be the case of Herman Kahn. See *Thinking about the Unthinkable* (New York: Horizon, 1962), Chapter 7.

a modest one when the confrontation between the chief contenders is not a head-on collision. In addition, there are those who believe that the spread of nuclear weapons makes a continuation of the game more, rather than less, probable.[5] Only future events and coming tests will show which one of these concepts is closest to the truth.

2. A second group of questions concerns the *mission* of the force.

A. A first question is one that remains academic at present: will the international force be a permanent one ready to be used whenever a central political authority decides that the conditions for the force's employment are met; will it be an *ad hoc* force set up in and for an emergency; or will it be the kind of stand-by force to which Chapter VII of the Charter referred, i.e., a force to be mobilized whenever a political decision to this effect would be made, but whose constitution would have been carefully prepared in advance and in detail? A subsidiary question in the case of a permanent force concerns its location in between conflicts — where would it be stationed?

B. In a world of states the relationship between the force and the parties involved in a dispute or crisis is of fundamental importance. The issue, to put it broadly, is that of consent.

(1) Does the force intervene with the consent of those parties, or against the will of one (or even all) of them? In the former case, even if the consent is a grudging one and has been wrested only by diplomatic pressure of a stringent sort, and even if one of the purposes of the force is actually to expel a state or a group of states from a position or an area (as in Suez with respect to England, France, and Israel, or in the Congo with respect to Belgian troops) the mission of the force can be termed interposition or neutralization. If at the outset or in the course of the operation the relation becomes an adversary one, the force's symbol is no longer the fireman. Depending on the point of view, it is either the policeman-in-action-against-a-delinquent or the pyromaniac: we are in the hypothesis of collective security (a military operation against a state and on behalf of a victim) or of collective action (a military operation either against a domestic trouble-maker or — a somewhat less easily imaginable hypothesis — against a group of feuding states that forcibly resist international intervention). The

---

[5] This is the case of General Pierre Gallois; see his *Balance of Terror* (Boston: Houghton Mifflin, 1961).

term "police," which is often used with reference to international forces, is both ambiguous and misleading. It is ambiguous because there is a great difference between police activities which are peaceful and police operations which involve the use of force. Domestically as well as in the international milieu, it is misleading because in either case the relation of the "policeman" to the "citizen" (whether law-abiding or delinquent) has nothing in common with the relation of an international force to a state or even a rebel group.[6]

(2) In the case of a non-adversary relationship, the issue of consent appears again at the other end of the operation. Can the host state determine freely the termination of the force's mission, does the force's withdrawal have to be negotiated with the political authority that controls the force, or can the operation continue even after the host state has withdrawn its consent?

C. The next set of questions concerns the *specific functions* of an international force.

(1) Preliminary questions refer to the nature of the conflict. If the role of the force is an adversary one, there are two key questions. First, who is the enemy (or who are the enemies): a major power, an ally of a major power, a small state? Second, is the conflict an international one (and in this case, does the force have a mandate as the rescuer of one side) or a domestic one (insurrection, secession, civil war) in which the force carries out a mandate against one of the factions? Or is it a mixture of domestic and international strife? The distinction between domestic and international conflicts and the nature of the contenders are also important if the force's role is a peaceful one.

(2) The scope and content of the mission may vary considerably. In the case of collective security or collective action, what are the military and the political objectives assigned to the force, and does it have to observe certain restraints either in the choice of arms, or in the selection of targets, or in the geographical scope of its operations? In the case of a peace force an important aspect of its mission is the stage at which it intervenes. Its function may be to insulate a local conflict from

---

[6] As I. L. Claude has pointed out, the relation between even a world government and a rebel group would be more like that between a national government and a minority, than like that of a government to an individual trouble-maker. (*Power and International Relations* [New York: Random House, 1962].)

outside intervention (Middle East, Congo); to separate warring nations or factions; to supervise a truce and to prevent the parties from coming to blows again; to carry out or supervise the implementation of a specific solution.

(3) It is also important to ask in each case whether the role of the force is an essentially negative or a positive one: does the mission consist of repelling an invasion, insulating an area or a problem, preventing or stopping an outbreak of violence, or does it consist of carrying out a substantive solution of the underlying dispute either by force (cf. the reunification of Korea under the resolution of October 7, 1950) or by the mere pressure of the force's presence? The experiences of the UN have demonstrated both the frustration of purely negative definitions whenever the parties were still locked in battle and the political difficulty of positive definitions in a divided and explosive world. In Korea after 1951, when there was no more talk of unifying the country by force, the problem of how to put an end to the war after the military status quo had been approximately restored plagued the operation, just as the assignment of negative missions to the UN Congo operation (ONUC) complicated the Congo force's task in the midst of a civil war. On the other hand, the resolution of October 7, 1950, brought about an escalation of the Korean War which weakened political support for the operation in the General Assembly, and ONUC's use of the right of self-defense so as to carry out the positive task of reunifying the Congo under Mr. Adoula's government was highly controversial.[7] Mr. Hammarskjöld's interpretation of the limits and possibilities of the UN made him prefer not only non-adversary interventions to adversary ones but negative tasks to positive ones.

3. A third group of questions concerns the *operations* of the force.

A. The problem of political support is obviously essential. Even in the case of a force at the service of a world government, national differences will certainly not vanish right away, and it will not be possible to discuss "one world" as if it were a merely a state writ large. *A fortiori*

---

[7] The fact that even in the resolution of November 14, 1961, the use of force was explicitly authorized only for the negative purpose of expelling mercenaries from Katanga of course added fuel to the controversy. But the very caution of the document indicates the political difficulty of obtaining support for more positive definitions, as well as the practical difficulty of remaining on the cautious side of the line.

an international system of separate states would have to be examined pretty much in the way in which students of the UN have analyzed the postwar world, no matter how strong the powers of the international authority in charge of controlling the force. The most important questions that have to be asked are:

(1) What states approved the resort to the force and the definition of its mission; what states opposed it; what states abstained?

(2) How have support, opposition, and abstention evolved during the operations?

(3) What is the nature and extent of financial support? The scrutiny of political support is not enough; there may be a discrepancy between political and financial backing, and the financing of the force must be studied separately.

B. The *composition* of the force raises another set of important questions.

(1) Professor Schelling's chapter[8] discusses the size of the force. It may be rash to assume that the size and the mission will always fit together perfectly. Like all measurements of power in world politics, the notion of size is a relative one: the impact of the force depends on the ratio between its own size and that of the forces it has to tame, separate, or deter. One of the main troubles of ONUC was the disproportion between a force that was large by UN "peace force" standards on the one hand and the size of the former Belgian colony and the complexity of the force's mission on the other. Conversely, the larger the force, the more its sponsors may be tempted to make it play a major "positive" task — a temptation that may account in part for the Soviets' insistence on limiting the size of the world force in the negotiations on Article 43 of the UN Charter.

(2) The political composition of the force is equally important. One may ask first who provides its members. At San Francisco it was assumed that peace would be maintained primarily by the "big policemen"; in recent years it has been necessary to keep the big powers out and to ask the small states to provide the emergency forces.[9] A choice between a force supplied by states geographically distant from the

8 See pp. 212-235.
9 See I. L. Claude, "The UN and the Use of Force," *International Conciliation*, March 1961 (No. 532).

trouble spot and a force composed of neighbors would also be full of consequences. Appearance and reality do not always coincide: a force whose men and commanders are drawn from small states but whose equipment, means of transportation, and weapons are provided by a major power has, within the international competition, a meaning quite different from that which the champions of international neutralization and "vacuum filling" would like to reserve to international force. Secondly, one should ask who determines the political composition of the force, and in particular how much of a veto does the host state have (if the relationship is a non-adversary one), and how free are the participants to withdraw from the operation when they see fit.

C. This brings us to a last set of problems, which can be summed up by the oldest question of political science and the ultimate question of political strategy: *who commands?*

(1) Since a force is always at the service of a policy, the question means, in the first place, what is the authority that decides to resort to the force, defines its mission and its composition? Three possibilities appear. The authority may be a coalition of states which go through a process of bargaining comparable to the process of coalition-building in national multiparty systems.[10] On the other hand, it may be one major state that obtains a mandate to serve as the political brain of the operation or takes the initiative and succeeds in getting the main lines of its policy approved by the necessary majorities (Korea serves as a precedent here). Or the political command may be shared between a body of state delegates — in which either one of the two formulas just described operates — and an international executive distinct from state delegates. This last solution evokes the UN Emergency Force (UNEF), the UN Observer Group in Lebanon of 1958 (UNOGIL), and ONUC; but in its first stages at least a world government would probably have to conform to that model also, just as the European Communities actually divide political authority between the supranational organs and the councils of ministers. Obviously the respective powers of the international executive and of the body of state agents may vary enormously. The relations between the two institutions, how-

---

10 The relevant precedents would be the Boxer expedition and the discussions among the Allies on strategy and on a unified command during World Wars I and II.

ever, are of decisive importance since there is a definite connection between the nature of this relation and the kind of international force that is likely to emerge or to operate. The more the international executive depends on the states for political and financial support, i.e., the less freedom of action he enjoys, the more reluctant the state may be to create large and permanent forces under the third formula, out of fear that the executive would use the men and money available to him in order to emancipate himself or, should large forces become necessary at some point, the more likely may be resort to one of the other two formulas of control.

(2) The question of military command and of civilian-military relations is also important. Is the military commander an international civil servant, or a national officer who wears an international hat for the duration of the enterprise? Appearance and reality may be at odds once again: if the political control of the operation is of the second type, the degree of international autonomy of the commander may be very low or purely fictitious. In all cases other than that of a permanent army, the division of authority between the international commander and the various national commanders of the contingents involved must also be studied closely.

II

So many combinations between the hypotheses distinguished above are possible that they defeat the attempt to set up a few models of international forces. True, most of the factors I have listed are interdependent; but because there are so many factors, the number of possible outcomes is just as high as that of the combinations of the different and interrelated causes of potential conflicts.

Nevertheless, all proposals for international force, whether modestly presented as efforts at preventive interposition of the sort described in Mr. Hammarskjöld's last annual reports, or advocated by heralds of collective security, or advanced by champions of world government, are based on one belief and pointed in one direction. It is the belief that "international anarchy" carries increasingly intolerable risks due to the dangers of traditional self-help in a thermonuclear world. It is in the direction of greater centralization of power, for even the dispatch of a small military observer corps to supervise a truce between minor states is an advance over either uncontrolled violence or pure and simple diplomatic intervention by third parties.

Some may argue that the proponents of an international order less dangerous than the present one rush in the wrong direction — that centralization of power means a more rather than a less bitter contest for control, and more rather than less of the scourge of intervention. There is indeed some truth in the argument. However, we shall assume that neither the isolation of each from all, envisaged by Rousseau,[11] nor the antithesis between peace and enforcement developed by Mr. John Burton[12] make much sense: the former is ruled out by history and technology, the latter rests on a truncated conception of the causes of conflicts. Consequently, the question that must be examined is this: how much centralization of power can realistically be introduced into the present international system? Since one cannot forecast the impact of cataclysms, let us assume that thermonuclear war will not break out in the near future. Let us assume also that even if nuclear weapons continue to spread, the distance between the super powers and the nuclear *parvenus* will remain considerable for quite a while; and let us remember that even if steps are taken toward explicit arms control or disarmament agreements,[13] we would still be dealing with a world of armed nations, competing ideologies, heterogeneity in state structures, regimes and levels of developments; consequently none of the sources of conflict described by Professor Bloomfield[14] would dry up.

1. The present international system makes extremely unlikely the setting up of a permanent international force or of a stand-by force of the kind envisaged in Chapter VII of the Charter.

A. There are important reasons which militate against both those types of forces.

[11] See Stanley Hoffmann, "Rousseau on War and Peace," *American Political Science Review,* June 1963 (Vol. 57, No. 2).

[12] See his *Peace Theory* (New York: Knopf, 1962).

[13] For reasons that will be discussed more fully below, I do not believe in the possibility or success of ambitious explicit agreements of that sort until *after* a radical transformation of the present system (to be defined below) has already begun.

[14] See pp. 24-46.

(1) The most fundamental reason is not, perhaps, what I. L. Claude calls the essence of sovereignty: the state's right to be unpredictable.[15] In the present competition, which is of a revolutionary nature, a state may be quite willing to mortgage this right and to combine its forces with others — but only to the extent to which it feels gravely threatened by an enemy that is concretely identified. The more lasting this enmity is thought to be, the more sacrifices to the common defense — or to common deterrence — are likely to be accepted. The existence of a clear-cut common enemy may dictate a joint policy, to be served by a combined or integrated military force; but the nation's common interest in avoiding all-out war is too abstract and too vague to dictate a sufficiently precise common policy that a permanent or stand-by force could uphold. A world force that would be above and beyond the very real lines of enmity that crisscross the world is inconceivable. A world force that would protect effectively all those who feel threatened against all their potential enemies is a contradiction in terms. A world force that would give a seal of approval to one particular set of states against another, while disregarding other patterns of hostility, would not be a world force. The circumstances which doomed Chapter VII have not been transcended. In the present international system (and in any other system of competing states) the establishment of a permanent or stand-by force requires either the consent of the major powers or the willingness of many of the lesser ones to side with some of the major states against the other camp.

(2) A permanent or stand-by force established by consent of the major powers could only be the expression of those common interests in survival, moderation of conflicts, and mitigation of the arms race that commentators never tire of describing as the "real" interests of the contenders. Unfortunately, reality — as shown by the nations' behavior — is more complex. The common interest in peace and prosperity is one thing, the creation of a common force quite another. When the competition entails a risk of world destruction, each super power may well give up the use of force at those levels and in those places where the danger of escalation is too formidable; but this is not to be confused either with giving up the threat to use force nor — even less

[15] Claude, *Power and International Relations*, p. 121.

— with the establishment of a world force to repress and replace the nations' resort to arms.

It is not easy to support, say, NATO and a common force at the same time. As long as the competition between the major powers lasts, each one can hardly act as if its allies were more dangerous than their common enemy, and the pressure that those allies put on the major ally when they suspect it of becoming flabby in the defense of the alliance's joint interests makes any explicit recognition of the super powers' common interests more rather than less difficult. A mutual desire for a *détente* is thus more likely to take the form of unilateral, parallel (and easily reversible) measures of restraint rather than the setting up of joint forces or of a "third force" explicitly and permanently backed by the first two.[16] As long as the major powers are engaged in a contest that may hopefully remain peaceful but is nevertheless total in the sense of being an idealogical competition as well as a power struggle, they are unlikely to set up a force which none of them could be sure to control and which could be used against the interests of one of them — or even against their common ones. For if it is true that the possession of a nuclear arsenal tends to inhibit the super powers' freedom of action and to upset the traditional hierarchy in some respects,[17] and as it is true that the expenses of a world force would fall heavily on the super powers, the desire of each one of them to be protected both against its chief rival and against small power irresponsibility would definitely weigh against the creation of a permanent or stand-by force.

(3) As for such a force established by a coalition composed of one major power, its allies, and the bulk of the "nonaligned" states, it would be a kind of NATO force writ large (and probably made small). The aims of such diverse nations and interests converge openly at times and may perhaps be said to coincide in the long run and in a very general way, but such a convergence is not guaranteed in advance for all con-

---

[16] See Stanley Hoffmann, "Restraints and Choices in American Foreign Policy," *Daedalus*, Fall 1962, pp. 668-704.

[17] Developments after the 1962 Cuban crisis confirm this analysis. There is one additional advantage of informal restraints over explicit agreements: violations are less likely to produce crises. For law operates as a plate glass window: breaking it makes noise and brings out the police, whereas throwing a rock across an open field draws less attention.

crete cases. Many of the non-communist nations either would refuse to support a scheme that would consecrate the East-West conflict as the dominant one, even though their own sympathies may be on the Western side, or in any event would wish to continue the neutralist game whose essence it is to preserve a nation's freedom to flirt with both sides and be courted by both. Thus, a coalition force of this type would all too easily be denounced as a recipe for world war.

Nor is it clear that powers of the middle rank, even if they are allied to a super power against a common enemy, would support a scheme that would enshrine — in fact if not in words — a duopoly in the sense of a permanent division of the world, each half being led by one major state. De Gaulle's objections to what he calls America's monopoly in the Western camp are a warning. In a multipolar system a lesser unit can become a major player if it plays the game well enough; in a bipolar one a lesser state, in order to become a big contender, must try to change the rules of the game. A permanent or stand-by force risks being an instrument at the service of the status quo, and the middle rank powers (without whose consent no such force could be created in the absence of big power agreement) would probably object on three counts: their fear of strings imposed by their chief partner; their fear of being deprived of the freedom of choice that they need in order to raise themselves to the top level (and that may entail some military blackmailing ability); and the concrete grievances (territorial, economic, etc.) which they would be afraid of having to give up in the event of a world force they do not control.

B. More specific arguments can be used against each of the two kinds of "non-improvised" forces that could be envisaged.

(1) An international standing army is out of the picture. Problems of composition and stationing would be insoluble, and the question of loyalty would arise in its most acute form. For an army must be at the service not merely of an ideal but also of institutions that give some flesh to the ideal. If such an authority could be established in a way that would not make it a major stake in the nations' contests, our troubles would by definition be ended. We have not reached Erewhon yet. It is impossible to see how today's contenders would agree on creating such a monster. It is impossible to see how, should they have

agreed on it in a fit of cosmic absent-mindedness or in a state of shock, the army would meet Professor Morgenthau's two tests.[18] What would be the reliability of a force in which totalitarians and non-totalitarians may be juxtaposed, or, if it were drawn exclusively from the reservoir of small, nonaligned states, in which an insidious battle for control would be just as permanent as the army? What would be the effectiveness of a force whose mission would stagger from the Scylla of terms so vague that its functions would appear nebulous to the Charybdis of terms concrete and pointed enough to give the force a sense of purpose, but at the price of militant partiality? The precedent of mercenaries is a very dubious one. Not only were they hardly instruments of world order, but they predated the age of national loyalty. A permanent standing army may be conceivable in a post-nationalist age when world politics would be much more moderate than in the past century. The way the world looks now brings to mind President Kennedy's rueful remark that things are likely to get worse before they get better.

(2) A world force composed of national contingents earmarked by the states and kept ready for international use, by making less impossible demands, would make the problems of political authority and loyalty appear less formidable. A European community which was still in the making and which did not have precise and positive common foreign and military policies was not able to give birth to a European army. But the degree of cooperation created in NATO by the common, well-defined military threat has been sufficient to permit NATO to be satisfied with much more limited military integration than had been envisaged for EDC, and consequently, NATO's decision-making procedures can be much shakier than those which EDC would have required.

However, the very spectacle of NATO provides us with two warnings. First, at the level of the world as a whole (or even of the non-communist world) the sense of a common, concrete threat vanishes. Secondly, even within NATO a joint negative interest does not erase important disagreements in political and military strategy due to divergent assessments of the means to the common end, to conflicting geostrategic priorities, and to the members' different positive purposes,

---

[18] See pp. 175-186.

which correspond to differing visions of the world *after* the final success of the common enterprise; hence, a complex inter-allied battle for control.

The establishment of an international stand-by force would run into the bog in which the negotiators of 1946-1947 sunk along with Chapter VII and, should a disarmament agreement be in the making, the insistence on the need for such a force as the corollary of a gradual elimination of arms race, arms threats, and armed attacks is likely further to complicate matters. For, in the first place, the establishment of a force of this kind presupposes one of two things: either there has to be a decision by the relevant states to let an international organ, such as the UN Security Council, decide in each case whether to mobilize the force and for what reason; or else there has to be a fully worked-out agreement defining in advance and in detail the kinds of circumstances in which the force could be used and the kinds of missions it could perform in each case. In the former case it is hard to imagine that nations whose enthusiasm for compulsory jurisdiction is on the whole well checked would let an international organ play what might be Russian roulette with their interests without "adequate guarantees" which, being incompatible, would be pretty hard to define to everyone's satisfaction. In other words, there would be a pre-emptive battle for control of the decision-making organ, of which postwar debate about the veto (when the Security Council was that organ), contests for two-thirds majorities (when the General Assembly became the battlefield), and discussions about a troika (when the Secretary-General's role increased) have given us a foretaste. But in the second possibility it is easy to predict that either the states would fail to agree on a meaningful definition, both exhaustive and precise enough (just as they have failed to define agression), or else the agreement on a document would not really settle anything, and in case after case a battle royal would break out around the issue as to whether or not the events fell into one of the slots of the agreement.

Let us, however, assume secondly that a stand-by force has been created under one of those formulas. Permanence would still risk being either a facade or a farce. The effectiveness of the force would be rather unpredictable because, although a stand-by force would seem much preferable to an improvised one, no two conflicts are really alike. For a stand-by force to be well prepared in every possible case it would need contingents as numerous and an arsenal as rich and diversified as those of the only states that can presently afford to devise omnibus strategies — the super powers.

As for the force's reliability, it would also be dubious. Should a conflict break out between the major states or between a major state and a close ally of the other one, a political choice would still have to be made between the risks of a collective security operation and a mere attempt at neutralization. It is all too likely that a world force could move in to "insulate" the area only if the major powers had first decided to let the force come in as a face-saving device, i.e., if the test of strength has not ended in a war or in a humiliating capitulation of one of the contenders. The availability of the device makes resort to it easier; however, it is hard to imagine the major powers agreeing in advance either *never* to test their strength or nerves again, or to settle ritually *any* such test in so suave a fashion.

Should a conflict break out in an area in which the major powers are not directly and militarily involved, they might well agree to let a peace force of the UNEF or ONUC type intervene, but again the decision would have to be made at the time of the emergency. It is hard to imagine them agreeing in advance *always* to let a third party — say, the Secretary-General — make the determination, or agreeing in advance *never* to send contingents of their own nationals into an area. It is of the essence of international uncertainty that one cannot predict whether a conflict will remain of a certain type, compatible with great power abstention, or whether it may not pose such risks for a major state that its direct intervention will become the lesser peril. It is hard to imagine the major states drawing up in advance a list of "noncompeting" countries — the permanent Procrustean bed of world order — for it is of the essence of the international competition that a list of this sort must be either dramatically short (with bad consequences for efficiency) or thoroughly unreliable. On the other hand, it is hard to imagine the major powers agreeing in advance *always* to include their nationals in the force; for it is also of the essence of the contest that each major power will try to keep its adversary out of a certain area, or to prevent it from consolidating whatever foothold it may already have.

Nor is it easy to imagine the smaller powers committing themselves in advance to well-defined patterns of action. The failure of big-power talks on Article 43 may have spared the super states the embarrassment of endless discussions with the smaller ones over Chapter VII, and the experience of the "Uniting for Peace" resolution has confirmed that solemn generalities do not determine concrete cases. Since the resort to international neutralization is most likely in crises affecting immediately the smaller states, few are likely to sign or to support a blank check for a procedure that, however neutral in intent and well devised to keep the over-all balance of force intact, may nevertheless affect quite unevenly the parties locally involved.

Thus the idea of the stand-by force runs into two sets of obstacles. The larger powers, because they have a preponderance of military strength, are unlikely to erect any institution capable of interfering with their own conflicting attempts at shaping the world they want. The smaller states, because they do not have enough power to shape their own future, are unlikely to accept any institution that may at worst condemn them even more to the role of pawns and at best remain indifferent to and independent from attempts at resolving fairly their substantive difficulties and disputes; nor, for that matter, are the big powers united enough to impose permanently such a scheme.

2. None of this means that within the present international system states will not be able to agree on the occasional establishment of international forces. The lessons of past years are more complex. On the one hand, even so mild a "stand-by" authority as the Peace Observation Commission has been reduced to a slumber much like death; on the other, the Members of the UN have set up forces of various sizes and missions. The political circumstances that have made them necessary may be with us for a long time to come.

A. The nature of the system seems to rule out one kind of force: the collective security force. If there is a genuine international community, collective security operates through a reflex of solidarity, expressing a common interpretation of common interests, which triggers the reaction against a violator of the common law, who is clearly seen as a delinquent. In a world less certain of the ultimate common good but still capable of agreeing on procedures and rules of the game, collective security becomes the modern version of the mechanism of imbalance that kept down the ambitions and the gains of trouble-makers (large or small) in balance of power systems — the mechanism by which an alliance of states tries to suppress attempts to upset the balance, undertaken by states that are seen as temporary adversaries, but not as necessarily evil or permanent enemies.

Today's international milieu is very far removed from the harmonious but theoretical model of a community. Alliance situations are realized, but two factors tend to dissociate alliances from collective security. The existence and the diffusion of nuclear weapons, along with the resulting danger of escalation, have made a resort to conventional force in inter-bloc relations less likely. The enlargement of the UN has made the one exception to this statement, Korea, quite definitely unique, for it is probable that no majority could now be found to give a seal of UN legitimacy to the military operations of one alliance. Collective security against a major power or its close allies is just about as impossible as the drafters of the Charter calculated: the risks are too high, the likelihood of majority support is too small, the dilemma of preparation is too insoluble. For it is impossible either to prepare in advance an operation against one of the major members of the organization or to improvise in an emergency an effective operation against a super power. Against it or its allies the only international forces that may perform military functions (at an obvious risk) are the coalesced forces of an alliance.

Outbreaks of violence among or within smaller nations, or in the last colonial or quasi-colonial areas, may well provide a majority of UN Members with the temptation of resorting to collective security or collective action, especially if the crusading spirit of anticolonialism can be enlisted. However, the twin dangers of competitive great power intervention and of politically and financially destructive great power opposition[19] would rise in such a way that peace forces for interposition and neutralization, inspired by the UNEF and ONUC precedents, with missions defined perhaps in more positive terms but stopping

---

[19] One can envisage that the United States would support interposition forces in case of serious troubles in Angola or, say, South Africa; it is hard to imagine the United States backing a collective security expedition against an ally or a close partner of an important ally.

nevertheless short of the collective use of force, remain the most likely prospect. For in the present world the nature of the delinquency is often not clear-cut enough, and even when there is sufficient agreement against the delinquent or the trouble-maker, a collective-intervention force runs the risk of disturbing even more the precarious balance of terror or power.

B. The kinds of international forces that remain possible are thus *ad hoc* forces of interposition which could be established and dispatched whenever:

(1) The major powers explicitly agree on measures in an area in which they are not militarily involved to prevent a conflict from escalating or to prevent some of their respective allies from dragging the world into disaster.

(2) One major power succeeds in convincing a majority of states to intervene in a conflict of the type described under (1) despite the opposition of the other major power. This opposition may complicate the undertaking, but if the area of the conflct is not one in which the opposing power is deeply committed and involved, the majority is less likely to be intimidated — especially if the other major state is skillful in presenting the operation as an effort to shut out bloc competition. An enterprise of this sort becomes an exercise in ambiguity. The lesser states hope that this insulation from the main contest will take place; the major state which encourages that hope wishes nevertheless to consolidate its own position by posing as the champion of the small; its antagonist hopes that there will be enough difficulties to thwart the ambitions of its rivals — while wishing perhaps also that the operation would succeed just enough to prevent a dangerously direct confrontation. The volatile character of this brew of expectations explains why configurations of such a sort may reproduce themselves from time to time but can hardly be codified.

(3) The major powers agree to entrust an international force with a task of supervision after an agreement on a problem affecting their immediate and essential interests in areas of direct involvement. So far, despite suggestions concerning Berlin, there have been no such cases.

C. Forces of interposition remain however subject to some serious limitations.

(1) The forces' efficiency and reliability continue to depend on the

nature and the size of the tempests they will have to master. As the Congo showed, even a sizable force may be in trouble if the problem it deals with keeps getting more formidable, like the Sphynx's questions. Paradoxically, insofar as collective security operations are ruled out, large scale inter-nation wars would not be the worst kind of tempests that forces of interposition would have to face, since those forces would intervene only after the belligerents had agreed to suspend hostilities. But major internal or colonial upheavals are both more unmanageable and more to be expected. The idea of organizing a UN force for Algeria at any point during the seven-year rebellion staggers the imagination; in case of serious trouble in east and south Africa, the prospects for UN forces are hardly rosier. Whenever the force is asked to intervene in a situation in which the major contenders have not agreed on the force's principle and mission, the operation will be in danger even if the host state — legally the sole authority but politically one among several contenders — has formally assented. The force will constantly risk gliding from interposition to an adversary relationship, and being too small for either case; on the other hand, any increase in its size will make of its control and of the definition of its mission a bigger stake.

The consequences for the force's morale are obvious. Even if the formal definition of its task remains, in Dr. Dicks' words,[20] simple and unpolitical, the realities would be complex and controversial. For, as the Congo again showed, simplicity is a function of the situation rather than of the drafting of the basic resolutions, and the genuine alternatives are not political versus unpolitical, but generally accepted versus hotly contested. Large domestic upheavals and ferocious colonial battles may still have to be resolved through the gruesome, time-honored process of the violent confrontation of the parties, as Proudhon had warned a century ago. And any step beyond insulation from the outside world might suck the force into the maelstrom.

(2) A second limitation is the financial one. The bigger the expedition, the more the force may have to depend for its material and financial support on the super powers or on one of them. The political consequences are obvious. At present and in the foreseeable future the

[20] See pp. 236-256.

super powers seem unwilling to support jointly undertakings designed
to keep them out of an area or capable of favoring one camp against
the other. Operations that depend on the financial good will of one
of the super powers can pretend to be efforts at interposition rather
than expressions of an alliance only as long as they are kept small; past
a certain threshold, the major power tends to be worried lest the degree
of political control it has over the operation not match the expenses it
incurs,[21] and the smaller states tend to get fearful about the political
slant of the enterprise. The financial troubles of ONUC made the
states more aware of the importance of financial security for international forces but not more capable of agreeing on the means of providing it. Consequently, although the circumstances enumerated under
B. are likely to recur, the Members of the UN may become more hesi-
tant than in the past to plunge into political waters with no financial
bottom.

3. None of these reservations suggests that a passage to a more
moderate international system will not improve the prospects of international force.

A. However, in this gradual shift to moderation, the contribution
of international force, while far from negligible, may well remain
modest. The primary condition, to put it simply, is the end of the
Cold War as the all-pervading tension. Such a change implies both a
progressive decline of ideology, i.e., an end to the proselytism of communist dogma,[22] and a return to a multipolar situation. As long as
there is a clash of radically antagonistic philosophies of domestic and
world order, the fear of nuclear war will be the main source of wisdom,
the only firm common standard in the game. Should a multipolar
world emerge, the chief contenders of today would be forced to recognize the limits of their ambitions and prospects, and such felt restraints
might corrode their ideological ardor. Obviously, whatever consolidates
those parts of the world that lie outside the main camps and keeps the
military competition of those camps away from such areas favors mod-

---

[21] The same is true in UN economic development institutions.

[22] The ideological East-West battle is an asymmetrical one. As I have written
elsewhere (see p. 199, footnote 16, above) the United States "is an ideological
contender by necessity rather than choice." See Raymond Aron, *Paix et Guerre
entre les Nations* (Paris: Calmann-Lévy, 1962), Chapter XXII.

eration in the long run. Here international forces of the kinds I have described as possible have a role to play. However, aid to underdeveloped countries and the stalemating of communist expansion through the maintenance of the "balance of terror" and through military alliances are likely to contribute even more to the appearance of new poles of power outside (and also within) each camp, and to the erosion of ideology.

Moreover, the period of change will also be one of tension: a risk of disintegration for one camp, the frustrations of a loss of control for the leader of the other (although the general direction would be the one it had desired), the trials and errors of nuclear diffusion, the continuing heterogeneity in levels of development, and the hazards of the population explosion are among the forces of trouble. Even if all those are under control, the gap between the advanced nuclear powers and the others will not be closed soon, and a decline of ideological fervor in one part of the communist camp cannot be equated with the end of ideology throughout that camp.

B. A more moderate system will probably find more ways of using an international force. A world which technology is shrinking, in which the fear of nuclear war or nuclear rearmament would still be a common concern, but which would no longer be torn by conflicts as revolutionary as the present ones, would not only be guided by a more generally accepted set of rules of the game, it would also need a higher degree of centralization of power.

(1) Two tendencies would thus converge to favor international forces. First, explicit agreements on arms control or disarmament would have become possible. As long as the political competition has an intensity and a scope as great as today, faith in arms control requires a belief in the capacity of the duopolists to agree explicitly against their respective allies, or a belief in their willingness to coerce those allies, a belief in the possibility of divorcing arms from politics, and a belief in the transcendence of ideological and geographical asymmetries by common interests identically experienced.[23] Only in a more moderate

---

[23] For a witty and fine distinction between merely common interests and joint ones, see C. B. Marshall, "Notes on Conferencemanship," *New Republic*, February 16, 1963 (Vol. 148, No. 7).

system could such hopes begin to be vindicated. At that point arms control agreements could be policed by international forces.

Secondly, the main powers in a moderate system tend to be more able and willing to act together in order to prevent small states from upsetting the status quo: the hierarchy becomes again more important than the bloc alliances. Given such a big power consensus, the capacity of the smaller states to resist the pressure from above would decrease, and prospective upstarts would have an advantage in promoting their interests through cunning rather than force. An international military force could be the secular arm of the international legitimacy the big powers would want to enforce.

(2) However, such hopes are not only what the Germans call *Zukunftsmusik*; they must also be tempered by the following considerations. First, there seems to be an inverse ratio between the existence of "permanent" (or let us say lasting) alliances and that of important international forces. A permanent force capable of playing the role theorists of collective security had earmarked for it presupposes an end of alliances that may well be incompatible with a system of separate states. It is easier to imagine a permanent force of interposition.

Secondly, it is just as easy to imagine that contests about its mission will arise in each concrete case, and that the political authority which will supervise its operations will be a major stake in the international competition. For a joint desire to limit the mischief that lesser states can produce, or even a joint desire by the majority of the big powers to prevent a misguided member of the elite from reaping excessive gains through unilateral action,[24] has rarely gone without a private

---

[24] This traditional mechanism of imbalance against a stray great power could not function again if that power were in possession of means of mass destruction. A multipolar world in which all the major states would be full-fledged nuclear powers (i.e., had effective invulnerable deterrents capable of inflicting unacceptable damage on any enemy) would not be a moderate one — to say the least (Aron, *op. cit.*, doubts that such a system could function or that today's super powers would tolerate its emergence). Thus the hypothesis discussed in the text presupposes some degree of arms control. I agree with the champions of arms control when they point out that without such measures moderation will be impossible to achieve; I do not believe, however, that those measures are likely to be explicitly defined and applied so long as the basic conditions of a return to moderation, described in the text as an end of the Cold War, have not been met. Thus we agree about the need, but differ about timing and prerequisites.

ambition on the part of each of the "responsible" major powers to win special advantages within the concert of the great. Arms control or disarmament measures may not alter this situation, for although the major states will have even more of a joint interest in preserving a hierarchy that the mere superiority of their arsenals may not ensure anymore, the fear of cheating or rearmament by one of them and the desire to escape or to reduce those controls that might hamper one's own freedom of action would also have increased. If the West European community may be cited as a precedent or model for a more moderate world system, one can envisage a general delegation of authority from the major states (and the others) to the common executive, full exercise of this authority by the executive in instances of low political explosiveness, and a battle for control whenever the political implications of action are high.

Thirdly, the world force's efficiency would remain as dependent as ever on the success of efforts at solving the substantive issues that would have made its intervention necessary. A system in which these substantive issues persisted indefinitely and whose statesmen would dispose of awesome international bayonets to sit on would be just as uncomfortable — and self-defeating — as previous examples. The less adequate the procedures for the settlement of disputes, the less satisfying to the parties the results achieved through such techniques, then the more resort to international force will be required — but the more unstabilizing its long-run effect will be. In a revolutionary system sitting on powder kegs may be defended as a precaution; in a moderate one it is at best a temporary expedient.

THOMAS C. SCHELLING

Strategy: A World Force in Operation

The relation of an international military authority to the industrial (once nuclear) powers in a disarmed world is an intriguing one. We should not expect much success in finding an ideal strategy for it. It is hard enough to find one for the United States, Britain, or the Soviet Union in the familiar world of competitive military force.

And unless we expect a nationally disarmed world to be a stagnant one — hardly likely in the first few decades, if only because of the novelty of the environment — it might not be wise even to look for an enduring strategy for the international force. If national disarmament and an internationalization of military force are ever accomplished, it will probably not be as a revealed religion but as a political-military experiment. We had better not burden the organization with the need to know in advance the solution to all its strategic problems, or even what all those problems will be.

The "strategy" of an international armed agency is not just its military techniques. It is also its "foreign policy." The problem is not only one of equipping and training an efficient force that can conquer a country or halt some hastily mobilized army. It includes whom to invade, when, on what provocation, with what "war aim," or whom to defend against what. It involves who the "enemy" would be in a world in which it may be politically awkward to talk about enemies and in which "enemies" may not always be nations but governments or civil-war factions within nations, or movements not identified with territories and nations. The distinction between civil war and international war, not too clear at present, may become less clear. Those who argue today whether it is better to be red or dead may have to decide whether disarmament is worth a war in arriving at a policy for the international force.

If we think of an international authority as a "police force — to use a term that is often applied — the correct analogy is not overtime parking and burglary, but school integration, general strikes, looting in the wake of a disaster, election frauds, labor racketeering, collusive price fixing, and the problems of jury rigging, police kickbacks, and the third degree. The "policing" function is not just a matter of blue-suited men on motorcycles, but the entire issue of law and order and individual rights. For our international military authority, we do not even know yet what "laws" it will be asked to enforce. And in making its plans to restrain an aggressor or to dampen hostility the international authority may not be allowed the conceptual advantage of a clearly identified "criminal."

We have at least three areas to explore. One is the *organization* of the force — how it is staffed and financed, where it is housed, where it buys its supplies, and what "security" functions it performs other than tactical military functions. The second is its *foreign policy* — what it is supposed to deter, to compel, or to obstruct, and what its military relations are to be with nations and with other international agencies. Third are the *techniques* by which the threat or application of military (or non-military) violence is to be used to support that policy.

"Strategy" may suggest that we should confine ourselves to the third area. And so we should, if we could, leaving organization and foreign policy to other studies. But the strategy of our international authority, like that of a nation, is constrained by its economic base and internal organization. The strategy of an island nation differs from that of a continental power; the strategy of a rich nation differs from that of a poor one; and the strategy of a unified nation differs from that of one plagued by civil war or dissidents. A nation's strategy depends on whether it can keep secrets, whether its enemies can, and whether it can bluff its enemies, surprise them, keep them guessing, or promote discord among them. The strategy of a nation depends on its vulnerability to sabotage, to paralysis of decision, to inter-service rivalry, and to the desertion or revolt of its troops. The same applies to an international force. We do not know whether an international military organization whould have independent financial means of support, secure access to supplies, and its own intelligence service. We do not know because it has not been decided. And some of these decisions should depend on their implications for the organization's strategy.[1]

THE ORGANIZATION OF THE FORCE

A good place to begin is with money. We need some idea of how much money the force would require. This depends on which "force" we are talking about — a single international force, a strategic force separate from a tactical or limited-war force, a deterrent force separate from intervention force, or a force that can confront major powers as distinct from the force used to monitor small countries. If it is to be a force that can deter, repel, or conquer one major power or all of them at the same time, it is likely to be expensive enough to dominate the budget.

It will presumably need an "invulnerable nuclear deterrent," probably a more flexible and diversified deterrent than the major powers require now, with some redundancy as a safeguard against defection and sabotage. It will need good armed reconnaissance and worldwide surveillance and some military capability in space. It may also have to consider more selective, discriminating action than national forces have considered necessary. If it is to have a capacity to invade and conquer large and small countries without (or with little) use of nuclear weapons, it will need well trained, well equipped airborne and amphibious troops. And it would probably have to maintain standards of quality and comfort that would meet the highest existing national standards. Such a force would probably cost something closer to $25

[1] Something else not decided — and the language of this chapter must, for that reason too, be ambiguous — is how the international armed forces will fit into some larger organization. There will be some parliamentary or formalized diplomatic body at the top, and there has to be some executive authority, military or civilian, over the armed forces or over each separate service or command. Whether there will be some executive-administrative body above the armed forces (as with the United Nations Secretariat) or parallel to them (or even subordinate to them for purposes of procurement, research, etc.), whether the international armed forces will be purely military or jointly military and civilian, how much autonomy they will have — even whether, like the Roman senate during Hannibal's invasion, a distrustful political authority will appoint a partnership of generals who rule on alternate days — must go unstipulated.

billion than to $10 billion (nearer to half the American than to twice the British present defense budget).

During the first decade or so of the arrangement there will be a number of countries that can mobilize more than a million men under 35 who have had military training. Some countries, like the United States, China, Britain, or Japan, would require amphibious invasion (unless Canada or Russia accorded unmolested access) or airborne attack. If prolonged war with selective strategic bombing is not to be inevitable, if victim countries are not to be invaded by their main rivals as allies or recruits of the international force, if the force is not to be exhausted in its first campaign and lose control, and if it is to deter adventurism or panic rearmament in other countries while attending to its victim, the force will have to have sizable, professional, peacetime ground-air-naval capability. (In fact, a military organization that can *really* threaten to keep the peace and to prevent rearmament may look so large and so expensive that it is politically unacceptable.)

This cost — $10 to $25 billion — is not just financially significant. It is strategically significant. The money will come mostly from a very few countries — the large industrial countries. In fact, it will come from precisely those countries that are the main potential "enemies" of the strategic force. It will come either through national contributions, through taxes levied by an international agency, or through business enterprises owned by the international agency and operating in those countries. The financial vulnerability of the force to a few major countries is therefore important.

Parliaments have traditionally been reluctant to give military establishments financial autonomy, sometimes on grounds that a self-sufficient military force can be a threat to political institutions while a short financial tether can ensure civilian control. A parliament can starve a military establishment into submission to its wishes (or can provoke, by its attempt, a coup or civil war). So can an international military establishment be starved by a major contributor nation or by several major contributors. It can be starved selectively if some of its contributors can hold up appropriations for particular functions or capabilities.

Not only is this a threat to the military force — a vulnerability to non-violent financial blockade — but it raises questions about the force's authority. Has the military force (or the agency that controls it) the right to collect the taxes to support itself? Can it use military violence to extract the money it needs to maintain itself? Is financial delinquency a *casus belli*? And may the military organization negotiate in the event of a few financial defections, for higher contributions from more willing countries, possibly by the implicit promise of favors to come?

A possibility is to make the armed organization financially independent. It might manage some strategic industries — international airlines and canals, for instance. It might acquire patent rights arising out of its military assets and its research and development, licensing them for commercial use. It might be granted real estate, so that it, too, can become a territorial entity. But it seems unlikely that the armed organization could live off its own assets, though a good many commercial benefits may come out of the multiple technical activities and properties that accrue to the force. But if it depends in part on its own earnings, may it use violence to protect its properties located within nations and to assure their profitable operation? Like the salt tax of earlier times, a few critical monopolies, perhaps especially related to foreign trade, might give a good deal of non-violent leverage to the force. Whether it would want to use it, of course, is another matter.

Next consider how the military authority will spend its money. Most powerful nations have possessed within their territories the industrial base of their war potential. Even countries as dependent on foreign trade as Britain and Japan manufacture most of their own weapons. Control of the industrial base and critical supplies is strategically important to a military force. Without its own industrial base, an international force designed to cope mainly with the big industrial powers would be dependent on its likely enemies not only for money but also for war materials and for research and development of new military capabilities.

Embargo is thus a weapon that can be used against the international force — not just deliberate hostile embargo, but malingering slowdowns and induced difficulties of delivery. Subtle sabotage could be a problem. In a crisis, if a strike occurs at a German or American plant producing re-entry vehicles for the international Polaris force, or if a high incidence of defectives shows up in the delivery of some critical weapons, the organization may have a sticky problem on its hand. And if there is a straightforward denial of access, the international force (or its controlling authority) has to decide not only whether a *casus belli* exists but how long it can afford to negotiate before it feels the pinch of supplies.

Some deliberate dispersal and redundancy of supply would look attractive to the force. It may want to be dependent on no single country for any important military item. It may want to be assured of excess capacity around the world so that, in a crisis, it can forego the output of particular countries. But this raises two problems. One is the high cost of duplicate facilities for complicated items. The second is that a latent "Nth country problem" would be aggravated.

Much that has been said about production and procurement applies to research and development, for which the force would also be dependent on its most likely enemies. If it is to finance all its own research and development outside the major industrial countries, this will probably be at a high cost both in outlay and in reliability. Probably the best that can be hoped for is that some kind of "oligopolistic competition" among three to six major industrial powers would keep the force from being too dependent on any single country or alliance.

In any case, the international force would have to think about the reliability and security of alternative contractors. The letting of a long-term weapon contract will almost surely lead to conjecture as to the political and security motives for choosing one country rather than another. (A country that is interested in the weakening or discrediting of the international force may be tempted to consider bad technological advice to achieve its purpose.) This consideration in turn raises the question whether the force will contract through governments or with private firms, and since the force may want some immunity from strikes and other disruptions in the privately organized economies, the answer is likely to be that it contracts through governments unless it invests in its own 'internationalized" arsenals and laboratories on neutral soil.

The loss of industrial secrecy under a worldwide disarmament arrangement might substantially spread military technology around the world. This spread would be relevant to a possible resumption of the arms race as well as to violation of the rules of disarmament. To pose the question in extreme form: how many countries have the right to

share in providing nuclear weapons to the international force? Do the
present nuclear powers retain, under the heading of "industrial security," the nuclear secrets they possess? Must they share them with each
other? Is the technology to be disseminated throughout an "open
world" that at some stage, by breakdown or re-negotiation, may begin
to rearm itself?

We should keep in mind that it is difficult in any country to divorce
military considerations from domestic economics. Any organization
that has ten or twenty billion dollars of procurement to undertake will
be obliged to think about depressed areas, balance of payments problems, equity in the distribution of contracts, and the industrial growth
of more than a hundred countries. What we now call "lobbies" and
"military-industrial complexes" may not be purified out of existence
by the internationalization of military procurement. And if the United
States and the Soviet Union are still in the race to see who will be first
on Mars, it is unlikely that an international military procurement
organization could stay aloof, and be universally considered aloof, from
the impact of its procurement on the relative space technologies of the
two countries.

In addition to financial, logistical, and industrial questions, there
are some questions of political and administrative organization that
would affect the strategy of the force. One is whether it should have its
own military intelligence service or should rely on some open "inspection" system to which all nations have equal access. Can it have "spies,"
and not just "inspectors"?

A second is whether it can keep its military plans and deployments
secret from the countries that it works for. Political as well as military
secrecy and surprise are involved, because the countries that might be
the subjects of military action by the international force would also be
represented in the organization. If they know exactly what kind of
attack to expect and when, which actions will trigger a response and
which will be allowed, or when a military deployment is a bluff and
when it means business, the international force will be unlike a
national force in its relation to the enemy.

Particularly if the force engages in any kind of "bargaining" — in
deterrent threats or ultimatums — it might be embarrassed to have its
internal decisions and plans known to its adversary. And if, say, it were

about to launch a preemptive invasion intended to be as efficient and bloodless as possible, surprise might be crucial.

Within nations, military organizations usually have secrets that are not available to the voters, political representatives, nor even the entire cabinet. Presumably the chief executive of a country has the right to any information he wants, but he may not know what he wants or whether it exists. The occurrence of military coups and revolts demonstrates that secrets can be held within a military organization. And there can be a legitimate recognition, particularly in times of crisis or war, that since any sharing of secret information with civilian authorities may compromise security, those who have a right to know certain things may prefer not to exercise it.

So we can properly imagine the military organization's having its own intelligence system separate from the intelligence arrangements of the "political authority," or the "inspection force," or whatever else there is. We may also suppose that it can have the legal right to make secret war plans. Whether it could keep secrets in fact, given its non-national personnel system and its political relations with other international agencies, is not easy to say. The answer probably depends on how far one is willing to compromise certain political principles in the interest of military effectiveness. If the organization is confined to a very few nationalities in its top ranks — the nationalities that reflect the former nuclear powers — it may be possible to keep information from the representatives of a hundred other countries. But there is still a problem in keeping secrets from potential adversaries among the major powers.

As Germany, Russia, or the United States becomes a possible target for military action, its representatives may have to be eased out of positions of confidence, their "security clearance" withdrawn, perhaps in a way that did not tip them off to what was happening. This would be difficult, even if one relied on very specially indoctrinated senior personnel who were allowed a good deal of autonomy. If their plans were reviewed by higher civilian authority, the same problem would arise there.

The nature of the problem is suggested by our own government: only the Congress can declare war. If the international force is to be responsive to some representative arrangement, the countries that are most likely to be enemies of the force are precisely the ones most likely to be strongly represented in the legislative branch. The problem is a little like that of a Congressional declaration of civil war against, say, New England. Bargaining between the federal government and a secessionist bloc of states under the threat of war, the development of operational military plans, and particularly any action based on surprise, would be affected by the presence in the Congress of legislators from New England who could not be constitutionally excluded from debate.

While the most tangible problems here may be those of operational secrecy, the more important ones relate to bargaining. Imagine that during the Cuban crisis the Russians by right had had a man sitting beside the President in the White House who not only knew what information was available to the President but also could overhear all the policy discussions. Just what risks to take, how far to let things go, with what limited objectives to take action if action were taken, what minimum Soviet responses would meet our demands, and all that — these are things that one usually wants to keep the potential enemy from knowing.

Of course, it can sometimes help to let the enemy know certain things. If in the Cuban crisis the Russians really miscalculated, and if it was in both our interests that they not miscalculate, it might have been better if they had had better knowledge of how the United States was going to react. When one is not bluffing, it helps if the adversary can authentically learn the fact. (But unless it had secret intelligence in addition, it could not be sure it wasn't being left out of something.)

At some stage, some formality like "declaration of adversary relation" might be required in order to put a country on notice and to exclude it from the inner councils of the organization. The question arises whether at that point the country could cancel its obligations to put up money, sell goods, permit access, provide information, and participate in political-military planning. This not only has to be considered a procedural question, but also as a factor inhibiting the determination of an adversary relationship. How does a legislature deal with illegal secession or civil war by some of those represented in it? (The filibuster comes to mind.)

These questions of security, surprise, and command are affected by another organizational question: whether there is to be a single international military force or several for different purposes. If the latter, what are to be the control and coordination arrangements between the several military organizations?

American forces are now represented in NATO, but there are United States commands, including the Strategic Air Command, to which the North Atlantic Treaty Organization (NATO) countries have had no access by virtue of the NATO treaty. Similarly, an international "strategic force" that is mainly oriented toward deterring the major industrial nations might be quite separate from other international forces whose functions are lower in the scale of violence, oriented toward different areas of trouble, and possibly less concentrated among a few main governments.

From the point of view of military organization, one would probably set up a strategic command separate from the force that is to cope with smaller-scale violence, denying the latter force access to the former. But such a separation of functions does not solve the political problem of who controls the strategic force: whether it tends to be considered the agent of, or the enemy of, the major industrial nations that formerly were (and potentially are) major nuclear powers. If, for the reasons of finance, technology, industrial power, security, and military experience already mentioned, the strategic command is the captive of the United States and the Soviet Union, it may be regarded as a monopoly of force by the great powers. But if control over the strategic command is widely spread, "democratically" or "popularly" diffused among many lesser countries, it may become essentially a device by which a few big nations are policed militarily for the benefit of the small ones. Control over the strategic command will be determined by the arrangements made for its financing, staffing, procurement, and so forth.

THE FOREIGN POLICY OF THE FORCE

These considerations bring into focus the novel position of the force in a disarmed world. We usually think of the Western alliance and the Soviet bloc, or the United States and the Soviet Union, as the principal potential enemies that may need to be deterred, detained, or kept disengaged *from each other* by an international force. But in a disarmed world the United States and the Soviet Union are likely to have a common interest in mantaining their superior mobilization base for the event of war or rearmament. Whether or not they collaborate, they may be of a mind on a number of issues in opposition to lesser countries (including their former allies). Certain preparatory actions that might be considered grounds for military threat and intervention might be available only to the major nations, perhaps the largest two. Threats of intervention might be directed not at one of these countries at the urging of the other, but at both of them at the urging of many other countries, or at the autonomous discretion of an international authority itself. Their maintenance of a technical mobilization base for rearmament, either deliberately or as a natural consequence of industrial and scientific activity, might be an example of such an issue.

Whether the force will be primarily the agent of great or small nations will affect its military strategy, because a main ingredient of that strategy will be threats of intervention. Beliefs about which threats are real and which bluffs, what kind of violence is threatened, and what the likelihood is that the violence will be contained or will get out of hand — these will depend on who controls it. War with a major country or bloc will always be dangerous business no matter what uniform the attackers wear.

An example of such a crisis of credibility is NATO at the present time. There has been much discussion of which deterrent threat will be more credible to the Russians — a United States deterrent "umbrella," independent national deterrents, or a fifteen-nation NATO deterrent. There are also disagreements over the nature of the Soviet threat to be deterred — a large-scale Soviet attack, small Soviet mischief, or Soviet response to an unpremeditated outbreak of violence (like Hungary) — for which appropriate NATO deterrents can be designed. Strategy depends not only on what is credible, but also on what contingencies and actions it is politically possible to contemplate and to plan.[2] And these in turn depend on where political control over strategy lies. Deterrence strategy is at least as much political as military,

---

[2] NATO is seriously precluded from acknowledging certain contingencies and making plans for them by the political sensitivity of the issues. Similarly it is often reported that the Russian and Chinese communists feel constrained — or used to feel constrained — to argue by "proxy," using Yugoslavia or Albania as euphemistic code words for Russia and China.

at least as much concerned with command structure as with the destructive potential of a military force.

There is another important question about the separation of commands. It seems unlikely that an international strategic force would intervene often against major powers. It would be too serious an event. A force may frequently intervene in smaller-scale affairs, of which the Congo, Laos, the Arab-Israeli dispute, Goa, or a Castro revolution might be examples. If there is a single force, its experience is likely to be dominated by small wars, brush fire engagements, police actions, and so forth. Its budgetary orientation may reflect the crises that it is called on to manage during its first several years, unless a "strategic" force is separately emphasized.

At the same time, if we reflect on how an international force might deal with, say, Vietnam, we do not know whether the job would fall under the strategic command or the limited-war or counter-insurgency command. An international force might be no more willing, perhaps less willing, than the United States to support a local force against externally supplied and externally indoctrinated insurgents. An international force might identify the target as Hanoi, Peiping, or Moscow, not the Laotian-Vietnamese border. And if it wanted credibly to threaten that it would not forever tolerate an externally supported revolt but would sooner or later use its military coercive power on North Vietnam or China, it would surely have to coordinate its local actions with its strategic plans. In other words, if most local problems are part of a strategic contest between East and West (or some such blocs) and if a significant element in local wars is some elusive participation of major powers, the relation between local and strategic responsibilities becomes an important matter of policy. It is not a foregone conclusion that in the interest of peace and quiescence the international force should pretend that local violence is a local problem when it is not.

THE TECHNIQUES OF THE FORCE

The techniques by which violence or the threat of violence would be used by the international strategic command should depend on the policy it is supposed to carry out. Even with a fairly explicit idea of what the force is supposed to do, such questions as whether continued disarmament will be worth a war cannot be answered in advance.

The least ambitious purpose that might be served by an international strategic command would be ceremonial. The major nuclear powers might like to support a façade, a pretense that an international force is aimed at them as well as at smaller countries. They might commit themselves to the notion of an international force capable of policing the entire world against everything, adhere nominally to their verbal commitments, and be quite slow about setting up any actual capability. (Some proposals for NATO nuclear forces may serve as illustrations of such an "international" force.) A force might, for example, consist of "national contributions" and solemn declarations by all parties that the progressive integration of the world would bring the force closer and closer to true unification and some eventual autonomy.

At the other extreme the most ambitious goal is probably a force whose primary function is to maintain its military supremacy against all possible adversaries. The critical thing here is the irreversibility of the arrangement. The armed authority would be charged with the mission of making sure that only by sufferance could any nation withdraw from the arrangement and rearm itself. The primary objective of such an organization would not be the deterrence or prevention of war among "disarmed" nations, but the deterrence or prevention of rearmament. As long as significant rearmament was forestalled, the international force would still be in business. It might not win all its wars; it might not prevent wars; but at least it would have the ultimate capability to do so. And as a last resort it could launch preventive war and military occupation against its potential enemies.

A less ambitious objective is to police disarmed nations against the temptations toward violence and aggression, protecting disarmed nations either by active defense or deterrence of attack. This is an easier role to fill because it implies weaponry and tactics effective against disarmed nations and applied in support of an international status quo. The difference between deterring war and deterring rearmament might be compared with the difference between deterring Soviet attack on Europe and deterring Soviet resistance to an armed "rollback" of the Iron Curtain. One is external and passive; the other is internal and active. Rearmament for major industrial countries would be largely an "internal" affair. Except for countries quite vulnerable to blockade, rearmament could be stopped only by force or coercion inside a country, not by containment at its borders.

An important role to consider for an international strategic command is that of a *buffer force*. Instead of being responsible for preventive war against a country that initiated rearmament, it might maintain a protective deterrent shelter within which other countries could catch up. Such a buffer force might not even be obliged to enter an arms race if it could exercise a sufficient deterrent influence — hold a "balance of power" and keep the situation stabilized until the rearmament of other countries had superseded their dependence on the force. Part of its purpose would be to induce or to permit countries to rearm with a view to stabilized deterrence and self-defense rather than with a view to pre-emptive action. The role of such a buffer force in the event of war itself might not be to win against all countries or against those that start it, but just to make winning a war costly and uncertain for the side that starts it. The international authority might, in other words, pursue a "minimum deterrence" strategy against war itself while providing shelter in the early stages of a rearmament race.

Its role might then be comparable to that of the American armed forces since the end of World War II. The United States has tried to deter, to contain, to guarantee, and otherwise to preserve peace and the status quo. It did not undertake and apparently did not seriously consider preventive war against a nuclear-arming Soviet force. An international force might be equally reluctant or unable to consider preventive war in the face of a large nation's persistent armament program.

If the military organization is intended to guarantee its own supremacy and the irreversibility of the disarmament arrangement by deterring rearmament if it can, and forcibly stopping it if deterrence fails, we get a very different strategy. We get a strategic force absolutely committed to preventive war in the interest of peace and disarmament. (It is even committed to it in the interest of the subjects of the country that it might preventively attack.) And it would confront a dilemma.

The dilemma is that war is war; and to act prematurely, impatiently, and without negotiating not only might create needless violence and damage but also would be a major political act. If instead the force procrastinates, negotiates, provides "one more chance," and waits for internal political decisions or a change of government, it may be confronted with an increasingly difficult military situation. As it waits it will be confronted with an enemy of increasing strength and an increasingly unattractive war, while its threat to initiate a forestalling war becomes less persuasive, and other countries become anxious and hedge against rearmament themselves.

The three main kinds of military action that the force could take against a united country would be pain, conquest, and obstruction. By "pain" I mean sheer coercive damage. Nuclear or other weapons might be used to inflict civil damage at a rate sufficient to induce the government to change its mind and bend to the will of the international authority. By "conquest" I mean invasion or occupation sufficient to put the international authority into the role of occupying power. By "obstruction" I mean military action designed to retard a country's rearmament, to make it more costly than the country could manage, to spoil it altogether or to impede it sufficiently to prevent a major threat to the security of other countries. This might be done either by selective bombing or by selective invasion and occupation of key facilities.

Activities aimed at causing confusion, revolt of the population, civil war, or *coup d'état* could come under any of these three headings but would, of course, involve different tactics.

It is not obvious that we should want a force, even were it charged with the most ambitious responsibilities, to have excellent capabilities to carry out those missions. We might prefer the international force itself (or the nations controlling its decisions) to be deterred by at least some prospect of difficulty or even failure. We might, in other words, want the force itself to be under strong incentive to consider military intervention only as a last resort.

Militarily we can distinguish at least three different kinds of deployment for the international strategic force. In one, strategic weapons and personnel would be kept in neutral territories — on the high seas, in special areas reserved to the international force (perhaps island bases), or perhaps distributed in enclaves in some politically acceptable proportions. Except for contingents that happen to be within the victim country, the international armed force would then be in the same position that national armed forces usually are with respect to war: to conquer they have to penetrate enemy territory.

In a second mode of deployment, forces could be kept deliberately within the countries that are most likely to be "enemies." This would mean keeping strategic forces within the larger industrial countries. It might include the option of moving more forces into a country toward which threats were being made or with which war was imminent. Moving extra forces into the United States or the Soviet Union would of course be a major political move and might be subject to restriction of access. The purpose of being within the country, other than cere-monial, would be to minimize the cost and delay of invasion, occupa-tion, or selective destruction — i.e., of war. Particularly for non-nuclear invasion — a quick capture of strategic points in the country — mobile forces already within the country, properly distributed, might enhance the likelihood of quick success. The force could occupy Moscow more reliably with ground forces located thirty miles away than by relying on airborne troops in bad weather. An amphibious landing on the coast of Japan, France, or the United States would be harder than just moving troops already located within these countries.

The third mode of deployment — and it might look a little unmili-tary — would be to put critically vulnerable parts of a country's econ-omy and essential services directly into the hands of an international force. If the force can control the supply of water, electricity, fuel, transport, and communication to American, German, or Soviet cities, it might minimize strategic bombing, selective occupation, and other violence. To coerce a country, like the landlord who shuts off the util-ities when a tenant refuses to move, the force could put on the squeeze by shutting down services. Rather than bomb electric power installa-tions the force might press a key that sets off a charge of dynamite already installed.

If one really believed in the reliability and permanence of an inter-national arrangement, such schemes for providing the authority with "hostages" might be more efficient, even more humane, than provid-ing it with bombers and shock troops. One could even go further and let the force have a monopoly of critical medicines to use for bacterial warfare on a transgressor country. As soon as it starts an epidemic, it sends its medical units in to make sure that no one suffers who cooperates. Those who oppose it — military forces, government leaders, or anyone else — are without essential vaccines and must decide for themselves whether to stay at large and suffer or to surrender to be cured.

These gimmicks undoubtedly suffer from novelty, even from meanness, and would not be acceptable. They probably also go too far in assuming that the scheme is really for keeps. They give the international force too great an assurance of easy victory. The cards should be stacked in favor of the international force, but not with complete reliability. The decision to intervene by force in a sovereign country should always be a hard one. Furthermore it is worth some extra cost to keep the forces of organized violence out of sight, in reserve, and confined by tradition. No matter how strongly the entire arrangement is opposed to military traditions, uniformed troops are likely to seem more civilized than schemes patterned on the "protection" rackets or a paternalistic big brother.

Nevertheless there may be something in the notion of "prior occupation," i.e., of having strategic forces already located where they can accomplish "strategic" missions by simple tactical means — throwing switches and using only the conventional weapons of armored infantry.

The "enemy" of the force may also look for unconventional techniques of deterrence. One, which works especially well in a totalitarian country, would be a government's using its own population as hostages. If a Chinese government could threaten to hold out in such a way that an international force would have to kill large numbers of Chinese, either directly or in the economic consequences of strategic bombing, the force and its political leadership might be substantially deterred.

A threat of this sort might be implicit in any country's determination to rearm unless stopped by military action. Such a determination presents the international authority with the dilemma mentioned earlier. Shall it inflict war damage on a violator, or should it abandon the disarmament agreement in the interest of peace? It hardly seems possible to answer this question in advance. The United States government did use Union forces to prevent secession by the Southern states from an agreement they had entered voluntarily, but the basic arrangement had been in effect for over four score years and was a good deal more than a disarmament agreement.

If the victim has nuclear weapons or can acquire them, it can threaten reprisal of its own. Against whom? If the international force has no homeland — no women, children, or industrial assets toward which it feels a strong attachment — there may be no way to hurt it except to engage it militarily. But the force will be acting at least with the acquiescence, and almost surely at the urging, of other major powers. If the victim has nuclear weapons that it can deliver on countries, it need not threaten to seek out the Quonset huts of an international island-based force; it can threaten to detonate weapons in Russia, China, Britain, Ghana, America, or wherever the military move against it originates politically.

Where might the United States, Japan, or the Soviet Union acquire nuclear weapons for reprisal? One possibility is that it retained them, contrary to agreement, in secret and secure locations. If other countries are believed to have hedged in this way, even the "honorable" countries may feel obliged to do likewise. (It is not out of the question that an agreement would even provide for some "minimum deterrent" buffer stock of weaponry, at least in the early stages.)

But if we assume — unreasonable though it may be to assume — that no country has its own nuclear weapons, there are still ways to get them. *Somebody* has them and knows how to use them. If they cannot be stolen from the force by burglary, they may be stolen or access provided by an insider. In a crisis nuclear weapons belonging to the international agency but located within particular countries might be captured or production and assembly facilities taken. Finally, for the most honorable of reasons, part or all of the international strategic nuclear force might secede in favor of the intended victim.

There are those who believe that military officers could be recruited and indoctrinated with exclusive loyalty to the international authority and that their reliability would be unquestioned. It is worthwhile to question whether this is desirable; even so, one must wonder whether it could be accomplished, particularly within the first few decades of the arrangement. Flag officers of the organization are likely to have been loyal and outstanding military officers who had served national governments. It would take the organization some twenty or thirty years to recruit youngsters under twenty, put them through the equivalent of Annapolis, and raise them in an international military tradition to flag rank.

Furthermore, it should not be a foregone conclusion that this kind of abstract loyalty can be bred into military officers, especially if they are born and raised in important countries that command their affection as well as their early allegiance. And even if it can, it remains to be proved that the best personnel of an international force are men who, after reaching maturity, can turn their backs on their homelands and "emigrate" into a government that has no population, no territory, no cultural tradition, and no family ties. The capacity to incur allegiance to an abstract organization, or even to "mankind" generally, may not be a capacity highly correlated with the other qualities we want in our senior military officers or even our junior ones.

But supposing that this abstract loyalty is desirable and that the international authority should appear to have promoted it successfully, we still could not be sure of it. It will be hard to cultivate officers finer than Robert E. Lee, whose devotion to his country has, to my knowledge, not really been questioned. He confronted a dilemma at the peak of his career — one that he could surely never have anticipated by a prior decision — and had to decide where his highest allegiance lay.

We still refer today to the Civil War as a conflict between North and South, rather than between America and the South; a military showdown between an international force and a major country may not appear as a showdown between the United States and mankind, or Russia and mankind, or a United Western Europe and mankind. It may appear as an East-West conflict or a European-Asian conflict, with an international force controlled by one bloc against another.

Similarly, military coups and civil wars throughout history — even in some of the most civilized and idealistic nations — have often found national military establishments not unified on one side or the other. One has to consider therefore the possibility that, in a major showdown between an international force and an important country or a bloc of countries, some of the international military forces or personnel would side with the victim country. They might refuse to take military action against it; they might split off and join it; or they might attempt to take over the international organization itself. So there *are* ways that countries in defiance of the international force could acquire weapons, including some of the best.

If we assume, then, that major countries may get nuclear weapons, "counter-deterrence" against the international authority or its supporters through threat of nuclear reprisal is meaningful. Furthermore, the delivery of these weapons might not be difficult if the nations are themselves substantially disarmed.

It is not likely that the international force would provide every country with an air defense or ballistic missile defense network against the possibility of nuclear attack. (Besides adding tens of billions to the possible cost, an effective system of active defense would look so militarized that countries might prefer to maintain small, national, nuclear deterrent offensive forces instead.) Thus a Soviet Union that got control of some nuclear-missile submarines or bomber aircraft with nuclear weapons and wanted to threaten western Europe or the North American hemisphere might pose a threat against which the international force could provide no direct shelter. The force might hope to *deter* such an attack; but if the result is just mutual deterrence, it has failed in the mission of capturing or disarming the delinquent country.

For a major industrial country a technique of defense against the international force might be sabotage. For two reasons the force might be susceptible. The first, already adverted to, is its likely inability to maintain tight internal security of the kind that national military forces hope to maintain. The problems of security clearance and personnel selection, together with the multi-national political access to information, would pose acute problems. And in an acute crisis of national loyalties the same possibilities of military defection mentioned earlier might provide opportunities for sabotage. In fact "honorable" sabotage of strategic forces might be easier, safer, and more conservative than revolt or defection by military forces.

A second vulnerability to sabotage is in the production process. A military force that buys complex equipment in the major industrial countries might risk certain vulnerabilities that had been embedded in the equipment it purchased. One may suppose that acceptance of complex equipment would be conditional on inspection by officers of a nationality other than the producers'. Nevertheless an "encrypted" vulnerability might be built into certain equipment — that is, secret vulnerabilities that did not affect the reliability of the equipment but could be triggered by those who knew about them. (This might be more likely in unique pieces of equipment — the central command-control headquarters of the international authority or the electronics of a missile force.)

Except for retaliation and sabotage, disarmed countries should be vulnerable to attack by a professional, well equipped, international force. In fact, preventive conquest might be militarily simpler for the force than defense of one country against another. If large numbers of ill-equipped American reservists invade Canada, the force can probably stop them most effectively by occupying critical parts of the United States, taking over or immobilizing government facilities, communications, and other essential services.

Non-violent resistance may be a problem for the force. What can be accomplished by non-violent resistance to the force depends on what the international force is after. That in turn raises the question of the "war aim" of the force when it does take action against a major adversary.

If the most feasible and most humane military action available to the force is pure conquest (military occupation of a country's government) the force will be good at achieving total victory — unconditional surrender — but not lesser objectives. Is the country then to be occupied indefinitely? Is a regime put in that is favorable to the nations that backed the international force? Or are the illegal facilities dismantled, the miscreants punished, and the country turned loose again? The extent of popular resistance may depend on what is expected to happen after the country has suffered a humane blitzkrieg.

It is worth noting that the temptation for the force to launch preventive occupation may be as strongly motivated, perhaps more strongly motivated, when two competing power blocs are both violating the agreement. In fact a force that can painlessly convert a bipolar cold war into victory for one side by invading and conquering either power bloc may ignite the same apprehensions that the possibility of pre-emptive attack does now. If somebody is eventually going to be conquered by the international force, pre-emptive control of that force by one side or the other may begin to appear imperative.

CONCLUSION

To speak of these contingencies may seem contrary to the spirit of a disarmament agreement and a peace-keeping world military organization. The whole arrangement only makes sense if there are decent prospects for the cooperation of the major powers. To suppose that something like the present East-West struggle continues, or that other competing power blocs emerge to continue a cold war, and that some major country or bloc provokes the international force into action, may seem like imagining the worst. In fact, not just imagining the worst but contradicting the premise on which it is all established.

But we are discussing the "strategic problems" of the force. One may hope that the eventual actions of any such military force are purely ceremonial, that its strategic problems never become real. But to the extent that it is meant to be a real force, capable of handling actual problems, we have to ask what those problems might be.

Two tentative conclusions can be put forward. First, it is unlikely that an international strategic command would have a completely reliable, credible capability to intervene and to stop any rearmament of a major industrial power. Its "deterrent" against rearmament will certainly be subject to some doubt. It will suffer from some of the same disabilities as a national deterrence force. As a coercive military organization it will be quite imperfect.

Second, it would probably be unwise and unsafe to have it any less imperfect. The international force can itself be a threat to peace, even to disarmament, and surely to the freedom and independence of nations. The more nearly omnipotent it is, the less reassurance it would provide. The greater its military superiority over individual nations, the more it can be viewed as a potential "enemy" by the nations that it is set up to guard. The more decisive its potential role, the more crucial becomes the capture of its political control or its disablement by those who cannot hope to control it.

If we are to have someday an international military force, we probably want one that is itself deterred. To create an instrument of painless world conquest, one that can overcome both passive and active resistance of national governments and national populations, might be to create extraordinary political instability. Indivisible, centralized, coherent power may be a good deal less conducive to peace and reassurance than a more diffuse, less decisive, less tempting instrument of control.

A world disarmament arrangement is unlikely to be viable if it requires a "perfect" strategic military force to deter violation and secession. Unless a quite imperfect deterrent can be believed adequate to forestall competitive violation, the arrangement should be abandoned or postponed.

Suppose an international strategic force were as likely to split apart as to stay together under crisis. Suppose it were believed appreciably vulnerable to various forms of sabotage. Suppose that individual nations could get hold of nuclear weapons and a capacity to deliver them on population centers. Suppose there were doubts whether the political arrangements were conducive to the force's timely action in a crisis — at least as many doubts as have ever been raised about American intervention on behalf of Europe. What is the consequence?

The consequence may be a significant deterrent, a deterrent based not on the certainty of decisive intervention but on a likelihood of intervention too great to ignore. A deterrent force does not have to *guarantee* that it can win the engagement.

This brings us back to the concept of "buffer." Instead of threatening to intervene against the rearming nation the force might be charged only with maintaining enough deterrence against war itself to permit other nations to take steps for their own protection. In the event of a rearmament race the international buffer force would try to ensure that no nation or group of nations could get a decisive headstart over its rivals.

Particularly since deterrence may depend on the absolute reprisal damage with which a nation can threaten an aggressor, not on just relative strengths, an international buffer might deter a rearming country's aggression long enough to permit other countries to develop at least "minimum deterrent forces" by themselves.

Under this concept the international force might even be authorized to assist in the laggards' rearmament. By simply threatening to facilitate the defensive, deterrent rearmament of the laggards (turning over its own production facilities to them, providing technical assistance, or giving some of its own weapons to them) the force might reduce the attractiveness to any nation of rushing back into an arms race. If this were the expected outcome of a rearmament race, there might appear little advantage in initiating such a race and no desperate haste to join a race that may or may not have begun.

How definitely and exactly can we hope to specify what the force is supposed to do? Can we rule out certain functions, such as its assisting laggards in their own rearmament? Can we make sure in advance that it will intervene (or that it will not intervene) in certain kinds of rearmament? Can we decide that it should engage in nuclear reprisal against a country that starts war, but not against a country that starts rearmament; or, choosing the opposite, can we guarantee that it will use nuclear weapons to deter or obstruct rearmament but not against a country that initiates conventional war?

I suspect we cannot. We can talk about the alternatives and can perhaps arrange weaponry, deployment, doctrine, political controls, and national military capabilities in a way that enhances the likelihood of certain decisions and reduces the likelihood of others. But no one can say in advance whether those who enjoy political control of the force will have the resolve, temerity, prudence, audacity, restraint, brutality, responsibility, or whatever else it takes, to launch war when they ought to, to threaten it credibly, to limit war properly if it occurs, or to abstain in the face of temptation. It is unlikely that we can deny the nations that politically control the force any ability to disband it, to redistribute its assets, or to charge it with grand new responsibilities that were never dreamed of before.

What could be decided in advance, and ought to be decided, is whether the force is to be viewed as an experiment in power politics or as a religious institution. If every war is a holy war, if the force cannot admit compromise or even occasional defeat, if every flaw in its strategy is to be construed as a doctrinal contradiction, if its leadership is to be considered the embodiment of disinterestedness and saintliness, and if any affront to the force is to be considered heresy, the demands on strategy will be exorbitant. The one thing we cannot do is to design a military force and strategy to support a doctrine of absolute self-righteousness.

HENRY V. DICKS

The International Soldier —
A Psychiatrist's View

I. INTRODUCTION

This chapter attempts to envisage potential conflicts of loyalty in the minds of soldiers of a future international peace force and to review some of the means and steps by which such conflicts might be eased or prevented. For it is a fundamental of collective action that for any group to be effective in pursuing its object its members must be reasonably free from crises of loyalty.

Man has long known that any armed force in action is only as strong as its group cohesion — its morale. As Napoleon put it: "*A la guerre les trois quarts sont des affaires morales. La balance des forces réelles n'est que pour un quart.*" But it was not until World War II that military thinkers, aided by the developing psychological sciences, began to spell out some of the conditions and factors governing military morale and formulated something like this list:

(1) Belief or faith in the cause for which the troops are asked to fight and die.

(2) Conviction of personal and group worth, as shown in the esteem accorded to their forces by the backing population and by the high command.

(3) Confidence in the leadership, especially at the face-to-face level.

(4) Good selection — i.e., the fitting of personal aptitudes to the technical tasks and demands required by the unit's role in

battle. This can be held to include a conviction of one's skill and mastery in the role.

(5) Confidence in the superiority and plentiful supply of technical equipment (arms, vehicles, etc.).

(6) Good personal logistic support — food, billets, welfare, medicine, fuel, home links, comforts.

Items 5 and 6 may be interpreted as derivatives of 2 and 3. Any authority or "backer" of troops who esteemed them well and any good commander would see to it that the supplies were the best possible in all respects. One need not waste time in considering what would be the morale of a starving, ill-equipped UN detachment used on doubtful legal grounds against a well-fed, better equipped national army full of self-righteousness! Most of this essay, therefore, will be taken up in considering how items 1 to 4 could be applied to a UN force from the experience of analogous provisions in other forces.

When the conditions of good morale are stated in this way, it becomes easy to see how bound up with our theme are "belief in the cause" and a "conviction of personal and group worth." The "good cause" of recent wars for which national armies have loyally fought has been the defense or the greater glory of the nation-state. National loyalty and belief in the cause were then almost identical. And what, in psychological terms, is "identity" but the sense of finding oneself and one's role affirmed as "good" or "worthwhile" by one's government and people in answer to the subjective question "What am I like?" The sense of identity requires a congruity of a person's values with his actions and their acceptance by society.

It appears, then, that the UN "cause" — the peace of the world — must become a powerful motivating sentiment analogous to patriotism; and it follows that the crucial task in the welding of supranational or international armed forces is the substitution of new, international loyalties for national loyalties.

At this point it becomes pertinent to distinguish between national loyalty and nationalism. The distinction will be of some importance in a potential or hypothetical international force. Whereas national loyalty and pride are, in the writer's view, entirely compatible in an individual or group with a wider identification, militant nationalism is not. The former could be illustrated by a young man who has already "found himself," has established his identity by his secure belonging to a reference group, for example his own family, and who can thus meet the wider world with self-confidence; the latter by an insecure young man, ambivalent about his reference group and unsure of his identity, full of mingled feelings of secret inferiority and compensatory, narcissistic self-assertion, with a "chip on his shoulder." The two young men present different risks as recruits for an international force. Aggressive nationalism in the individual would be among the most troublesome difficulties in the creation and effective operation of international projects, especially any such project as a UN armed force acting as the guardian of international law and order vis-à-vis a nation guilty of aggression under the banner of righteous nationalistic aims.

The question is how we might overcome such loyalty troubles in a UN force. But we ought first to examine the pessimistic assumption that national allegiance must constitute a serious weakness in a supranational armed force. Is it possible that we have looked at the motivations of soldiers only in the light of recent wars, when the professional military were greatly outnumbered and all but submerged by the vast armies of non-professional soldiers whose military attitudes and incentives were chiefly those of aroused national loyalty and national identification? We might get a different picture if we consider the problem in the light of "peacetime" forces, dominated of course by professional career soldiers,[1] who would constitute the bulk of any UN force whether temporary or permanent.

II. THE PROFESSIONAL SOLDIER'S ATTITUDES

Military history suggests that the profession of arms has been exercised with valor and proficiency in causes which bear little relation to the national loyalties of the warriors involved. Generals and soldiers have fought and died for empires, religions, and ideologies which were not part of their native background. The motley armies of Tilly and Wallenstein in the Thirty Years' War contained professional mercenaries, little touched by the ideological struggle, who fought and died for loyalty to their generals.

[1] To save tedium, all groups of fighting men will be called "soldiers," whether naval, marine, air force, or ground force.

The former British Indian Army, which (like France's former co-lonial contingents) was recruited from a number of peoples, provides a recent example of the capacity of professional soldiers, even though precluded from the pinnacles of the profession, to identify with and render splendid service for the cause of a remote ruler under competent yet alien leadership. We also recall the "mercenaries" of heroic stature: the O'Higginses and Cochranes, the Barclay de Tollys and MacMahons — foreign professionals who commanded alien national or revolution-ary armies or navies with at best only the mild approval of their motherland. Scrutiny of their stories might well reveal conflicts of early loyalties or doubts about identity, some perhaps not laudable. The Foreign Legion illustrates what mixed motives may converge to as-semble and to weld diverse deviants into a dedicated force.

It appears that professional soldiers constitute a transnational pro-fessional group in the sense that artists or engineers or doctors do. As the latter have desciplined their talents, so the career soldiers have ac-cepted discipline of their combative tendencies. Moreover, from the study of several groups of professional soldiers certain features of the motivations, personality dynamics, and self-perception of military men emerge which make up a "military profile" which has surprising con-stancy over wide cultural and national differences. It makes profes-sional soldiers of different national and racial origins more akin to each other than many of them would be to some sub-groups of their own peoples.

It is the writer's opinion that professional soldiers — especially en-listed men — do not choose their roles primarily out of national loyalty. They choose their job because it offers satisfaction for their personal needs. They are no more and no less loyal or nationalistic than their civilian fellow-citizens. It is the political currents of our present phase of history which by and large encourage some nationalistic, authori-tarian men to choose the role of brave defender of the nation as a suitable outlet for their super-patriotism or ethnocentricity. Soldiers are, in fact, often more objective and less bigoted about their enemies and can identify with them more readily than the nationally conscious civilian.

The Identity of the Soldier

Morris Janowitz has recently described the typical attitudes and motivations of professional officers especially in the highest ranks at the Pentagon in the United States.[2] Even in this relatively "new" corps, formed moreover in a revolutionary setting, Janowitz finds the typical military ethos of Europe well ingrained. The virtues of chivalry and gentlemanly conduct, of personal loyalty to the commander-in-chief, and the acceptance of the brotherhood of disciplined men are characteristic. To this I would add the strong bonds, more typical of enlisted men, within the particular unit (a ship's company, a tank regiment, an air squadron) that identifies the members. In some of the older European as well as Asian armed forces with long traditions of allegiance to a king or feudal overlord these characteristics stand out even more clearly than in the United States. The identity or self-image which is shared by and links the military professions everywhere is among the oldest distinctive life styles in the world. It was described in the tenets of the *Kshattriya* (warrior) caste of ancient India, and in the chivalry which enabled a Crusader baron to establish a sense of gentlemanly understanding with his Saracen opponent.

Military professionalism embodies a congruence of the social role with personal needs for a manly life of sport and risk, and for being perceived as a standard-bearer of certain virtues. These virtues include both command and loyal obedience, orderliness, and the spurning of materialist or corrupt self-interest. These often — but not always — go with non-political conservatism and a high degree of simple religious faith. We have lately seen radical military fraternities in some new countries take over control as "saviors" of their people.

In World War II the operation of the military code of behavior was seen at its best in the small face-to-face combat teams: the bomber crew, the tank crew, the infantry squad manning a pill-box or forward position; the company of a motor torpedo boat or a submarine. Here "the cause" or the political issues were only marginally in mind. It was the loyalty to the leader and to the comrades, the trained mastery of

2 Morris Janowitz, *The Professional Soldier* (New York: Free Press of Glencoe, 1960). See especially Chapter 2.

fear, the intense experience of brotherhood and mutual commitment which made what the Germans called *das fronterlebnis* a life-long memory of a man's "finest hours." Military forces everywhere, despite the introduction of machine technology which approximates the skills of a large proportion of soldiers to those of their civilian counterparts, have preserved this central core of their professional ethos by the unifying marks of the military specialist — the smart drill and uniforms, saluting, and so on — which are the symbol of special brotherhood.

III. THE SOCIAL INTEGRATION OF A MILITARY FORCE

If there is truth in our assertion that the professional soldier has certain nearly universal attitudes toward his role and certain personal values around which his identity and self-image are built, then the task of creating an international military constabulary or peace force becomes at the human level that of enlisting and conserving the loyalties of a sufficient number of such soldiers. How this might be done will be discussed under four headings: (1) the creation of a high command and general staff; (2) recruitment and personnel policy for a permanent force, with some references also to short-term task groups; (3) conflicts of national or ideological loyalties within both of these; and (4) the problem of deracination.

1. Creation of a High Command

The creation of a world military constabulary dedicated to world peace has been a dream of internationalists since the days of the League of Nations. Since that time we have had experience with loaned detachments of national forces pooled to serve the UN in this way, the most significant being the Korean operation, in which the command structure seems to have functioned effectively. With political progress, a permanent military staff advising and planning for the UN may supersede the improvised forces whose staff officers and units could be recalled at the whim of their governments.

Assuming that political and legal sanction for creating a permanent force under the orders of UN executive organs has been worked out and agreed, the selection and briefing of a high command and general staff will be the key problem. If this body is well formed, it will itself create a force suitable for its mission within the limits of civilian and budgetary control. Ultimately the authority of the UN (or of a world government) will come to depend on the loyalty and dedication of this elite body; and its power will be the greater the more the UN replaces sovereign states as the holder of military means of coercion. Checks against abuse of this power, however, need to be worked into its structure.

Where shall we look for people who are sufficiently senior to form first a planning staff and next a field force, and who possess in highest degree the virtues of professional officers? How can this be done without arousing suspicions among the presumably still extant differing ideological camps which might have agreed, grudgingly and on logic rather than from burning idealism, to such a force? There has been wisdom in nominating commanders for *ad hoc* UN troops from among small or uncommitted countries even when their operational experience or skill had not been proved. Can we conceive of a stage of political objectivity or mature rationality when the UN would agree to delegate to an expert body of behavioral scientists the preparation of a "job analysis" and personality criteria for such selection, and then to invite them to cooperate in choosing this all-important staff perhaps from a list of willing "possibles" nominated by member nations? The methods exist and are now in use in the sphere of industrial and military personnel selection. Their use for our purpose would seem essential.

In the light of what was said earlier about the nature of the military code, we need not anticipate severe conflicts of loyalty or difficulties of adaptation in such chosen volunteers to the new commander-in-chief, i.e., the symbolic or real head of the UN. This, one ventures to think, might even be easier with military personalities than with civilians at corresponding level.

To what image of a universal "good cause" shall we ask our hypothetical guardians of the peace to devote their faith? We can perhaps define their role as that of maintaining, as a last resort when other means have failed, standards of civilized political behavior to be defined in UN statutes. On this "good cause" we may hope for agreement from all ideological and national camps. We may liken this aim of an international staff to that of the uniformed constabulary or police of most countries, who watch for and have authority to prevent breaches of the peace irrespective of the importance or motives of the people committing the acts.

It is the civil power which gives the authority and subsequently adjudicates. As Janowitz[3] argues in the case of the United States officer corps of the future, such a constabulary role is the only possible one to assign to an international force. It alone gives its military elite the sense of guardianship of law and order "on behalf of all the peoples," irrespective of which nationality or territory is involved in breaches, as well as the "built-in" loyalty to civil powers and legal process. Its pride would be in the successful and humane elimination of political and military delinquency against the world order. There could be no old-time "glory" to boast over.

The assimilation of these essentially protective, "parental" values — so well displayed, for example, by many a middle-aged, tolerant London policeman — will be the essential learning process for the international high command. It is in this spirit that they should proceed to build the forces for which their civilian masters will grant them money and sanction.

Given the assurance of the other factors we enumerated as necessary for high morale, namely a relation of mutual trust and esteem with the civilian heads of the UN, a secure and dignified level of remuneration, pension provisions, and not too much interference or cheese-paring at the budgetary or technical autonomy level, one can be optimistic about the prospect of attracting military personalities of high caliber to a task which they might well judge to be more interesting and challenging for the essential qualities of the dedicated disciplined professional soldier than a time-serving job at home.

2. The Creation of a Permanent International Force

The formation and nourishing of a permanent force of highly trained, mobile soldiers may be more difficult than recruiting generals and staff officers. One factor favoring recruitment might be the reduction in the level of national forces in countries which accept disarmament, hence making available large numbers of trained officers and enlisted men from such countries for the original force. On the score of

[3] *Ibid.*, Chapter 20.

role perception and honorable identification with it, it is desirable that, at least to begin with, the top jobs should be filled by able soldiers of smaller nations — e.g., the Swedes, the Thais, the Mexicans — whose parent country will be universally accepted as not aspiring to world domination, and whose soldiers have for a long time accepted the role of guardians rather than prestige-creators. It would seem essential too that at the stage when a permanent international high command is allowed to exist by the concert of nations, its personnel should be committed to the UN by the terms of employment and not merely loaned by national forces for a brief period. If the demobilized men were enrolled as "foundation members" with the consent and blessing of their own governments, the primary conflict of loyalty would be minimized. Many good soldiers tend to take the line of least resistance, which is to continue in a congenial role promising some extra rewards. There was no difficulty in Britain in manning various post-World War I control and plebiscite forces on a semi-international level. Let us admit that a considerable number of such men will be time-serving mercenaries, the kind who form the core of most regular armed forces. If the top policy control is safe, we can accept them.

The major problem is how to maintain their cohesion by identifying them with a cause not so easily accepted by such men as the simple one of national power. Let us examine this question under the heads of the major factors listed earlier as contributing to high morale. In addition, we should consider the advantages and disadvantages to morale of units composed on an ethnic basis as against those made up of soldiers recruited at random from anywhere.

(a) *"The good cause."* What matters is that in any recruiting campaign as well as throughout training the utmost care should be taken to remind all ranks of their high mission and role. "Where there is no vision, the people perish." In a world in which, so we hope, the military virtues derived from another age will be less and less esteemed, it will be a difficult task to foster the conviction in such a force that it is respected rather than regarded as an archaic minority. In democratic settings especially, soldiers are apt to be personally somewhat on the defensive, hence tending to counter-contempt of democratic values. The soldierly personality is one in which subordination and domination are polarized. It will require the use of much psychosocial skill to reconcile the integration of members of the force and their role values with the pacific surrounding population. The good cause has to be shared by both, but chiefly by the military as its human symbol. We shall recur to this theme later. Here we only stress the crucial importance to morale of the image or sense of identity which such soldiers will feel themselves to embody in the popular mind.

There is an inner conflict of identity common among soldiers (and policemen) especially in peacetime. It is compounded of certain dimly perceived insights of the average man's hate of authority figures, and of their own identification with, or submission to, the paternal superego. There results some guilt feeling at being on the side of the boss. Many an intelligent officer will disarmingly say to academic or professional people: "I am only a plain, bluff soldier," implying an apology for having chosen a low-ranking and despised tough occupation, with an underlying note of defiance and pride. He feels that his dedication to valor, extraversion, and life on limited pay should mark him as a leader but that others will not grant this.

(b) *Need for sense of worth.* The foregoing remarks bring us to the second important factor in maintaining morale in a regular standing armed force in a civilian world — especially in peacetime. From the point of view of military cohesion all armed and police forces need a sense of forming a special *corps d'élite.* The semi-segregation of the military community is a necessary part of this if the boundaries of their inner group *mores* and loyalties are not to dissolve. And so even national armed forces are, in the main, a community apart. They and their families live in barracks, cantonments, or camps and have a largely self-contained social life, a condition which gives rise to conflicting feelings on the part of the civilian community. The civilian, when he is permitted to visit military installations or when soldiers parade on national holidays, has a sense of national pride in the armed forces. But at other times he commonly looks on the military as living in comparative idleness, with every convenience provided for it at the taxpayer's expense; and he resents its necessary presence.

Ambivalent feelings toward an international force will be much more marked. Contingents of such a UN force will have to be stationed at strategic points in various parts of the globe where they will be in a sense an alien body in the midst of the population; and special efforts at good public relations will be necessary to overcome the mutual sense of strangeness and even of "occupation." The image required for good relationships of this future world constabulary with the host population will be one of self-containment, but a friendly, calculated fraternal one.

There are several measures which the force could take to reduce ambivalence and make itself respected and even welcomed by the people among whom it is placed:

 (i) The force should possess good liaison officers, including experts in the culture patterns of the area.

 (ii) The force should be an economic advantage to the area in which it is located. It ought to purchase supplies when possible locally, including leisure facilities.

 (iii) The manpower and technical resources of the force should be made available for the benefit of the area. Emergencies such as natural catastrophes or epidemics are only the most obvious examples. The force's engineers could also be employed for constructing drainage, building bridges, and road-building, while its medical and educational staffs would be available to treat, train, and educate underdeveloped populations and upgrade their local services.

Thus the force should be perceived not only as a guardian of peace and a symbol of benevolent authority but also in some sense as UN technical aid, as a sort of resourceful Peace Corps. This kind of relationship, if cultivated with full regard for the self-respect of both parties, will be a help in building the right image of their role both in the soldiers and in the surrounding population.

We must expect a degree of strain in the soldiers even when these good conditions are realized. Few ordinary people can tolerate long spells of expatriation even in married quarters. Two and a half years without change has been considered the maximum in static units a long way from home. And few populations will take readily to having outside groups quartered in their midst, especially if these have higher living standards than themselves, until they understand and share the purposes of the strangers — which will take time.

 (c) *Face-to-face leadership.* It is not only under combat conditions that face-to-face leadership assumes supreme importance in a soldier's life. We have always known, and now have the evidence from studies of group relations, that the dynamic which binds groups is not chiefly the common task but the shared, family-like loyalty to the leader, which also cements the bonds between the "brothers" in affection and rivalry with one another. This shared identification is seen most clearly in the military group, where it points up the need for careful selection of the junior officers who will mature into captains. It is at platoon and company level that it is essential to create an image of the trusted unit leader role, and this image should be consistently used for recruitment appeals in all countries from which it is decided to seek volunteers. The "profile" of the required qualities must be rigorously applied in choosing candidates. The appeal of the role is likely to be considerable to the kind of young man who might previously have volunteered for his nation's overseas service as an administrator, soldier, or educator. Additional figures who can decisively influence the morale of men are the unit medical officer and the senior non-commissioned officers, who must be carefully selected at first entry and on promotion.

In this connection both politico-social education in the values which the force exists to defend and uphold and the inculcation of the correct attitudes toward the civilian population, whether friendly or the people of a country against whom action is contemplated or going on, are important. Moreover, they must come from the men's own officers. The so-called "education" officer "from above" who goes from group to group is only grudgingly accepted by most soldiers, and his words are discounted as coming from an outsider.

At staff and high echelon levels provision should be made for a guidance or educational directorate with responsibility for morale and human relations which would hold seminars for suitable junior officers. The courses should have the same degree of priority and prestige as technical training and other graduate study. At this level there is ample scope for participation of civilian political and social science experts.

(d) *Technical skill and superiority.* These are mentioned again to emphasize the value which soldiers attach to the quality and quantity of their equipment and supply. One need only recall the *élan* of the "invincible" Nazi *Luftwaffe* until it met the British Spitfires, whose pilots in their turn felt tremendous uplift of fighting spirit when they knew that they could outgun and outmaneuver the Germans. In the same way, though soldiers complain of incessant training in arms and tactics, this high pitch of skill also gives them a good feeling of being "a crack team," especially if backed by adequate aptitude selection which has a role to play here as at command levels.

(e) *Welfare.* This aspect of morale building includes food, housing, mails, and medical services as well as constructive leisure. The latter comprises further education for its own sake and for helping men on leaving the services to obtain skilled employment in civilian life; it must comprise arrangements, including financial aid, for the soldier's re-integration with his own people on completion of contract. These things, which ought to be in the program of any civilized military force, should be made explicit in the contracts of service in an international force. They could be the responsibility of UN force liaison offices in all parts of the world, who would integrate their social follow-up services with similar services at the national level.

(f) *Symbolism and ceremony.* The value of non-rational elements in creating a self-image of worth and group allegiance should not be overlooked. Such elements include the design of special flags, badges, and uniforms and ceremonies ranging from solemn induction to public appearances on parade on suitable occasions — e.g., UN Day and other anniversaries connected with the growth of the world community.

Doubtless some system of awards for good service, bravery, or other distinction would be instituted. The bestowals should optimally be made by representatives of the civil power, who should also show other signs of live concern for and pride in their armed force.

The foregoing are some of the ways in which soldiers serving any given force can be helped to build and maintain a good image of themselves and to feel pride in the unit to which they belong. These methods create conditions which favor good morale and group cohesion in military forces anywhere. Their observance in a new international force *sui generis* is doubly necessary.

We must now attempt a more difficul feat of imaginative prediction and try to weigh the advantages of random individual recruitment on the Foreign Legion model as against those of embodiment by ethnic units — the Gurkha model.

3. Blended or Pure?

From the point of view of morale our concern is with the basic unit of affiliation, the unit with which a man can easily identify at a face-to-face level — let us say the company (200) of land troops, the air squadron, or the crew of a small warship. For operational purposes land units may need to be up to battalion (800) strength. Higher formations in a hypothetical regular UN force will necessarily consist of units internationally composed. In any such force a linguistic and communications problem will exist at all levels, not to mention the problems caused by differing ethnic culture patterns reflected in dietary and religious customs, in attitudes to other people and to authority, and so on. Technological change, secularization, and convergence of patterns of urban life are softening some of these differences, but it would be a mistake to underrate them. Attempting to alleviate them, however, by too narrow selection in hopes of avoiding trouble with communications or "culture clash" might well result in the image of the force as a "Western," or a "white" or an "Asian" enclave and thus in the sacrifice of universal acceptance.

It could be argued that in advanced countries with many avenues of skilled work and upward mobility open to its universally literate populations the armed forces in peacetime have been regarded as "backward" institutions. They have often attracted to their ranks the less resourceful and independent personalities save in times of major unemployment. Yet the military life was often a school where self-respect, discipline, and technical skills were learned. The service was also the mother symbol and nurturant home for many orphans and products of broken families or adolescent revolt. In less developed countries the armed forces, on the contrary, are often the best school that enterprising and independent youth can find. To them military service is an opportunity for modernizing — of learning the three R's, acquiring technological knowledge, having a higher standard of living than at home in the mud village. Nurtured in the universally diffused traditions of military honor and efficiency, the armed forces of such countries often truly represent the most "civilized" and modern-thinking elite group. By the same token, UN soldiers from such countries could become agents of social change and modern ideas for their homeland.

A valuable function of the UN force would be that of a school for men from diverse climes and races brought together and held by a common task-commitment and shared identifications, learning to be "modern men" and rubbing a lot of prejudices and archaisms off each other. They will start with certain similarities — the wish to be soldiers because this answers a personality need. The question is one of how to cushion the culture clash, how to encourage this new image without causing confusion and maladaptation leading to loss of identity in many simple men.

(a) *Units are homogeneous (the Gurkha model).* The advantage of embodiment in ethnic units is that men with strong elemental national identification or culture peculiarities can join a unit which is not frighteningly new or strange. They will be with their own kind, have their own sort of food, welfare, and patterns of authority. Recruitment of such units for a UN force might be facilitated by the attraction of friends from the same region. The logistic problem would be simplified if a station-quartermaster knew he had to produce typical diets for a unit of Hindus or for a unit of Nigerians. Although presumably for commands and communications the force would have one or two compulsory languages mastered by officers, senior non-commissioned officers, and signalers, the life and discipline in the face-to-face units could be conducted in the vernacular. Religious observances and familiar customs would be kept up.

National identity problems might be lessened. The universal "good cause" and high mission of the whole force could still be inculcated by the educational influence of belonging to it, as stressed by the general regime and symbolism already discussed. National loyalties could be turned to good account in healthy inter-unit rivalries and competition for smartness and efficiency and in sports. A given unit could be withdrawn from any military action against its own nationals with its threat of crises in loyalty.

The disadvantages of ethnic units might be a lessened over-all identification with the force, a greater ethnocentric resistance to "modernizing" and becoming a true international soldier. Mass disaffection or rioting might be more likely and more difficult to control. Whereas in a Foreign Legion type of unit such clashes might be confined to a few hotheads, in the ethnic type two companies — say of Danes and Indonesians — might well become a real problem if inter-unit hostility broke out. We recall the recent trouble in the "homogeneous" British Army of the Rhine between a unit of Scots and Lancashire men!

At a higher level, if we suppose that the rival ideologies at present dividing humanity were still active, albeit covered over to the extent of permitting service of the respective nationals in a UN force, ethnic units might bring with them solid political attitudes, prestige claims, and intolerance which might seriously conflict with the objective and non-political role of the force. This is another aspect of the dilemma discussed earlier. How does one incorporate into the force men with lifelong exposure to totalitarian indoctrination, especially if their rulers see to it that only "the right ones" are permitted to "volunteer"?

(b) *Units are of individuals (the Foreign Legion model)*. It was stated earlier that the release of many soldiers, both officers and enlisted men, from national forces might offer a ready nucleus of a field force. Such men would volunteer individually and from personal motives ranging from international idealism to mental laziness, the attraction of good pay, and the prospects of adventure. To select and enroll them into units culturally compatible and not too heterogeneous would require language training and a regime — the creation of a climate of tradition — so broad and characterless as to make identifications rather problematic. The Foreign Legion had a clear image to model itself on and give loyalty to — namely the French officers and the President of France. In an international force only exceptional characters somewhat polyglot, rootless, or dedicated, are likely to benefit by finding a new identity in a UN force.

We cannot risk the force's becoming a refuge for psychopaths. If, however, it was found that there were enough tough and yet stable military types, such recruits would become the most mobile and dedicated elite group of the force. They would not be bothered by national affiliations or customs since they would be seeking a worthwhile new identity. It is likely that many of them would be deviants, including various political defectors, whose personalities would create disciplinary difficulties when their high expectations were thwarted; but others would be types who would in any case become soldiers, seamen, or colonial pioneers.

On balance it would seem sensible to expect the main structure of the force we envisage to be on a Gurkha model but there should be some experimental units on the Foreign Legion model. In these latter we may have one of the necessary alembics to produce the man of the future, whose home is the world, and who is capable of modifying parochial stereotypes and archaisms on his return to his native land.

4. *Conflicts of Ideologies and Identity*

We must now turn to what is perhaps the thorniest problem in trying to blend a motley crowd of men reared in widely differing societies and ideologies into a cohesive, disciplined military force. This may take place in the fairly near future, while the world is still profoundly divided as to values and political goals and in the consequential molding of children to assimilate them.

We said that we could make the ethos of the force non-political, technical, and professional, hoping to gain the allegiance of all to the primary task of enforcing law and order as an instrument in the hands of the civilian executive organs of the UN. We postulated that these organs would act impartially under law and demonstrate the justice and legality of the cause. One can further assume that common training and unit life would foster solidarity and some lasting identifications overriding the more parochial ones. But these parochial loyalties — nationalist and ideological — will be deeper. Even among genuine volunteers, who might come forward precisely because of their revolt against some aspect of their national policies or way of life, the clash with others who might denigrate their country could mobilize unsuspected depths of national feeling. This is most likely to happen in Foreign Legion mixed units — between soldiers originating in different great power countries or between one of them and "unaligned" nationals who detest their pretensions and envy them their national background and power.

Within limits of good fellowship and deeper ties, such barrack room arguments and fights have educational value; and it might be possible to structure such conflicts in debates as part of morale building and training in world citizenship under good leadership. Nonetheless, as long as great power alignments and rivalries exist, a force at UN disposal cannot be permitted to be but another reflection of them. Therefore the wiser plan is initially to confine recruitment not only of staff but also of officers and enlisted men to smaller non-competing countries as was done in the case of the *ad hoc* task forces at Gaza or in the Congo. It would be easier and even prestigious for nationals of small countries to identify with the new world-constabulary concept. Only in the improbable or at least presently unforeseeable event of power politics having manifestly been abandoned in favor of social engineering everywhere could this ordinance be cautiously modified in favor of some experimental toleration of "mixed" units and "great power" ethnic units. The results on the members' identity and morale problems should be carefully assessed as a piece of social research. This caution is preferable to the likely alternative of the staff having to discharge unassimilable men or to disband whole units on grounds of national or political fanaticism, actions which would lead to very awkward and unfortunate charges of partiality in the councils of the UN by offended national delegates.

While any organization must reserve the right to terminate the services of misfits, a UN force should take great care to draft its regulations in terms which will minimize this risk. The desirable goal is a morale structure which includes and respects conflict and tries to deal with it by assimilation. Discharge should be on behavior, not on views. The unit climate should be able to tolerate a few fanatics and agitators.

5. *The Problem of Deracination*

Some social thinkers have been exercised by demoralization resulting from individuals being uprooted from their accustomed milieus and transplanted into strange social and geographical surroundings. Such demoralization, with loss of sense of identity and personal worth, which is called "deracination," is well known to occur not only in forcibly displaced persons. It happens also in volunteers — for example lonely students from remote or underdeveloped countries overwhelmed by the impact of a great Western city, or disenchanted emigrants who have left their native country with a vision of some promised better life. It happens even in UN personnel and especially their families, who can suffer from considerable loss of "belongingness" and from homesickness after a long spell of expatriation in what have been called the "international ghettoes" of Geneva or New York.

To what extent is deracination a danger to the potential forces we are considering? It would be foolish to underrate the severe personal maladaptations — depression, loss of initiative, resentment, and so forth — which may eventually break to the surface in some people under conditions of expatriation and which lead to disaffection, irrational griping, and desertion. In the introductory section we alluded to two models of behavior, using the paradigm of a secure young man with a good home background incorporated in his personality in contrast to an insecure young man from a problem family who on the surface might seem tougher, more ready to abandon his roots and assert his independence. We know with certainty which of these two is likely to be the better risk as a soldier — the one with sound roots. Hence my stress on good selection and on the need for ethnically homogeneous basic units for our force. The potential sufferer from deracination symptoms is one who unconsciously seeks in each new situation "a better father and mother" and — of course — becomes repeatedly disenchanted because his quest was a projection to the outer environment of an essentially inner, psychic malaise. He began without safe roots; the move to another milieu, intended as a cure by him, emphasized the trouble.

The problem might be most acute for those potential recruits to the UN force whom we described as already somewhat rootless, polyglot characters, who are sometimes the products of forced population movement (such as the sons of anticommunist, east European refugees). It is for the avoidance of such dangers on a large scale that we have tried to build into the envisaged group structure some safeguards against the sense of rootlessness. In contrast to the civilian groups mentioned above, our force was imagined as consciously providing a "parental" function by its personnel policy and by advocating a mainly ethnic pattern for its basic units. It is not proposed that the United Nations should subvert men from their motherlands or drive out their good feelings of national pride and identity, although we hope that they will become good UN men. We have attempted to incorporate into our planned service life respect for the customs and folkways of our soldiers (i.e., their national identity). They would be surrounded by their compatriots, and in static conditions by their families living in suitable cantonments. The contract of service would be for a limited period, during which home furlough and facilities for easy communication with home would be provided. At the end of his period of service a soldier would normally expect to be repatriated with his dependents (if any) and given help to establish himself in his native land as a more educated, modern person with new skills.

It might happen that some men will have become strangers and feel deracinated only on returning to a home which they had outgrown. The same danger arises in national forces, in civilian pioneering projects — in fact, anywhere where people are exposed to new experiences and horizons. We should therefore be prepared to meet the problem but not inflate it. If we can create a focus of international loyalties in men also securely rooted in their own backgrounds, a brotherhood of men-at-arms dedicated to making a safer world, we should not be deterred by the moderate risk involved. The anxieties we feel may well be akin to those aroused in us by the kindred idea of "surrender of national sovereignty" — abolishing "safe" boundaries and so imperiling our sacred national identities — those perilous archaisms of the pre-nuclear age.

IV. CONCLUSION

It remains to sum up what is necessarily a tentative essay in applying the lessons learned from morale problems of national armed forces to a hypothetical international constabulary.

We have proposed that national identity and loyalty do not of themselves constitute a powerful obstacle to securing the services of professional soldiers. Such soldiers' personality structure could be shown to rest on the individual's image of a good self, his identity, and his sense of worth — not so much on primarily national allegiance (with which in recent history it has become confused) as on an almost universal code of professional conduct and honor. We have also attempted to relate the maintenance of this good image to the acknowledged conditions favoring high morale in military force — the cement without which such a structure does not long survive as an effective instrument.

We have suggested that, in order to lessen conflict between national and international loyalties in future UN soldiers, they should be drawn from countries not in the great-power struggle, whether national or ideological; that they should be given a simple nonpolitical task as the cause with which to identify; and that they should be offered such conditions and publicly perceived status as would assimilate them to a well esteemed constabulary rather than to an army of the old sort. They should be trained to be bringers of peace, order, and modernization to the regions in which they may be stationed, somewhat recalling the great civilizing impact which came as the still visible by-product of Rome's legions upon the barbarians.

In order to reduce conflicts of identity in individual soldiers we have proposed that the initial basis for forming the face-to-face units should be an ethnic one. This would provide a halfway house between international loyalty and continued awareness of belonging to the national or ethnic reference group. With these and general welfare measures it could be anticipated that a regular international force, unified around good leadership and well designed education and symbolic functions, could be made viable. The problem of penetration of the force by solid, national, ideological groups may perhaps be avoided by reliance on a simple agreed statute of impartial aims and temporary exclusion of soldiers from the camps of great powers who are likely to be the chief carriers of the ideologies and pretensions conflicting with the international order.

Deracination was seen as a danger chiefly if the force recruited, without careful selection, men already somewhat footloose who were seeking escape from inner insecurity and were prone to disaffection. The service could be constructed to deal fairly satisfactorily with the problem of deracination, which was perhaps raised partly because of the opposite fear of loss of national sovereignty if we permitted the international force to become a reality. If the force came into being it could, in competent hands, be made into a workshop for creating a truly modern, international man who would never be the same again after experiencing its fellowship.

APPENDIX

UNITED NATIONS PEACE FORCE

An address to the Harvard Alumni Association,
delivered in Cambridge, Massachusetts, June 13, 1963,
by the Secretary-General of the United Nations,

U THANT

The development of an international order, enshrined in an accepted code of world law and guaranteed by an effective world police force, has long been a human aspiration. This dream is based upon the very reasonable idea of projecting the stability and orderliness of a well-governed State onto the relations between nations.

In the history of most nation-States, there came a time when the feuding of a few powerful interests or personages, in disregard of the welfare of the majority, and the ensuing chaos and disaster, became intolerable. From this situation, there was the evolution in due course of a strong central authority, based on popular representation, a sound system of law and a reliable police force. In our world, we reached a similarly intolerable situation many years ago and have twice in this century paid a terrible price for having failed to draw the necessary conclusions.

Most sensible people now agree that some reliable system of ensuring world peace is essential. But, as in most situations involving great and conflicting interests and very large numbers of people, there is all the difference in the world between the need and the practical fulfilment of the need. That fulfilment will be a long and complicated process, requiring a degree of confidence and understanding which we have not yet established in our world.

Few would deny that, if we are to look forward with confidence to the future, we have to take a great step forward in regulating the relations of nations and produce workable institutions for that purpose. One should not, however, underestimate the difficulties of such a step or the inevitable risks which attend it.

Nations and Governments, taking a great step forward, face imponderables and unknown dangers which no research or scientific test can resolve, for these unforeseeable events will be the result of the actions, reactions and interactions or hundreds of millions of human beings, and the human mind and human behaviour are still perhaps the most mysterious and awe-inspiring force in our world. Statesmen are wise, therefore, to view the future with caution and to examine proposals for fundamental change with more than usual care.

While we are making this step forward towards a new world order, we need guarantees, we need moderating influences and we need some commonly operated and accepted agency to share the risks and make the necessary tests and experiments, and even mistakes. Certainly we need an agency through which the necessary confidence and contact among nations can be built up and maintained. The United Nations is the nearest thing we have to such an agency, and I believe that it is beginning to play an important role of the kind I have just described.

It is no doubt true that there are certain great problems, such as the struggle between the greatest powers and the related problem of disarmament, which may be with us for a long time and which, perhaps, cannot be tackled head-on by the United Nations. We must, of course, do everything that we can to avoid adding fuel to the great power struggle.

There are, however, a large number of important problems and situations which *can* usefully be tackled and, if this is done, the greatest problems themselves can be isolated, if not resolved. We should, in this process, begin to develop the necessary institutions and practices by which, at a later stage, a more stable world order can be ensured.

I am going to talk today about one particular aspect of our problems, namely, peace-keeping and the use of international peace forces by the United Nations. Due partly to the lack of unanimity among the great powers ever since 1946, and partly to the radical change in the nature of war resulting from the development of atomic and hydrogen weapons, there has been a gradual change in thinking on questions of international security in the United Nations.

There has been a tacit transition from the concept of collective security, as set out in Chapter VII of the United Nations Charter, to a more realistic idea of peace-keeping. The idea that conventional military methods — or, to put it bluntly, war — can be used by or on behalf of the United Nations to counter aggression and secure the peace, seems now to be rather impractical.

There also has been a change in emphasis from the use of the military forces of the great powers, as contemplated in the Charter, to the use, in practice, of the military resources of the smaller powers, which has the advantage of not entangling United Nations actions in the antagonisms of the cold war.

Although there has been one collective action under the aegis of the United Nations — Korea — and although in 1951 the Collective Measures Committee, set up by the General Assembly under the Uniting for Peace resolution, actually published in its report a list of units earmarked by

Member States for service with the United Nations in actions to counter aggression, actual developments have in practice been in a rather different direction.

The nature of these developments is sometimes confused, wittingly or unwittingly, by an attempt to relate them to the use of force to counter aggression by the Security Council provided for in Chapter VII of the Charter. In fact, the peace-keeping forces I am about to describe are of a very different kind and have little in common with the forces foreseen in Chapter VII, but their existence is not in conflict with Chapter VII. They are essentially *peace* and not fighting forces and they operate only with the consent of the parties directly concerned.

In this context, it is worth noting that *all* of the permanent members of the Security Council have, at one time or another in the past 15 years, voted in support of the creation of one or other of these forces, and that none of them has in any case gone further than to abstain from voting on them.

Since 1950, the United Nations has been called on to deal with a number of critical situations of varying urgency. The most urgent of these have been what are sometimes called "brush-fire wars", meaning, I take it, small conflagrations which, unless controlled, may all too easily ignite very much larger ones.

If we briefly look through the United Nations experience with this kind of operation, we can see that from small and informal beginnings a useful body of precedent and practice has grown up over the years of using military personnel of Member States on peace-keeping operations. In Greece in 1947, the United Nations Special Committee on the Balkans found that professional military officers were invaluable as an observer group in assessing the highly complicated and fluctuating situation. The Security Council itself set up an observer group of military officers in India and Pakistan to watch over the Kashmir question. This observer group, which was set up in 1948, is still operating.

A much larger use of military observers by the United Nations was made when, in July 1948, the first truce agreements in the Palestine war were supervised on the ground by some 700 United Nations military observers working under the United Nations Mediator and the Chief of Staff. This team developed into the United Nations Truce Supervision Organization after the armistice agreements between Israel and her Arab neighbours were concluded in the period from February to July 1949.

This organization of officers from many countries still plays a vital role in keeping the peace in the Middle East and in reporting on and dealing with incidents which, though small in themselves, might all too easily become the cause of far larger disturbances if not dealt with. Its indefatigable members in their white jeeps are now a familiar and welcome part of the Middle Eastern landscape.

A peace-keeping organization of a different nature made its appearance as a result of the Suez crisis of October 1956. Confronted with a situation of the utmost urgency in which two of the permanent members of the Security Council were directly involved, the General Assembly voted for the urgent creation of a United Nations force. This was essentially *not* a force designed actively to fight against aggression.

It went to Egypt with the express consent of the Egyptian Government and after the other parties concerned had agreed to a cease-fire. It was designed not to fight but rather to allow those involved to disengage without further disturbance. It allowed for the peaceful resolution of one of the most dangerous crises which had faced the world since the Second World War. It also, incidentally, allowed for the clearance by the United Nations of the Suez Canal, which had been blocked during the previous military action.

The United Nations Emergency Force in the Middle East has for six years watched over the borders of Israel with the United Arab Republic in the Gaza Strip and through the Sinai Desert. It also watches over the access to the Gulf of Aqaba and to the Israeli port of Elath. What was once a most troubled and terrorized frontier has become peaceful and prosperous on both sides, and the very presence of the United Nations Force is both an insurance against a resumption of trouble and a good excuse not to engage in it. It presents us with one serious problem. To maintain an army of over 5,000 men costs money, but at present the parties concerned have no wish to see it removed.

In 1958 another very tense situation, with quite different origins, occurred in Lebanon. After the success of UNEF, there were suggestions in many quarters that another United Nations force should be collected and dispatched to that country. Here, however, the problem, though aggravated by external factors, was essentially a domestic one.

The Security Council therefore set up a three-man observer group and left the Secretary-General considerable latitude as to the methods to be employed to make this group effective in watching over the possibilities of infiltration from outside. A highly mobile group of 600 officers was quickly organized to keep watch from ground and air, while the crisis itself was resolved by negotiation and discussion. By the end of 1958, it was possible to withdraw the United Nations Observer Group from the Lebanon altogether.

The greatest and most complex challenge to the United Nations in the peacekeeping field arose a few days after the Congo gained its independence from Belgium on 30 June 1960. The general proportions of this problem are sometimes obscured by a wealth of dramatic detail and are worth restating. Harassed by mutiny, lawlessness and the collapse of public order and services from within, and afflicted by foreign military intervention as well as by ominous threats of other forms of interference from without, the new Government of the Congo appealed to the United Nations for help.

The Security Council committed the United Nations to respond to this appeal and thus made the Organization not only the guarantor of law and order and the protector of the Congo against external interference from any source, but also the adviser and helper of a newly independent State which had had virtually no preparation for its independence.

By filling, in the space of a few hours, the very dangerous vacuum which existed in the Congo in July 1960, the urgent danger of a confrontation of the great powers in the heart of Africa was avoided and the territorial integrity of the Congo preserved. The new leaders of the Congo have been given at least a short breathing-spell in which to find their feet. Despite its shortcomings, which must be judged in the light of the fearsome complexity of the problem, the United Nations Operation in the Congo is, in my opinion, a promising and encouraging experiment in international responsibility and action.

The blue helmets of the United Nations Force are known throughout the Congo as the symbol of security. Its soldiers have given protection at one time or another in the last three years to almost every Congolese public figure and almost every group, both African and non-African, when danger and violence threatened them. It is worth noting that, now that the withdrawal of the United Nations Force in the Congo is in sight, the deepest regret, and even alarm, is expressed by the very groups who used to be its most hostile critics and detractors.

In the Force, soldiers from other African countries work side by side in this vast tropical country with those from farther away. Their loyalty to the United Nations, their team spirit and comradeship have been an inspiration to all those who value the peace-keeping role of the United Nations.

I will end my catalogue with two more operations, one of which has already been successfully concluded, and which also involved an unprecedented role for the United Nations. I would like to refer first to the transfer of West Irian from Dutch rule, through a temporary period of United Nations executive authority, backed by a United Nations Security Force, to the administration of Indonesia. This entire operation has taken place with the agreement of the parties concerned, and in consultation with them.

The second is the dispatch to Yemen of an observer team as a basis for the disengagement of the United Arab Republic and Saudi Arabia from the affairs of Yemen. This operation will be paid for by the two parties concerned, and has been undertaken at their request and that of the Government of Yemen.

Although these are peace forces, service in them is hard and can be dangerous. In the Middle East, the United Nations has registered casualties not only from accidents and disease, but from mines. Both there and in

West Irian, as also in Yemen, the terrain and the climate are inhospitable. In the Congo, we have had, unfortunately, serious casualties from unwanted fighting as well as from other causes, and I very much hope that we shall have no more.

I have only mentioned here the peace-keeping activities which have involved the use, in one way or another, of military personnel. If I were to mention the many other tense situations in which the United Nations, and my office in particular, have been used as a meeting-ground and as an instrument for mediation and peaceful settlement, the list would be much longer.

To sum up, we have now had experience of three major peace-keeping forces and a variety of military observer and truce supervisory operations. Each of the three forces has been different in composition, nature and task, but they have shared certain common characteristics.

All three were improvised and called into the field at very short notice; all three were severely limited in their right to use force; all three were designed solely for the maintenance of peace and not for fighting in the military sense; all three were recruited from the smaller powers and with special reference to their acceptability in the area in which they were to serve; all three operated with the express consent and co-operation of the States or territories where they were stationed, as well as of any other parties directly concerned in the situation; and all three were under the direction and control of the Secretary-General acting on behalf of the organs of the United Nations.

These facts may now seem commonplace; it is a measure of the progress that has been made that even ten years ago they would have seemed very unusual.

By the standards of an efficient national military establishment, these forces have considerable disadvantages. Obviously, a force put together only after the emergency with which it is to deal is in full swing, will inevitably have some shortcomings. There is difficulty in recruiting at very short notice exactly the right kind of units for the work in hand, and in operating a force whose units and officers meet each other for the first time in the midst of a delicate operation. There are differences not only of language and tradition but of training, equipment and staff procedures. There are differences in pay and emoluments which, if not handled carefully, can cause considerable problems of discipline and morale. Staff-work and command are especially difficult where every decision has important political implications.

Although these contingents from Member States are under the operational control of the United Nations, disciplinary powers are still vested in the national authorities and this could be, although in fact it never has been, the cause of very serious difficulties for the United Nations Force Commander and for the Secretary-General.

The fact that the military establishments of the permanent members of the Security Council cannot be used cuts us off from the most obvious sources of equipment and personnel. The improvised nature of these operations also gives rise to various problems of logistics.

In our experience, these difficulties, which are inherent in the pioneering nature of these operations, have been offset by the enthusiastic co-operation of Member States and by the spirit and comprehension of the officers and men of the contingents which have made up the United Nations forces. It is an encouraging thought that in the military establishments of some 30 or more countries in the world there are now large numbers of officers and men who have served the United Nations with distinction in one or other of these operations and have added thereby a new dimension to their military experience.

The improvised approach also makes it possible on each occasion to make up the United Nations force from the countries which are, politically and in other ways, most suitable for the operation in hand, and at least the United Nations is not afflicted with the age-old problem of having on its hands a standing army with nothing to do.

In my opinion, a permanent United Nations force is not a practical proposition at the present time. I know that many serious people in many countries are enthusiastic about the idea, and I welcome their enthusiasm and the thought they are putting into the evolution of the institution which will eventually and surely emerge. Many difficulties still stand in the way of its evolution.

Personally, I have no doubt that the world should eventually have an international police force which will be accepted as an integral and essential part of life in the same way as national police forces are accepted. Meanwhile, we must be sure that developments are in the right direction and that we can also meet critical situations as and when they occur.

There are a number of reasons why it seems to me that the establishment of a permanent United Nations force would be premature at the present time. I doubt whether many Governments in the world would yet be prepared to accept the political implications of such an institution and, in the light of our current experience with financial problems, I am sure that they would have very serious difficulties in accepting the financial implications.

I believe that we need a number of parallel developments before we can evolve such an institution. We have to go further along the road of codification and acceptance of a workable body of international law. We have to develop a more sophisticated public opinion in the world, which can accept the transition from predominantly national thinking to international thinking.

We shall have to develop a deeper faith in international institutions as such, and a greater confidence in the possibility of a United Nations civil service whose international loyalty and objectivity are generally accepted and above suspicion. We shall have to improve the method of financing international organization. Until these conditions are met, a permanent United Nations force may not be a practical proposition.

But we have already shown that, when the situation demands it, it is possible to use the soldiers of many countries for objectives which are not national ones and that the soldiers respond magnificently to this new challenge. We have also seen that, when the situation is serious enough, Governments are prepared to waive certain of the attributes of national sovereignty in the interest of keeping the peace through the United Nations. We have demonstrated that a loyalty to international service can exist side by side with legitimate national pride.

And, perhaps most important of all, we have shown that there *can* be a practical alternative to the deadly ultimate struggle and that it is an alternative which brings out the good and generous qualities in men rather than their destructive and selfish qualities.

Although it is perhaps too early, for the reasons I have already given, to consider the establishment of a permanent United Nations force, I believe there are a number of measures which could be taken even now to improve on our present capacity for meeting dangerous situations. It would be extremely desirable, for example, if countries would, in their national military planning, make provision for suitable units which could be made available at short notice for United Nations service and thereby decrease the degree of improvisation necessary in an emergency.

I take this opportunity publicly to welcome and express my appreciation for the efforts of the Scandinavian countries in this direction. Denmark, Norway and Sweden have for some time now engaged in joint planning of a stand-by force comprising various essential components to be put at the disposal of the United Nations when necessary. It would be a very welcome development if other countries would consider following the lead of the Scandinavian countries in this matter.

At present, the activities of the United Nations are overshadowed by a very serious financial crisis, a crisis which stems directly from the costs of the special peace-keeping operations in the Middle East and the Congo and from the failure of some Members to pay their assessments for those operations. Although the sums of money involved are small in comparison to the sums spent by many countries on military budgets, they do, nonetheless, present a very serious financial and political challenge to the stability of the United Nations.

The United Nations is the sum of all its Members and, to develop in the right direction, it must maintain this global character. On the other hand, I am convinced that the Organization must maintain and develop its active role in keeping the peace. I therefore view with the gravest concern the prolongation of the financial crisis of the United Nations with its very serious political overtones, and I trust that we may see a solution of the problem before too long.

I am concerned at this financial crisis more particularly because I see, in the long run, no acceptable alternative method of keeping peace in the world to the steady and sound development of the peace-keeping functions of the United Nations. It is no longer possible to think rationally in terms of countering aggression or keeping the peace by the use of the ultimate weapons.

However improvised and fumbling the United Nations approach may be, we have to develop it to deal with the sudden antagonisms and dangers of our world, until we can evolve more permanent institutions. There has been already a great advance in the world towards co-operation, mutual responsibility and common interest. I have described some of the pioneering co-operative efforts made by the United Nations to keep the peace.

I believe that these efforts constitute vital steps towards a more mature, more acceptable, and more balanced world order. We must have the confidence and the means to sustain them and the determination to develop out of them a reliable and workable system for the future.

I am a firm believer in the organic development of institutions. I also firmly believe that, if the United Nations is to justify the hopes of its founders and of the peoples of the world, it must develop into an active and effective agency for peace and international conciliation by responding to the challenges which face it. May we have the courage, the faith, and the wisdom to make it so.

UNITED NATIONS EMERGENCY FORCE

*Summary study of the experience derived from
the establishment and operation of the force.
"Concluding Observations and Principles"
from the Report of the Secretary-General,*

DAG HAMMARSKJÖLD

A. OBSERVATIONS

148. In the preceding pages of this report a summary has been given of
the experience of the United Nations derived from the establishment and
operation of the United Nations Emergency Force. In advance of the conclusions, certain observations are called for regarding the specific circumstances in which the experience with UNEF has been gained, since those
circumstances definitely limit any detailed application of that experience
to the general problem of United Nations operations of this character. It
is useful, in this context, also to note and compare the subsequent experience with United Nations operations in relation to Lebanon and Jordan.

149. UNEF was brought into being to meet a particular situation in which
a United Nations force could be interposed between regular, national
military forces which were subject to a cease-fire agreed to by the opposing
parties. UNEF has continued to function along the "dividing line" between the national forces. It follows that in UNEF there has never been
any need for rights and responsibilities other than those necessary for such
an interposed force under cease-fire conditions. The Force was not used in
any way to enforce withdrawals but, in the successive stages of the withdrawals, followed the withdrawing troops to the "dividing line" of each
stage. It is also to be noted that the Force has functioned under a clear-cut
mandate which has entirely detached it from involvement in any internal
or local problems, and also has enabled it to maintain its neutrality in
relation to international political issues. The fact that UNEF was designed
to meet the needs of this specific situation largely determined its military

UN Document A/3943, October 9, 1958.

components, geographical composition, deployment and status, and also its effectiveness.

150. A further factor of significance in the evaluation of the UNEF experience is that in Gaza the Force is in an area having special status under the Armistice Agreement. In Gaza and elsewhere in its area of operations, UNEF has been able to function without any question arising of its presence infringing upon sovereign rights, on the basis that, at the invitation of the Egyptian Government and in accordance with the decision of the General Assembly, the United Nations assists in maintaining quiet on the Armistice Demarcation Line around the Gaza Strip and along the international line to the south. The Government of Egypt has co-operated by taking necessary steps to facilitate the functioning of UNEF in the Gaza area. The same is true of the position of the Egyptian Government in keeping its limited military units in the Sinai Peninsula away from the area in which the UNEF chiefly functions.

151. Obviously, some of the above-mentioned circumstances are of such a nature that it could not reasonably be expected that they would often be duplicated elsewhere. Nor can it be assumed that they provide a sufficient basis to warrant indiscriminate projection of the UNEF experience in planning for future United Nations operations of this kind. Indeed, the more recent experiences in Lebanon and Jordan serve only to emphasize the uniqueness of the UNEF setting, which, in part at least, explains the success of this pioneer venture. Neither in Lebanon nor in Jordan would it have been possible to interpose a United Nations force between conflicting parties. Nor would it have been possible in either of those situations to preserve a natural distinction between the presence and functions in various areas of any United Nations force and the presence and functions of government troops. In Lebanon, it is unlikely that a United Nations force could have operated without soon becoming a party to the internal conflicts among nationals of the country. In Jordan, the presence of a United Nations force has been regarded by the Government as difficult to reconcile with its own exercise of full sovereignty over the people and territory of the country. United Nations experience with these three Middle East operations justifies the assumption that, in each new conflict situation in which the United Nations might be called upon to intervene with military personnel, the nature of the actual organization required and its paramilitary aspects would be determined by the particular needs of the situation and could not, therefore, be anticipated in advance. Thus, for example, standby arrangements for a force designed for a UNEF-type operation would not have been of practical value in either of the situations in Lebanon or Jordan, where conditions required an approach in all relevant aspects quite different from that employed in UNEF.

152. The foregoing leads to the obvious conclusion that, in considering general stand-by arrangements for United Nations operations of the kind

d in this report, a course should be followed which would afford
‗‗‗‗erable degree of flexibility in approaching the varying needs that
may arise. This could be achieved if stand-by arrangements were to consist
of an approval of those general conclusions regarding principles which can
be reached in the light of the UNEF experience, and which would provide
a setting within which, with the necessary variations of approach, personnel in units or otherwise could be recruited and an operation organized
without delay and with full adjustment to the specific situation requiring
the action.

153. Further support for the position here taken is found in that the type
and rank of military personnel required, the need for specialists and for
supporting units, as well as the vehicle and equipment demands, as experience has shown, also vary so much from case to case that more far-reaching
and firm arrangements — as, for example, the maintenance of a nucleus
United Nations force of the type generally envisaged — would be without
great practical value and certainly would not warrant the substantial sacrifices involved. By way of illustration of this point UNEF has been able to
use enlisted men with short military experience under the command of
experienced officers; the recruitment of personnel for the United Nations
Observation Group in Lebanon has been limited largely to officers, who,
however, with few exceptions, did not have to be rigorously screened for
the mission; while the arrangements in relation to Jordan may involve, if
any, only a very limited number of military personnel, all of officer rank
but individually and carefully chosen for the purpose. Similar differences
are apparent as regards the need for matériel with UNEF being adequately
served by, in military calculations, a quite modest number of aircraft and
vehicles, while UNOGIL has had to operate with a considerably higher
ratio of planes and vehicles to the men involved, because of the specific
tasks with which it has been entrusted.

B. BASIC PRINCIPLES

154. In view of the impossibility of determining beforehand the specific
form of a United Nations presence of the type considered in this report,
which would be necessary to meet adequately the requirements of a given
situation, a broad decision by the General Assembly should attempt to do
no more than endorse certain basic principles and rules which would provide an adaptable framework for later operations that might be found necessary. In a practical sense, it is not feasible in advance of a known situation
to do more than to provide for some helpful stand-by arrangements for a
force or similar forms of a United Nations presence. In the following
paragraphs, certain principles and rules are laid down in the light of the
experience gathered in the past years, which, if they were to meet with the
approval of the General Assembly, would provide a continuing basis on
which useful contacts in a stand-by context might be established with

interested Governments, with the aim of being prepared for any requests which might arise from future decisions by the Assembly on a force or similar arrangement to deal with a specific case.

155. As the arrangements discussed in this report do not cover the type of force envisaged under Chapter VII of the Charter, it follows from international law and the Charter that the United Nations cannot undertake to implement them by stationing units on the territory of a Member State without the consent of the Government concerned. It similarly follows from the Charter that the consent of a Member nation is necessary for the United Nations to use its military personnel or matériel. These basic rules have been observed in the recent United Nations operations in the Middle East. They naturally hold valid for all similar operations in the future.

156. The fact that a United Nations operation of the type envisaged requires the consent of the Government on whose territory it takes place creates a problem, as it is normally difficult for the United Nations to engage in such an operation without guarantees against unilateral actions by the host Government which might put the United Nations in a questionable position, either administratively or in relation to contributing Governments.

157. The formula employed in relation to the Government of Egypt for UNEF seems, in the light of experience, to provide an adequate solution to this problem. The Government of Egypt declared that, when exercising its sovereign right with regard to the presence of the Force, it would be guided by good faith in the interpretation of the purposes of the Force. This declaration was balanced by a declaration by the United Nations to the effect that the maintenance of the Force by the United Nations would be determined by similar good faith in the interpretation of the purposes.

158. The consequence of such a bilateral declaration is that, were either side to act unilaterally in refusing continued presence or deciding on withdrawal, and were the other side to find that such action was contrary to a good faith interpretation of the purposes of the operation, an exchange of views would be called for towards harmonizing the positions. This does not imply any infringement on the sovereign right of the host Government, nor any restriction of the right of the United Nations to decide on termination of its own operation whenever it might see fit to do so. But it does mean a mutual recognition of the fact that the operation, being based on collaboration between the host Government and the United Nations, should be carried on in forms natural to such collaboration, and especially so with regard to the questions of presence and maintenance.

159. It is unlikely that any Government in the future would be willing to go beyond the declaration of the Government of Egypt with regard to UNEF. Nor, in my view, should the United Nations commit itself beyond the point established for UNEF in relation to the Government of Egypt. In these circumstances, I consider it reasonable to regard the formula

mentioned in paragraph 158 above as a valid basis for future arrangements of a similar kind.

160. Another point of principle which arises in relation to the question of consent refers to the composition of United Nations military elements stationed on the territory of a Member country. While the United Nations must reserve for itself the authority to decide on the composition of such elements, it is obvious that the host country, in giving its consent, cannot be indifferent to the composition of those elements. In order to limit the scope of possible difference of opinion, the United Nations in recent operations has followed two principles: not to include units from any of the permanent members of the Security Council; and not to include units from any country which, because of its geographical position or for other reasons, might be considered as possibly having a special interest in the situation which has called for the operation. I believe that these two principles also should be considered as essential to any stand-by arrangements.

161. Given the two principles mentioned in paragraph 160, in actual practice the area within which conflicting views may be expressed will in all probability be so reduced normally as to facilitate the harmonizing of the rights of the United Nations with the interests of the host country. It would seem desirable to accept the formula applied in the case of UNEF, which is to the effect that, while it is for the United Nations alone to decide on the composition of military elements sent to a country, the United Nations should, in deciding on composition, take fully into account the viewpoint of the host Government as one of the most serious factors which should guide the recruitment of the personnel. Usually, this is likely to mean that serious objections by the host country against participation by a specific contributing country in the United Nations operation will determine the action of the Organization. However, were the United Nations for good reasons to find that course inadvisable, it would remain free to pursue its own line, and any resulting conflict would have to be resolved on a political rather than on a legal basis. I would recommend that the basis thus laid in the case of UNEF be considered as the formula on composition applicable to similar operations in the future.

162. The principles indicated in the four points discussed above (paragraphs 155-161 inclusive) were either established by the General Assembly itself, elaborated in practice or in negotiations with the Government of Egypt. They have served as the basis for a status Agreement which applies to the United Nations personnel in the Force in Egypt. In its entirety, this status Agreement has stood up well to the test of experience. Its basic principles should be embodied in similar agreements in the future, and their recognition, therefore, would seem necessarily to form part of any stand-by arrangements for a force. The Agreement regarding the presence of UNOGIL in Lebanon, although much less elaborate because of the modest size of the operation and the fact that normal immunity rules

could be applied to the bulk of the personnel, also reflects the basic principles I have in mind.

163. The most important principle in the status Agreement ensures that UNEF personnel, when involved in criminal actions, come under the jurisdiction of the criminal courts of their home countries. The establishment of this principle for UNEF, in relation to Egypt, has set a most valuable precedent. Experience shows that this principle is essential to the successful recruitment by the United Nations of military personnel not otherwise under immunity rules, from its Member countries. The position established for UNEF should be maintained in future arrangements.

164. Another principle involved in the UNEF status Agreement, and which should be retained, is that the United Nations activity should have freedom of movement within its area of operations and all such facilities regarding access to that area and communications as are necessary for successful completion of the task. This also obviously involves certain rights of over-flight over the territory of the host country. These principles have been maintained in the case of UNOGIL. Their application requires an agreement on what is to be considered as the area of operations and as to what facilities of access and communications are to be considered necessary. On the assumption that, like UNEF, any similar United Nations operation in the future would be of assistance to the nation on whose territory it is stationed, it is not to be expected that the necessary process of agreement will give rise to any serious complications in the interpretation of the principle.

165. Apart from the principles thus established in negotiated agreements or formal decisions, a series of basic rules has been developed in practice. Some of these rules would appear to merit general application. This is true especially of the precept that authority granted to the United Nations group cannot be exercised within a given territory either in competition with representatives of the host Government or in co-operation with them on the basis of any joint operation. Thus, a United Nations operation must be separate and distinct from activities by national authorities. UNEF experience indicates how this rule may apply in practice. A right of detention which normally would be exercised only by local authorities is extended to UNEF units. However, this is so only within a limited area where the local authorities voluntarily abstain from exercising similar rights, whether alone or in collaboration with the United Nations. Were the underlying principle of this example not to be applied, United Nations units might run the risk of getting involved in differences with the local authorities or public or in internal conflicts which would be highly detrimental to the effectiveness of the operation and to the relations between the United Nations and the host Government.

166. A rule closely related to the one last-mentioned, and reflecting a basic Charter principle, precludes the employment of United Nations elements

in situations of an essentially internal nature. As a matter of course, the United Nations personnel cannot be permitted in any sense to be a party to internal conflicts. Their role must be limited to external aspects of the political situation as, for example, infiltration or other activities affecting international boundaries.

167. Even in the case of UNEF, where the United Nations itself had taken a stand on decisive elements in the situation which gave rise to the creation of the Force, it was explicitly stated that the Force should not be used to enforce any specific political solution of pending problems or to influence the political balance decisive to such a solution. This precept clearly imposes a serious limitation on the possible use of United Nations elements, were it to be given general application to them whenever they are not created under Chapter VII of the Charter. However, I believe its acceptance to be necessary, if the United Nations is to be in a position to draw on Member countries for contributions in men and matériel to United Nations operations of this kind.

168. Military personnel employed by the United Nations in paramilitary operations are, of course, not under the same formal obligations in relation to the Organization as staff members of the Secretariat. However, the position must be maintained that the basic rules of the United Nations for international service are applicable also to such personnel, particularly as regards full loyalty to the aims of the Organization and to abstention from acts in relation to their country of origin or to other countries which might deprive the operation of its international character and create a situation of dual loyalty. The observance of this rule is not only vital for good relations with the host country, it is also to the benefit of the contributing countries concerned, as any other attitude might involve them in responsibilities which would be undesirable in the light of the national policies pursued.

169. In setting up UNEF, the General Assembly appointed a Commander of the Force with the position of an international civil servant responsible for discharge of his task to the Assembly, but administratively integrated with the United Nations organization, and under instructions from the Secretary-General on the basis of the executive authority for the operation vested in him by the Assembly.

170. A somewhat different procedure was followed in the case of UNOGIL, where the Security Council delegated to the Secretary-General the responsibility for constituting the Observation Group. However, basically the same principle employed in UNEF is applied to UNOGIL, for the Group is responsible for the conduct of its business to the Security Council, while administratively it is under the Secretary-General, who is charged with its organization. A basically similar pattern finds reflection also in the arrangements being made by the United Nations in relation to Jordan.

171. The innovation represented by the constitutional pattern thus followed in recent United Nations field operations has, in experience, proved to be highly practical and, especially, politically of decisive importance, as it has provided for an integration giving the operation all the advantages of administrative co-ordination with the Secretariat and of the fully internationalized status of the Secretariat. As pointed out in my "Second and final report on the Emergency Force", on which the General Assembly based its decision to organize the Force, the appointment by the General Assembly of a Commander determined the legal status of the Force. The other arrangements, mentioned above, reflect the same basic concept.

172. In full recognition of the wide variety of forms which decisions on a United Nations operation may take in seeking to fit differing situations calling for such an operation, the underlying rule concerning command and authority which has been consistently applied in recent years, as set out above, should, in my view, be maintained for the future. Thus, a United Nations operation should always be under a leadership established by the General Assembly or the Security Council, or on the basis of delegated authority by the Secretary-General, so as to make it directly responsible to one of the main organs of the United Nations, while integrated with the Secretariat in an appropriate form.

173. Were soundings with Member Governments, based on the aforementioned legal and political principles and rules and on the regulations regarding financial responsibilities set out below, to show that a number of Governments in their planning would be willing to take into account the possibility of having to provide promptly — on an emergency basis, on specific appeal from the United Nations — men and matériel to a United Nations operation of the kind envisaged in this report, a question arises regarding the conditions under which such a desirable stand-by arrangement could be utilized.

174. Under the Charter, and under the "Uniting for Peace" resolution, a formal decision on a United Nations operation must be taken by the General Assembly or by the Security Council. It must be regarded as excluded that the right to take such a decision, in any general terms, could properly be considered as delegated to the Secretary-General. Short of an explicit decision by the General Assembly or the Security Council with a specific authorization, the Secretary-General, thus, cannot be considered as entitled to appeal to a Member nation for military personnel to be dispatched to another Member country in a United Nations operation.

175. The terms of the delegation in each operation thus far have set the limit of the Secretary-General's authority. Thus, for example, as apparent from the description of the new body, the decision relating to UNEF, which was to be implemented by the Secretary-General, qualified the operation as being one of a paramilitary nature, while the absence of an explicit authorization for the Force to take offensive action excluded the

organization by the Secretary-General of units for such action, and consequently, the units generally were equipped only with weapons necessary for self-defence. Had there been any remaining doubts in this respect, the legal basis on which the General Assembly took its decision would have made this limitation clear.

176. Similarly, the Security Council decision on the United Nations Observation Group in Lebanon qualified the kind of operation that the Secretary-General was authorized to organize by the very name given to the unit to be established. That name excluded the creation of a para-military force and imposed, in fact, such limitations on the operation as to call for great restraint regarding the arming of the unit and its right of self-defence.

177. The General Assembly decision concerning the arrangements in relation to Jordan was in such broad terms as to provide possibilities for the organization of any kind of operation, short of one possible only under Chapter VII. In this case, however, as in the case of UNEF, a certain incompleteness in the terminology of the decision was covered by the conclusions following from the legal basis on which the decision was taken.

178. Confirmation by the Assembly of the interpretation of the question of authority given above would be useful. This interpretation would signify that a Member country, in deciding upon a contribution of men or matériel to a United Nations operation on the basis of such stand-by understandings as may have been reached, could rely upon the explicit terms of the executive authority delegated to the Secretary-General in determining the use which could be made of the units provided; it being understood, naturally, that in the types of operation with which this report is concerned this could never include combat activity. There will always remain, of course, a certain margin of freedom for judgement, as, for example, on the extent and nature of the arming of the units and of their right to self-defence. In the case of UNEF, such questions of interpretation have been solved in consultation with the contributing Governments and with the host Government. The Advisory Committee on UNEF set up by the General Assembly has in this context proved to be of especially great assistance.

179. In the preceding paragraph I have touched upon the extent to which a right of self-defence may be exercised by United Nations units of the type envisaged. It should be generally recognized that such a right exists. However, in certain cases this right should be exercised only under strictly defined conditions. A problem arises in this context because of the fact that a wide interpretation of the right of self-defence might well blur the distinction between operations of the character discussed in this report and combat operations, which would require a decision under Chapter VII of the Charter and an explicit, more far-reaching delegation of authority to the Secretary-General than would be required for any of the operations

discussed here. A reasonable definition seems to have been established in the case of UNEF, where the rule is applied that men engaged in the operation may never take the initiative in the use of armed force, but are entitled to respond with force to an attack with arms, including attempts to use force to make them withdraw from positions which they occupy under orders from the Commander, acting under the authority of the Assembly and within the scope of its resolutions. The basic element involved is clearly the prohibition against any initiative in the use of armed force. This definition of the limit between self-defence, as permissible for United Nations elements of the kind discussed, and offensive action, which is beyond the competence of such elements, should be approved for future guidance.

180. The clear delimitation of the right to use force which has been set out above as a basic rule for the type of operations discussed in this report should dissipate any objections against the suggested stand-by arrangements which would be based on the view that they go beyond the measures which the Charter permits the General Assembly to take and infringe upon prerogatives of the Security Council. The principles outlined above put UNEF on the same level, constitutionally, as UNOGIL, for example, qualifying it so as to make it an instrument of efforts at mediation and conciliation. It may be noted in this context that UNOGIL has not given rise to any constitutional objections; the fact that the Group was created by the Security Council is in this case irrelevant, as the Council acted entirely within the limits of Chapter VI of the Charter, and as a similar action obviously could have been taken by the General Assembly under Article 22.

181. In the case of UNEF, the General Assembly decided to organize an Advisory Committee under the chairmanship of the Secretary-General, to assist the operation. In practice, this arrangement has proved highly useful. In principle, it should be accepted as a precedent for the future. Extensive operations with serious political implications, regarding which, for practical reasons, executive authority would need to be delegated to the Secretary-General, require close collaboration with authorized representatives of the General Assembly. However, it would be undesirable for this collaboration to be given such a form as to lead to divided responsibilities or to diminished efficiency in the operation. The method chosen by the General Assembly in the case of UNEF seems the most appropriate one if such risks are to be avoided. The Committee is fully informed by the Secretary-General and his associates. There is a free exchange of views in closed meetings where advice can be sought and given. But ultimate decisions rest with the Secretary-General, as the executive in charge of carrying out the operation. Dissenting views are not registered by vote, but are put on record in the proceedings of the Committee. It is useful for contributing countries to be represented on such an advisory committee, but if the contributing States are numerous the size of the committee

might become so large as to make it ineffective. On the other hand, it is obviously excluded that any party to the conflict should be a member. Normally, I believe that the same basic rule regarding permanent members of the Security Council which has been applied to units and men in the recent operations should be applied also in the selection of members for a relevant advisory committee.

182. In the administration of UNEF at Headquarters, certain special arrangements were made on an ad hoc basis to provide expert military guidance. Thus, a senior Military Adviser and three officer assistants were attached to the Executive Office as consultants. The Military Adviser, and the Under-Secretary representing the Secretary-General on current matters relating to the Force, were assisted by a group of military representatives from the countries providing contingents, sitting as an informal military advisory committee. Once the operation was firmly established, these arrangements could be and were reduced and simplified, but in the initial stage they proved to be of great value organizationally and also as an added means of maintaining close contacts with contributing Governments.

183. A parallel arrangement was that by which, for a period, a personal representative of the Secretary-General was stationed in the capital of the host country as a liaison officer directly in contact with the Government.

184. In view of the very great diversity likely to characterize the experience in practice of using United Nations units within the scope of this report, it is impossible to enunciate any principles for organizational arrangements at Headquarters or in the host country that should be made in anticipation of each case. There will always be developed, as a matter of course, the forms of liaison for which there will be a clear need.

185. The question, however, is of interest in this context, as it has a bearing on the problem whether or not such stand-by arrangements as those for which the principles and rules set out here would provide, would call for any kind of nucleus of military experts at United Nations Headquarters. At some stage, a standing group of a few military experts might be useful in order to keep under review such arrangements as may be made by Member Governments in preparation for meeting possible appeals for an operation. I would consider it premature, however, to take any decision of this kind at the present time, since the foreseeable tasks that might evolve for the Secretariat do not go beyond what it is now able to cope with unassisted by such special measures. Were a more far-reaching understanding than I have indicated to prove possible, the matter obviously would have to be reconsidered and submitted again in appropriate form to the General Assembly, which then might consider the organizational problem. Pending such a development later, the present working rule, in my view, should be that the Secretariat, while undertaking the soundings mentioned above and the necessary continuing contacts with the Governments, should not take any measures beyond keeping the situation under

constant review, so as to be able to act expeditiously, if a decision by the General Assembly or the Security Council should call for prompt action.

186. It may be reiterated in passing that the United Nations Secretariat has by now had extensive experience in establishing and maintaining United Nations operations involving military personnel and, without improvising or augmenting unduly, can quickly provide any operation of that nature with efficient communications service in the field and with Headquarters, with transportation and vehicles for local transport, with well-tested administrative and accounting systems and expert personnel to man them, and with effective procurement and security arrangements.

187. The financial obligations of Member countries to the United Nations are of two kinds. On the one hand, there are such obligations as are covered by the scale of contributions established by the General Assembly; on the other, there are certain voluntary commitments outside that scale, such as United Nations technical assistance or the United Nations Children's Fund. While, of course, contributions from individual Member nations to United Nations units for field operations may always be made on a voluntary basis, thus being lifted outside the scale of contributions, the principle must be that, as flowing from decisions of one of the main organs of the United Nations, such contributions should be subordinated to the normal financial rules. Any other principle would seriously limit the possibility of recruiting the necessary personnel from the most appropriate countries and achieving the best geographical distribution, since most countries are not likely to be in a position to assume the additional financial burdens involved and since, unless otherwise agreed, all contributing countries should be treated on the same basis.

188. In the initial stages of UNEF, Member nations assumed certain additional burdens beyond those which would follow from the application of normal rules governing contributions to the United Nations. Later, financial relations were adjusted so as to be based on full compensation for extra and extraordinary costs, financed under the normal scale of contributions. The underlying rule is that a contributing country, by such action, should not be subjected to financial sacrifices beyond those obligations which would be incurred if it were not contributing directly to the operation. On the other hand, naturally, contributing countries should not shift to the United Nations any costs which, in any case they would have had to meet under their normal domestic policy.

189. I believe that, as part of the stand-by arrangements, it should be established that the costs for United Nations operations of the type in question, based on decisions of the General Assembly or the Security Council, should be allocated in accordance with the normal scale of contributions. The United Nations in this way should assume responsibility for all additional costs incurred by a contributing country because of its participation in the operation, on the basis of a cost assessment which, on

the other hand, would not transfer to the United Nations any costs which would otherwise have been incurred by a contributing Government under its regular national policy.

190. With relation to the men engaged in one of its operations, the United Nations should naturally assume all responsibilities necessary to safeguard the normal interest of those so employed. Thus, they should be fully compensated by the United Nations for any losses of earning power or social benefits which may be suffered because of their service with the United Nations. In view of the great variety of regulations applied by various countries, it is impossible to go beyond this general statement of principle; the details would have to be worked out with each contributing Government, as appropriate.

191. With relation to a host Government, it should be the rule that as the United Nations units are dispatched to the country in the interest and with the consent and co-operation of the host Government, that Government should provide all necessary facilities for the operation. This, in principle, should be done without any compensation, in case such facilities are in the possession of the host Government itself. Thus, for example, contributions of government services or government-owned property placed at the disposal of the United Nations for its operation should not be subject to compensation.

192. Concerning the claims of private citizens in the host country, the applicable rule is that the United Nations should pay compensation for the use of their property or services, whenever the host Government would have been obligated to pay for similar services or uses. The question whether the United Nations, in its turn, should be reimbursed by the host Government for such outlays would properly be settled through negotiation, in the light of the circumstances in each separate case.

193. The approach indicated in this chapter suggests a way in which the United Nations, within the limits of the Charter, may seek the most practical method of mustering and using, as necessary, the resources — both of nations and its own — required for operations involving military personnel which may be conceived in response to the needs of specific conflict situations. The national resources likely to be available for such purposes, if our limited experience is a gauge, are no doubt substantial, but they cannot now be calculated or even estimated, and even their availability at any particular time would probably be subject to considerable fluctuation, for political and other reasons. Formalizing the principles and rules outlined above, however, would afford a strengthened basis on which to expedite the mobilization of voluntary aid towards meeting urgent need. Their approval by the Assembly, thus clarifying and regularizing important legal and practical issues, would also ensure a more efficient use of any aid extended to the Organization, were it again to have to appeal to Member nations for such assistance.

SELECTED UN RESOLUTIONS ON

EMERGENCY FORCES

UN GENERAL ASSEMBLY RESOLUTIONS
ESTABLISHING UNEF, NOVEMBER, 1956

*(Resolutions adopted without reference to a committee.
Question considered by the Security Council at its
749th and 750th meetings, held on 30 October 1956.)*

RESOLUTION 997 (ES-I)

The General Assembly,

Noting the disregard on many occasions by parties to the Israel-Arab armistice agreements of 1949 of the terms of such agreements, and that the armed forces of Israel have penetrated deeply into Egyptian territory in violation of the General Armistice Agreement between Egypt and Israel of 24 February 1964,[1]

Noting that armed forces of France and the United Kingdom of Great Britain and Northern Ireland are conducting military operations against Egyptian territory,

Noting that traffic through the Suez Canal is now interrupted to the serious prejudice of many nations,

Expressing its grave concern over these developments,

1. *Urges* as a matter of priority that all parties now involved in hostilities in the area agree to an immediate cease-fire and, as part thereof, halt the movement of military forces and arms into the area;

2. *Urges* the parties to the armistice agreements promptly to withdraw all forces behind the armistice lines, to desist from raids across the armistice lines into neighboring territory, and to observe scrupulously the provisions of the armistice agreements;

3. *Recommends* that all Member States refrain from introducing military goods in the area of hostilities and in general refrain from any acts which would delay or prevent the implementation of the present resolution;

[1] *Official Records of the Security Council, Fourth Year, Special Supplement No. 3.*

4. *Urges* that, upon the cease-fire being effective, steps be taken to re-open the Suez Canal and restore secure freedom of navigation;

5. *Requests* the Secretary-General to observe and report promptly on the compliance with the present resolution to the Security Council and to the General Assembly, for such further action as they may deem appropriate in accordance with the Charter;

6. *Decides* to remain in emergency session pending compliance with the present resolution.

562nd plenary meeting,
2 November 1956.

RESOLUTION 998 (ES-I)

The General Assembly,

Bearing in mind the urgent necessity of facilitating compliance with its resolution 997 (ES-I) of 2 November 1956,

Requests, as a matter of priority, the Secretary-General to submit to it within forty-eight hours a plan for the setting up, with the consent of the nations concerned, of an emergency international United Nations Force to secure and supervise the cessation of hostilities in accordance with all the terms of the aforementioned resolution.

563rd plenary meeting,
4 November 1956.

RESOLUTION 999 (ES-I)

The General Assembly,

Noting with regret that not all the parties concerned have yet agreed to comply with the provisions of its resolution 997 (ES-I) of 2 November 1956,

Noting the special priority given in that resolution to an immediate cease-fire and, as part thereof, to the halting of the movement of military forces and arms into the area,

Noting further that the resolution urged the parties to the armistice agreements promptly to withdraw all forces behind the armistice lines, to desist from raids across the armistice lines into neighboring territory, and to observe scrupulously the provisions of the armistice agreements,

1. *Reaffirms* its resolution 997 (ES-I), and once again calls upon the parties immediately to comply with the provisions of the said resolution;

2. *Authorizes* the Secretary-General immediately to arrange with the parties concerned for the implementation of the cease-fire and the halting of the movement of military forces and arms into the area, and requests him to report compliance forthwith and, in any case, not later than twelve hours from the time of adoption of the present resolution;

3. *Requests* the Secretary-General, with the assistance of the Chief of Staff and the members of the United Nations Truce Supervision Organiza-

tion, to obtain compliance of the withdrawal of all forces behind the armistice lines;

4. *Decides* to meet again immediately on receipt of the Secretary-General's report referred to in paragraph 2 of the present resolution.

563rd plenary meeting,
4 November 1956.

RESOLUTION 1000 (ES-I)

The General Assembly,

Having requested the Secretary-General, in its resolution 998 (ES-I) of 4 November 1956, to submit to it a plan for an emergency international United Nations Force, for the purposes stated,

Noting with satisfaction the first report of the Secretary-General on the plan,[2] and having in mind particularly paragraph 4 of that report,

1. *Establishes* a United Nations Command for an emergency international Force to secure and supervise the cessation of hostilities in accordance with all the terms of General Assembly resolution 997 (ES-I) of 2 November 1956;

2. *Appoints*, on an emergency basis, the Chief of Staff of the United Nations Truce Supervision Organization, Major-General E. L. M. Burns, as Chief of the Command;

3. *Authorizes* the Chief of the Command immediately to recruit, from the observer corps of the United Nations Truce Supervision Organization, a limited number of officers who shall be nationals of countries other than those having permanent membership in the Security Council, and further authorizes him, in consultation with the Secretary-General, to undertake the recruitment directly, from various Member States other than the permanent members of the Security Council, of the additional number of officers needed;

4. *Invites* the Secretary-General to take such administrative measures as may be necessary for the prompt execution of the actions envisaged in the present resolution.

565th plenary meeting,
5 November 1956.

RESOLUTION 1001 (ES-I)

The General Assembly,

Recalling its resolution 997 (ES-I) of 2 November 1956 concerning the cease-fire, withdrawal of troops and other matters related to the military operations in Egyptian territory, as well as its resolution 998 (ES-I) of 4

---

[2] *Official Records of the General Assembly, First Emergency Special Session, Annexes,* agenda item 5, document A/3289.

November 1956 concerning the request to the Secretary-General to submit
a plan for an emergency international United Nations Force,

Having established by its resolution 1000 (ES-I) of 5 November 1956 a
United Nations Command for an emergency international Force, having
appointed the Chief of Staff of the United Nations Truce Supervision
Organization as Chief of the Command with authorization to him to begin
the recruitment of officers for the Command, and having invited the Secretary-General to take the administrative measures necessary for the prompt
execution of that resolution,

Noting with appreciation the second and final report of the Secretary-
General[3] on the plan for an emergency international United Nations Force
as requested in General Assembly resolution 998 (ES-I), and having examined that plan,

1. *Expresses its approval* of the guiding principles for the organization
and functioning of the emergency international United Nations Force as
expounded in paragraphs 6 to 9 of the Secretary-General's report;

2. *Concurs* in the definition of the functions of the Force as stated in
paragraph 12 of the Secretary-General's report;

3. *Invites* the Secretary-General to continue discussions with Governments of Member States concerning offers of participation in the Force,
toward the objective of its balanced composition;

4. *Requests* the Chief of the Command, in consultation with the Secretary-General as regards size and composition, to proceed forthwith with the
full organization of the Force;

5. *Approves provisionally* the basic rule concerning the financing of the
Force laid down in paragraph 15 of the Secretary-General's report;

6. *Establishes* an Advisory Committee composed of one representative
from each of the following countries: Brazil, Canada, Ceylon, Colombia,
India, Norway and Pakistan, and requests this Committee, whose Chair-
man shall be the Secretary-General, to undertake the development of those
aspects of the planning for the Force and its operation not already dealt
with by the General Assembly and which do not fall within the area of the
direct responsibility of the Chief of the Command;

7. *Authorizes* the Secretary-General to issue all regulations and instructions which may be essential to the effective functioning of the Force, following consultation with the Committee aforementioned, and to take all
other necessary administrative and executive action;

8. *Determines* that, following the fulfilment of the immediate responsibilities defined for it in operative paragraphs 6 and 7 above, the Advisory
Committee shall continue to assist the Secretary-General in the responsibilities falling to him under the present and other relevant resolutions;

9. *Decides* that the Advisory Committee, in the performance of its

[3] *Ibid.*, document A/3302.

duties, shall be empowered to request, through the usual procedures, the convening of the General Assembly and to report to the Assembly whenever matters arise which, in its opinion, are of such urgency and importance as to require consideration by the General Assembly itself;

10. *Requests* all Member States to afford assistance as necessary to the United Nations Command in the performance of its functions, including arrangements for passage to and from the area involved.

567th plenary meeting,
7 November 1956.

RESOLUTION 1002 (ES-I)

The General Assembly,

Recalling its resolutions 997 (ES-I) of 2 November 1956, 998 (ES-I) and 999 (ES-I) of 4 November 1956 and 1000 (ES-I) of 5 November 1956, adopted by overwhelming majorities,

Noting in particular that the General Assembly, by its resolution 1000 (ES-I), established a United Nations Command for an emergency international Force to secure and supervise the cessation of hostilities in accordance with all the terms of its resolution 997 (ES-I),

1. *Reaffirms* the above-mentioned resolutions;

2. *Calls once again upon* Israel immediately to withdraw all its forces behind the armistice lines established by the General Armistice Agreement between Egypt and Israel of 24 February 1949;[4]

3. *Calls once again upon* the United Kingdom and France immediately to withdraw all their forces from Egyptian territory, consistently with the above-mentioned resolutions;

4. *Urges* the Secretary-General to communicate the present resolution to the parties concerned, and requests him promptly to report to the General Assembly on the compliance with this resolution.

567th plenary meeting,
7 November 1956.

RESOLUTION 1003 (ES-I)

The General Assembly,

1. *Decides* to place on the provisional agenda of its eleventh regular session, as a matter of priority, the question on the agenda of its first emergency special session;

2. *Refers* to its eleventh regular session, for consideration, the records of the meetings and the documents of its first emergency special session;

3. *Decides* that, notwithstanding paragraph 1 above, the first emergency

[4] *Official Records of the Security Council, Fourth Year, Special Supplement No. 3.*

special session may continue to consider the question, if necessary, prior to the eleventh regular session of the Assembly.

572nd plenary meeting,
10 November 1956.

UN SECURITY COUNCIL RESOLUTION
ON THE CONGO, JULY 14, 1960

The Security Council,

Considering the report of the Secretary-General on a request for United Nations action in relation to the Republic of the Congo,

Considering the request for military assistance addressed to the Secretary-General by the President and the Prime Minister of the Republic of the Congo (document S/4382),

1. *Calls upon* the Government of Belgium to withdraw their troops from the territory of the Republic of the Congo;

2. *Decides* to authorize the Secretary-General to take the necessary steps, in consultation with the Government of the Republic of the Congo, to provide the Government with such military assistance, as may be necessary, until, through the efforts of the Congolese Government with the technical assistance of the United Nations, the national security forces may be able, in the opinion of the Government, to meet fully their tasks;

3. *Requests* the Secretary-General to report to the Security Council as appropirate.

The resolution was adopted by the following vote:

In favor: Argentina, Ceylon, Ecuador, Italy, Poland, Tunisia, USSR, United States—8.

Against: None.

Abstaining: China, France, United Kingdom—3.

UN SECURITY COUNCIL RESOLUTION
OF AUGUST 9, 1960, ON THE CONGO

The Security Council,

Recalling its resolution of July 22, 1960 (S/4405), *inter alia,* calling upon the Government of Belgium to implement speedily the Security Council resolution of July 14 (S/4387) on the withdrawal of their troops and authorizing the Secretary-General to take all necessary action to this effect,

Having noted the second report by the Secretary-General on the implementation of the aforesaid two resolutions and his statement before the Council,

Having considered the statements made by the representatives of Belgium and the Republic of the Congo to this Council at this meeting,

Noting with satisfaction the progress made by the United Nations in carrying out the Security Council resolutions in respect of the territory of the Republic of the Congo other than the Province of Katanga,

Noting however that the United Nations had been prevented from implementing the aforesaid resolutions in the Province of Katanga although it was ready, and in fact attempted, to do so,

Recognizing that the withdrawal of Belgian troops from the Province of Katanga will be a positive contribution to and essential for the proper implementation of the Security Council resolutions,

1. *Confirms* the authority given to the Secretary-General by the Security Council resolutions of July 14 and July 22, 1960, and requests him to continue to carry out the responsibility placed on him thereby;

2. *Calls upon* the Government of Belgium to withdraw immediately its troops from the Province of Katanga under speedy modalities determined by the Secretary-General and to assist in every possible way the implementation of the Council's resolutions;

3. *Declares* that the entry of the United Nations force into the Province of Katanga is necessary for the full implementation of this resolution;

4. *Reaffirms* that the United Nations force in the Congo will not be a party to or in any way intervene in or be used to influence the outcome of any internal conflict, constitutional or otherwise;

5. *Calls upon* all member states, in accordance with Articles 25 and 49 of the Charter, to accept and carry out the decisions of the Security Council and to afford mutual assistance in carrying out measures decided upon by the Security Council;

6. *Requests* the Secretary-General to implement this resolution and to report further to the Security Council as appropriate.

UN SECURITY COUNCIL RESOLUTIONS
OF FEBRUARY 21, 1961, ON THE CONGO

[A.]

The Security Council,

Having considered the situation in the Congo,

Having learned with deep regret the announcement of the killing of the Congolese leaders, Mr. Patrice Lumumba, Mr. Maurice Mpolo and Mr. Joseph Okito,

Deeply concerned at the grave repercussions of these crimes and the danger of widespread civil war and bloodshed in the Congo and the threat to international peace and security,

Noting the report of the Secretary-General's special representative dated 12 February, 1961, bringing to light the development of a serious civil-war situation and preparations therefor,

1. *Urges* that the United Nations take immediately all appropriate meas-

ures to prevent the occurrence of civil war in the Congo, including arrangements for cease-fires, the halting of all military operations, the prevention of clashes, and the use of force, if necessary, in the last resort;

2. *Urges* that measures be taken for the immediate withdrawal and evacuation from the Congo of all Belgian and other foreign military and para-military personnel and political advisers not under the United Nations command, and mercenaries;

3. *Calls upon* all states to take immediate and energetic measures to prevent the departure of such personnel for the Congo from their territories, and for the denial of transit and other facilities to them;

4. *Decides* that an immediate and impartial investigation be held in order to ascertain the circumstances of the death of Mr. Lumumba and his colleagues and that the perpetrators of these crimes be punished;

5. *Reaffirms* the Security Council resolutions of 14 July, 22 July and 9 August, 1960, and the General Assembly resolution 1,474 (ES-IV) of 20 September, 1960, and reminds all states of their obligation under these resolutions.

[B.]

The Security Council,

Gravely concerned at the continuing deterioration in the Congo, and the prevalence of conditions which seriously imperil peace and order and the unity and territorial integrity of the Congo, and threaten international peace and security,

Noting with deep regret and concern the systematic violations of human rights and fundamental freedoms and the general absence of rule of law in the Congo,

Recognizing the imperative necessity of the restoration of parliamentary institutions in the Congo in accordance with the fundamental law of the country, so that the will of the people should be reflected through the freely elected Parliament,

Convinced that the solution of the problem of the Congo lies in the hands of the Congolese people themselves without any interference from outside and that there can be no solution without conciliation,

Convinced further that the imposition of any solution, including the formation of any government not based on genuine conciliation, would, far from settling any issues, greatly enhance the dangers of conflict within the Congo and threat to international peace and security,

1. *Urges* the convening of the Parliament and the taking of necessary protective measures in that connection;

2. *Urges* that Congolese armed units and personnel should be reorganized and brought under discipline and control and arrangements be made on impartial and equitable bases to that end and with a view to the elimina-

tion of any possibility of interference by such units and personnel in the political life of the Congo;

3. *Calls upon* all states to extend their full cooperation and assistance and take such measures as may be necessary on their part, for the implementation of this resolution.

INDEX